201 SUN SIGN BOOK

Forecasts by
Kim Rogers-Gallagher

Cover Design by Kevin R. Brown
Editing by Andrea Neff
Background with Sunflower: iStockphoto.com/ulimi
Sunflower: iStockphoto.com/nick73
Interior Zodiac Icons: iStockphoto.com/Trillingstudio

Copyright 2014 Llewellyn Publications
ISBN: 978-0-7387-2687-8
A Division of Llewellyn Worldwide Ltd., www.llewellyn.com
Llewellyn is a registered trademark of Llewellyn Worldwide Ltd.
2143 Wooddale Drive, Woodbury, MN 55125
Printed in the USA

Contents

2014

SEPTEMBER
S	M	T	W	T	F	S
	1	2	3	4	5	6
7	8	9	10	11	12	13
14	15	16	17	18	19	20
21	22	23	24	25	26	27
28	29	30				

OCTOBER
S	M	T	W	T	F	S
			1	2	3	4
5	6	7	8	9	10	11
12	13	14	15	16	17	18
19	20	21	22	23	24	25
26	27	28	29	30	31	

NOVEMBER
S	M	T	W	T	F	S
						1
2	3	4	5	6	7	8
9	10	11	12	13	14	15
16	17	18	19	20	21	22
23	24	25	26	27	28	29
30						

DECEMBER
S	M	T	W	T	F	S
	1	2	3	4	5	6
7	8	9	10	11	12	13
14	15	16	17	18	19	20
21	22	23	24	25	26	27
28	29	30	31			

2015

JANUARY
S	M	T	W	T	F	S
				1	2	3
4	5	6	7	8	9	10
11	12	13	14	15	16	17
18	19	20	21	22	23	24
25	26	27	28	29	30	31

FEBRUARY
S	M	T	W	T	F	S
1	2	3	4	5	6	7
8	9	10	11	12	13	14
15	16	17	18	19	20	21
22	23	24	25	26	27	28

MARCH
S	M	T	W	T	F	S
1	2	3	4	5	6	7
8	9	10	11	12	13	14
15	16	17	18	19	20	21
22	23	24	25	26	27	28
29	30	31				

APRIL
S	M	T	W	T	F	S
			1	2	3	4
5	6	7	8	9	10	11
12	13	14	15	16	17	18
19	20	21	22	23	24	25
26	27	28	29	30		

MAY
S	M	T	W	T	F	S
					1	2
3	4	5	6	7	8	9
10	11	12	13	14	15	16
17	18	19	20	21	22	23
24	25	26	27	28	29	30
31						

JUNE
S	M	T	W	T	F	S
	1	2	3	4	5	6
7	8	9	10	11	12	13
14	15	16	17	18	19	20
21	22	23	24	25	26	27
28	29	30				

JULY
S	M	T	W	T	F	S
			1	2	3	4
5	6	7	8	9	10	11
12	13	14	15	16	17	18
19	20	21	22	23	24	25
26	27	28	29	30	31	

AUGUST
S	M	T	W	T	F	S
						1
2	3	4	5	6	7	8
9	10	11	12	13	14	15
16	17	18	19	20	21	22
23	24	25	26	27	28	29
30	31					

SEPTEMBER
S	M	T	W	T	F	S
		1	2	3	4	5
6	7	8	9	10	11	12
13	14	15	16	17	18	19
20	21	22	23	24	25	26
27	28	29	30			

OCTOBER
S	M	T	W	T	F	S
				1	2	3
4	5	6	7	8	9	10
11	12	13	14	15	16	17
18	19	20	21	22	23	24
25	26	27	28	29	30	31

NOVEMBER
S	M	T	W	T	F	S
1	2	3	4	5	6	7
8	9	10	11	12	13	14
15	16	17	18	19	20	21
22	23	24	25	26	27	28
29	30					

DECEMBER
S	M	T	W	T	F	S
		1	2	3	4	5
6	7	8	9	10	11	12
13	14	15	16	17	18	19
20	21	22	23	24	25	26
27	28	29	30	31		

2016

JANUARY
S	M	T	W	T	F	S
					1	2
3	4	5	6	7	8	9
10	11	12	13	14	15	16
17	18	19	20	21	22	23
24	25	26	27	28	29	30
31						

FEBRUARY
S	M	T	W	T	F	S
	1	2	3	4	5	6
7	8	9	10	11	12	13
14	15	16	17	18	19	20
21	22	23	24	25	26	27
28	29					

MARCH
S	M	T	W	T	F	S
		1	2	3	4	5
6	7	8	9	10	11	12
13	14	15	16	17	18	19
20	21	22	23	24	25	26
27	28	29	30	31		

APRIL
S	M	T	W	T	F	S
					1	2
3	4	5	6	7	8	9
10	11	12	13	14	15	16
17	18	19	20	21	22	23
24	25	26	27	28	29	30

MAY
S	M	T	W	T	F	S
1	2	3	4	5	6	7
8	9	10	11	12	13	14
15	16	17	18	19	20	21
22	23	24	25	26	27	28
29	30	31				

JUNE
S	M	T	W	T	F	S
			1	2	3	4
5	6	7	8	9	10	11
12	13	14	15	16	17	18
19	20	21	22	23	24	25
26	27	28	29	30		

JULY
S	M	T	W	T	F	S
					1	2
3	4	5	6	7	8	9
10	11	12	13	14	15	16
17	18	19	20	21	22	23
24	25	26	27	28	29	30
31						

AUGUST
S	M	T	W	T	F	S
	1	2	3	4	5	6
7	8	9	10	11	12	13
14	15	16	17	18	19	20
21	22	23	24	25	26	27
28	29	30	31			

Meet Kim Rogers-Gallagher

Kim fell in love with astrology in grade school and began her formal education close to thirty years ago. She's written hundreds of articles and columns for magazines and online publications, contributed to several astrological anthologies, and has two books of her own to her credit, *Astrology for the Light Side of the Brain* and *Astrology for the Light Side of the Future*, both available from ACS/Starcrafts Publishing. Kim is the author of daily e-mail horoscopes for astrology.com, and her work appears in the introductory sections of *Llewellyn's Astrology Calendar*, *Llewellyn's Witches' Datebook*, and *Llewellyn's Witches' Calendar*.

At the moment, Kim is having great fun on her Facebook page, facebook.com/KRGFenix, where she turns daily transits into fun celestial adventures. She's a well-known speaker who's been part of the UAC (United Astrology Conference) faculty since 1996 and has lectured at many other international conferences.

An avid animal lover, Kim occasionally receives permission from her seriously spoiled fur-kids (and her computer) to leave home for a while and indulge her ninth-house Sagg Sun by traveling for "work"— that is, talking to groups about astrology (which really isn't work at all). In typical Sagg style, Kim loves to laugh, but she also loves to chat, which comes in handy when she does private phone consultations.

She is a twenty-year "citizen" of Pennsic, an annual medieval event, where she gets to dress up in funny clothes, live in a tent, and pretend she's back in the 1300s for two weeks every year—which, oddly enough, is her idea of a good time.

Kim can be contacted at KRGPhoenix313@yahoo.com for fees regarding readings, classes, and lectures.

New Concepts for Zodiac Signs

The signs of the zodiac represent characteristics and traits that indicate how energy operates within our lives. The signs tell the story of human evolution and development, and all are necessary to form the continuum of whole-life experience. In fact, all twelve signs are represented within your astrological chart.

Although the traditional metaphors for the twelve signs (such as Aries, the Ram) are always functional, these alternative concepts for each of the twelve signs also describe the gradual unfolding of the human spirit.

Aries: The Initiator is the first sign of the zodiac and encompasses the primary concept of getting things started. This fiery ignition and bright beginning can prove to be the thrust necessary for new life, but the Initiator also can appear before a situation is ready for change and create disruption.

Taurus: The Maintainer sustains what Aries has begun and brings stability and focus into the picture, yet there also can be a tendency to try to maintain something in its current state without allowing for new growth.

Gemini: The Questioner seeks to determine whether alternatives are possible and offers diversity to the processes Taurus has brought into stability. Yet questioning can also lead to distraction, subsequently scattering energy and diffusing focus.

Cancer: The Nurturer provides the qualities necessary for growth and security, and encourages a deepening awareness of emotional needs. Yet this same nurturing can stifle individuation if it becomes too smothering.

Leo: The Loyalist directs and centralizes the experiences Cancer feeds. This quality is powerfully targeted toward self-awareness, but can be shortsighted. Hence, the Loyalist can hold steadfastly to viewpoints or feelings that inhibit new experiences.

Virgo: The Modifier analyzes the situations Leo brings to light and determines possibilities for change. Even though this change may be in the name of improvement, it can lead to dissatisfaction with the self if not directed in harmony with higher needs.

Libra: The Judge is constantly comparing everything to be sure that a certain level of rightness and perfection is presented. However, the Judge can also present possibilities that are harsh and seem to be cold or without feeling.

Scorpio: The Catalyst steps into the play of life to provide the quality of alchemical transformation. The Catalyst can stir the brew just enough to create a healing potion, or may get things going to such a powerful extent that they boil out of control.

Sagittarius: The Adventurer moves away from Scorpio's dimension to seek what lies beyond the horizon. The Adventurer continually looks for possibilities that answer the ultimate questions, but may forget the pathway back home.

Capricorn: The Pragmatist attempts to put everything into its rightful place and find ways to make life work out right. The Pragmatist can teach lessons of practicality and determination, but can become highly self-righteous when shortsighted.

Aquarius: The Reformer looks for ways to take what Capricorn has built and bring it up to date. Yet there is also a tendency to scrap the original in favor of a new plan that may not have the stable foundation necessary to operate effectively.

Pisces: The Visionary brings mysticism and imagination, and challenges the soul to move beyond the physical plane, into the realm of what might be. The Visionary can pierce the veil, returning enlightened to the physical world. The challenge is to avoid getting lost within the illusion of an alternate reality.

Astrology Basics

Astrology is an ancient and continually evolving system used to clarify your identity and your needs. An astrological chart—which is calculated using the date, time, and place of birth—contains many factors that symbolically represent the needs, expressions, and experiences that make up the whole person. A professional astrologer interprets this symbolic picture, offering you an accurate portrait of your personality.

The chart itself—the horoscope—is a portrait of an individual. Generally, a natal (or birth) horoscope is drawn on a circular wheel. The wheel is divided into twelve segments, called houses. Each of the twelve houses represents a different aspect of the individual, much like the facets of a brilliantly cut stone. The houses depict different environments, such as home, school, and work. The houses also represent roles and relationships: parents, friends, lovers, children, partners. In each environment, individuals show a different side of their personality. At home, you may represent yourself quite differently than you do on the job. Additionally, in each relationship you will project a different image of yourself. For example, your parents may rarely see the side you show to intimate friends.

Symbols for the planets, the Sun, and the Moon are drawn inside the houses. Each planet represents a separate kind of energy. You experience and express each energy in specific ways. The way you use each of these energies is up to you. The planets in your chart do not make you do anything!

Signs of the Zodiac

The twelve signs of the zodiac indicate characteristics and traits that further define your personality. Each sign can be expressed in positive and negative ways. What's more, you have all twelve signs somewhere in your chart. Signs that are strongly emphasized by the planets have greater force. The Sun, Moon, and planets are placed on the chart according to their position at the time of birth. The qualities of a sign, combined with the energy of a planet, indicate how you might be most likely to use that energy and the best ways to develop that energy. The signs add color, emphasis, and dimension to the personality.

The Twelve Signs

Aries	♈	The Initiator
Taurus	♉	The Maintainer
Gemini	♊	The Questioner
Cancer	♋	The Nurturer
Leo	♌	The Loyalist
Virgo	♍	The Modifier
Libra	♎	The Judge
Scorpio	♏	The Catalyst
Sagittarius	♐	The Adventurer
Capricorn	♑	The Pragmatist
Aquarius	♒	The Reformer
Pisces	♓	The Visionary

Signs are also placed at the cusps, or dividing lines, of each of the houses. The influence of the signs on the houses is much the same as their influence on the Sun, Moon, and planets. Each house is shaped by the sign on its cusp.

When you view a horoscope, you will notice that there appear to be four distinct angles dividing the wheel of the chart. The line that divides the chart into a top and bottom half represents the horizon. In most cases, the left side of the horizon is called the Ascendant. The zodiac sign on the Ascendant is your rising sign. The Ascendant indicates the way others are likely to view you.

The Sun, Moon, or a planet can be compared to an actor in a play. The sign shows how the energy works, like the role the actor plays in a drama. The house indicates where the energy operates, like the setting of a play. On a psychological level, the Sun represents who you think you are. The Ascendant describes who others think you are, and the Moon reflects your emotional self.

Astrologers also study the geometric relationships between the Sun, Moon, and planets. These geometric angles are called aspects. Aspects further define the strengths, weaknesses, and challenges within your physical, mental, emotional, and spiritual selves. Sometimes patterns also appear in an astrological chart. These patterns have meaning.

To understand cycles for any given point in time, astrologers study several factors. Many use transits, which refer to the movement and positions of the planets. When astrologers compare those positions to the birth horoscope, the transits indicate activity in particular areas of the chart. The *Sun Sign Book* uses transits.

As you can see, your Sun sign is just one of many factors that describe who you are—but it is a powerful one! As the symbol of the ego, the Sun in your chart reflects your drive to be noticed. Most people can easily relate to the concepts associated with their Sun sign, since it is tied to their sense of personal identity.

Meanings of the Planets

The Sun

The Sun indicates the psychological bias that will dominate your actions. What you see, and why, is told in the reading for your Sun. The Sun also shows the basic energy patterns of your body and psyche. In many ways, the Sun is the dominant force in your horoscope and your life. Other influences, especially that of the Moon, may modify the Sun's influence, but nothing will cause you to depart very far from the basic solar pattern. Always keep in mind the basic influence of the Sun and remember all other influences must be interpreted in terms of it, especially insofar as they play a visible role in your life. You may think, dream, imagine, and hope a thousand things, according to your Moon and your other planets, but the Sun is what you are. To be your best self in terms of your Sun is to cause your energies to work along the path in which they will have maximum help from planetary vibrations.

The Moon

The Moon tells the desire of your life. When you know what you mean but can't verbalize it, it is your Moon that knows it and your Sun that can't say it. The wordless ecstasy, the mute sorrow, the secret dream, the esoteric picture of yourself that you can't get across to the world, or that the world doesn't comprehend or value—these are the products of the Moon. When you are misunderstood, it is your Moon nature, expressed imperfectly through the Sun sign, that feels betrayed. Things you know without thought—intuitions, hunches,

The Planets

Sun	☉	The ego, self, willpower
Moon	☽	The subconscious self, habits
Mercury	☿	Communication, the intellect
Venus	♀	Emotional expression, love, appreciation, artistry
Mars	♂	Physical drive, assertiveness, anger
Jupiter	♃	Philosophy, ethics, generosity
Saturn	♄	Discipline, focus, responsibility
Uranus	♅	Individuality, rebelliousness
Neptune	♆	Imagination, sensitivity, compassion
Pluto	♇	Transformation, healing, regeneration

instincts—are the products of the Moon. Modes of expression that you feel truly reflect your deepest self belong to the Moon: art, letters, creative work of any kind; sometimes love; sometimes business. Whatever you feel to be most deeply yourself is the product of your Moon and of the sign your Moon occupies at birth.

Mercury

Mercury is the sensory antenna of your horoscope. Its position by sign indicates your reactions to sights, sounds, odors, tastes, and touch impressions, affording a key to the attitude you have toward the physical world around you. Mercury is the messenger through which your physical body and brain (ruled by the Sun) and your inner nature (ruled by the Moon) are kept in contact with the outer world, which will appear to you according to the index of Mercury's position by sign in the horoscope. Mercury rules your rational mind.

Venus

Venus is the emotional antenna of your horoscope. Through Venus, impressions come to you from the outer world. The position of Venus by sign at the time of your birth determines your attitude toward these experiences. As Mercury is the messenger linking sense impressions (sight, smell, etc.) to the basic nature of your Sun and Moon, so Venus is the messenger linking emotional impressions. If Venus is found in the same sign as the Sun, emotions gain importance in your life and have a direct bearing on your actions. If Venus is in the same sign as the Moon, emotions bear directly on your inner nature, add self-confidence, make you sensitive to emotional impressions, and frequently indicate that you have more love in your heart than you are able to express. If Venus is in the same sign as Mercury, emotional impressions and sense impressions work together; you tend to idealize the world of the senses and sensualize the world of the emotions to interpret what you see and hear.

Mars

Mars is the energy principle in the horoscope. Its position indicates the channels into which energy will most easily be directed. It is the planet through which the activities of the Sun and the desires of the Moon express themselves in action. In the same sign as the Sun, Mars gives abundant energy, sometimes misdirected in temper, temperament, and quarrels. In the same sign as the Moon, it gives a great capacity to make use of the innermost aims, and to make the inner desires articulate and practical. In the same sign as Venus, it quickens emotional reactions and causes you to act on them, makes for ardor and passion in love, and fosters an earthly awareness of emotional realities.

Jupiter

Jupiter is the feeler for opportunity that you have out in the world. It passes along chances of a lifetime for consideration according to the basic nature of your Sun and Moon. Jupiter's sign position indicates the places you will look for opportunity, the uses to which you wish to put it, and the capacity you have to react and profit by it. Jupiter is ordinarily and erroneously called the planet of luck. It is "luck" insofar as it is the index of opportunity, but your luck depends less on what comes to you than on what you do with what comes to you. In the same sign as the Sun or Moon, Jupiter gives a direct and generally effective response to opportunity and is likely to show forth at its "luckiest." If Jupiter is in the same sign as Mercury, sense impressions are interpreted opportunistically. If Jupiter is in the same sign as Venus, you interpret emotions in such a way as to turn them to your advantage; your feelings work harmoniously with the chances for progress that the world has to offer. If Jupiter is in the same sign as Mars, you follow opportunity with energy, dash, enthusiasm, and courage; take big chances; and play your cards wide open.

Saturn

Saturn indicates the direction that will be taken in life by the self-preserving principle that, in its highest manifestation, ceases to be purely defensive and becomes ambitious and aspiring. Your defense or attack against the world is shown by the sign position of Saturn in the horoscope of birth. If Saturn is in the same sign as the Sun or Moon, defense predominates, and there is danger of introversion. The farther Saturn is from the Sun, Moon, and Ascendant, the better for objectivity and extroversion. If Saturn is in the same sign as Mercury, there is a profound and serious reaction to sensory impressions; this position generally accompanies a deep and efficient mind. If Saturn is in the same sign as Venus, a defensive attitude toward emotional experience makes for apparent coolness in love and difficulty with the emotions and human relations. If Saturn is in the same sign as Mars, confusion between defensive and aggressive urges can make a person indecisive. On the other hand, if the Sun and Moon are strong and the total personality well developed, a balanced, peaceful, and calm individual of sober judgment and moderate actions may be indicated. If Saturn is in the same sign as Jupiter, the reaction to opportunity is sober and balanced.

Uranus

Uranus in a general way relates to creativity, originality, or individuality, and its position by sign in the horoscope tells the direction in which you will seek to express yourself. In the same sign as Mercury or the Moon, Uranus suggests acute awareness, a quick reaction to sense impressions and experiences, or a hair-trigger mind. In the same sign as the Sun, it points to great nervous activity, a high-strung nature, and an original, creative, or eccentric personality. In the same sign as Mars, Uranus indicates high-speed activity, love of swift motion, and perhaps love of danger. In the same sign as Venus, it suggests an unusual reaction to emotional experience, idealism, sensuality, and original ideas about love and human relations. In the same sign as Saturn, Uranus points to good sense; this can be a practical, creative position, but more often than not it sets up a destructive conflict between practicality and originality that can result in a stalemate. In the same sign as Jupiter, Uranus makes opportunity, creates wealth and the means of getting it, and is conducive to the inventive, executive, and daring.

Neptune

Neptune relates to the deep subconscious, inherited mentality, and spirituality, indicating what you take for granted in life. Neptune in the same sign as the Sun or Moon indicates that intuitions and hunches—or delusions—dominate; there is a need to rigidly hold to reality. In the same sign as Mercury, Neptune indicates sharp sensory perceptions, a sensitive and perhaps creative mind, and a quivering intensity of reaction to sensory experience. In the same sign as Venus, it reveals idealistic and romantic (or sentimental) reactions to emotional experience, as well as the danger of sensationalism and a love of strange pleasures. In the same sign as Mars, Neptune indicates energy and intuition that work together to make mastery of life—one of the signs of having angels (or devils) on your side. When in the same sign as Jupiter, Neptune describes an intuitive response to opportunity along practical and money-making lines. In the same sign as Saturn, Neptune indicates intuitive defense and attack on the world, which is generally successful unless Saturn is polarized on the negative side; then there is danger of unhappiness.

Pluto

Pluto is a planet of extremes, from the lowest criminal and violent level of our society to the heights people can attain when they realize their significance in the collectivity of humanity. Pluto also rules three important mysteries of life—sex, death, and rebirth—and links them to each other. One level of death symbolized by Pluto is the physical death of an individual, which occurs so that a person can be reborn into another body to further his or her spiritual development. On another level, individuals can experience a "death" of their old self when they realize the deeper significance of life; thus they become one of the "second born." In a natal horoscope, Pluto signifies our perspective on the world, our conscious and subconscious. Since so many of Pluto's qualities are centered on the deeper mysteries of life, the house position of Pluto, and aspects to it, can show you how to attain a deeper understanding of the importance of the spiritual in your life.

Astrological Glossary

Air: One of the four basic elements. The air signs are Gemini, Libra, and Aquarius.

Angles: The four points of the chart that divide it into quadrants. The angles are sensitive areas that lend emphasis to planets located near them. These points are located on the cusps of the first, fourth, seventh, and tenth houses in a chart.

Ascendant: Rising sign. The degree of the zodiac on the eastern horizon at the time and place for which the horoscope is calculated. It can indicate the image or physical appearance you project to the world. The cusp of the first house.

Aspect: The angular relationship between planets, sensitive points, or house cusps in a horoscope. Lines drawn between the two points and the center of the chart, representing the earth, form the angle of the aspect. Astrological aspects include the conjunction (two points that are 0 degrees apart), opposition (two points, 180 degrees apart), square (two points, 90 degrees apart), sextile (two points, 60 degrees apart), and trine (two points, 120 degrees apart). Aspects can indicate harmony or challenge.

Cardinal Sign: One of the three qualities, or categories, that describe how a sign expresses itself. Aries, Cancer, Libra, and Capricorn are the cardinal signs, believed to initiate activity.

Chiron: Chiron is a comet traveling in orbit between Saturn and Uranus. It is believed to represent a key or doorway, healing, ecology, and a bridge between traditional and modern methods.

Conjunction: An aspect or angle between two points in a chart where the two points are close enough so that the energies join. Can be considered either harmonious or challenging, depending on the planets involved and their placement.

Cusp: A dividing line between signs or houses in a chart.

Degree: Degree of arc. One of 360 divisions of a circle. The circle of the zodiac is divided into twelve astrological signs of 30 degrees each. Each degree is made up of 60 minutes, and each minute is made up of 60 seconds of zodiacal longitude.

Earth: One of the four basic elements. The earth signs are Taurus, Virgo, and Capricorn.

Eclipse: A Solar Eclipse is the full or partial covering of the Sun by the Moon (as viewed from the earth), and a Lunar Eclipse is the full or partial covering of the Moon by the earth's own shadow.

Ecliptic: The Sun's apparent path around the earth, which is actually the plane of the earth's orbit extended out into space. The ecliptic forms the center of the zodiac.

Electional Astrology: A branch of astrology concerned with choosing the best time to initiate an activity.

Elements: The signs of the zodiac are divided into four groups of three zodiacal signs, each symbolized by one of the four elements of the ancients: fire, earth, air, and water. The element of a sign is said to express its essential nature.

Ephemeris: A listing of the Sun, Moon, and planets' positions and related information for astrological purposes.

Equinox: Equal night. The point in the earth's orbit around the Sun at which the day and night are equal in length.

Feminine Signs: Each zodiac sign is either "masculine" or "feminine." Earth signs (Taurus, Virgo, and Capricorn) and water signs (Cancer, Scorpio, and Pisces) are feminine.

Fire: One of the four basic elements. The fire signs are Aries, Leo, and Sagittarius.

Fixed Signs: Fixed is one of the three qualities, or categories, that describe how a sign expresses itself. The fixed signs are Taurus, Leo, Scorpio, and Aquarius. Fixed signs are said to be predisposed to existing patterns and somewhat resistant to change.

Hard Aspects: Hard aspects are those aspects in a chart that astrologers believe to represent difficulty or challenges. Among the hard aspects are the square, the opposition, and the conjunction (depending on which planets are conjunct).

Horizon: The word *horizon* is used in astrology in a manner similar to its common usage, except that only the eastern and western horizons are considered useful. The eastern horizon at the point of birth is the

Ascendant, or first house cusp, of a natal chart, and the western horizon at the point of birth is the Descendant, or seventh house cusp.

Houses: Division of the horoscope into twelve segments, beginning with the Ascendant. The dividing line between two houses is called a house cusp. Each house corresponds to certain aspects of daily living, and is ruled by the astrological sign that governs the cusp, or dividing line between the house and the one previous.

Ingress: The point of entry of a planet into a sign.

Lagna: A term used in Hindu or Vedic astrology for Ascendant, the degree of the zodiac on the eastern horizon at the time of birth.

Masculine Signs: Each of the twelve signs of the zodiac is either "masculine" or "feminine." The fire signs (Aries, Leo, and Sagittarius) and the air signs (Gemini, Libra, and Aquarius) are masculine.

Midheaven: The highest point on the ecliptic, where it intersects the meridian that passes directly above the place for which the horoscope is cast; the southern point of the horoscope.

Midpoint: A point equally distant to two planets or house cusps. Midpoints are considered by some astrologers to be sensitive points in a person's chart.

Mundane Astrology: Mundane astrology is the branch of astrology generally concerned with political and economic events, and the nations involved in these events.

Mutable Signs: Mutable is one of the three qualities, or categories, that describe how a sign expresses itself. Mutable signs are Gemini, Virgo, Sagittarius, and Pisces. Mutable signs are said to be very adaptable and sometimes changeable.

Natal Chart: A person's birth chart. A natal chart is essentially a "snapshot" showing the placement of each of the planets at the exact time of a person's birth.

Node: The point where the planets cross the ecliptic, or the earth's apparent path around the Sun. The North Node is the point where a planet moves northward, from the earth's perspective, as it crosses the ecliptic; the South Node is where it moves south.

Opposition: Two points in a chart that are 180 degrees apart.

Orb: A small degree of margin used when calculating aspects in a chart. For example, although 180 degrees form an exact opposition, an astrologer might consider an aspect within 3 or 4 degrees on either side of 180 degrees to be an opposition, as the impact of the aspect can still be felt within this range. The less orb on an aspect, the stronger the aspect. Astrologers' opinions vary on how many degrees of orb to allow for each aspect.

Outer Planet: Uranus, Neptune, and Pluto are known as the outer planets. Because of their distance from the Sun, they take a long time to complete a single rotation. Everyone born within a few years on either side of a given date will have similar placements of these planets.

Planet: The planets used in astrology are Mercury, Venus, Mars, Jupiter, Saturn, Uranus, Neptune, and Pluto. For astrological purposes, the Sun and Moon are also considered planets. A natal chart, or birth chart, lists planetary placements at the moment of birth.

Planetary Rulership: The sign in which a planet is most harmoniously placed. Examples are the Sun in Leo, Jupiter in Sagittarius, and the Moon in Cancer.

Precession of Equinoxes: The gradual movement of the point of the spring equinox, located at 0 degrees Aries. This point marks the beginning of the tropical zodiac. The point moves slowly backward through the constellations of the zodiac, so that about every 2,000 years the equinox begins in an earlier constellation.

Qualities: In addition to categorizing the signs by element, astrologers place the twelve signs of the zodiac into three additional categories, or qualities: cardinal, mutable, or fixed. Each sign is considered to be a combination of its element and quality. Where the element of a sign describes its basic nature, the quality describes its mode of expression.

Retrograde Motion: The apparent backward motion of a planet. This is an illusion caused by the relative motion of the earth and other planets in their elliptical orbits.

Sextile: Two points in a chart that are 60 degrees apart.

Sidereal Zodiac: Generally used by Hindu or Vedic astrologers. The sidereal zodiac is located where the constellations are actually positioned in the sky.

Soft Aspects: Soft aspects indicate good fortune or an easy relationship in the chart. Among the soft aspects are the trine, the sextile, and the conjunction (depending on which planets are conjunct each other).

Square: Two points in a chart that are 90 degrees apart.

Sun Sign: The sign of the zodiac in which the Sun is located at any given time.

Synodic Cycle: The time between conjunctions of two planets.

Trine: Two points in a chart that are 120 degrees apart.

Tropical Zodiac: The tropical zodiac begins at 0 degrees Aries, where the Sun is located during the spring equinox. This system is used by most Western astrologers and throughout this book.

Void-of-Course: A planet is void-of-course after it has made its last aspect within a sign but before it has entered a new sign.

Water: One of the four basic elements. The water signs are Cancer, Scorpio, and Pisces.

Using This Book

This book contains what is called Sun sign astrology; that is, astrology based on the sign that your Sun was in at the time of your birth. The technique has its foundation in ancient Greek astrology, in which the Sun was one of five points in the chart that were used as focal points for delineation.

The most effective way to use astrology, however, is through one-on-one work with a professional astrologer, who can integrate the eight or so other astrological bodies into the interpretation to provide you with guidance. There are factors related to the year and time of day you were born that are highly significant in the way you approach life and vital to making wise choices. In addition, there are ways of using astrology that aren't addressed here, such as compatibility between two specific individuals, discovering family patterns, or picking a day for a wedding or grand opening.

To best use the information in the monthly forecasts, you'll want to determine your Ascendant, or rising sign. If you don't know your Ascendant, the tables following this description will help you determine your rising sign. They are most accurate for those born in the continental United States. They provide only an approximation, but can be used as a good rule of thumb. Your exact Ascendant may vary from the tables according to your time and place of birth. Once you've approximated your ascending sign using the tables or determined your Ascendant by having your chart calculated, you'll know two significant factors in your chart. Read the monthly forecast sections for both your Sun and Ascendant to gain the most useful information. In addition, you can read the section about the sign your Moon is in. The Sun is the true, inner you; the Ascendant is your shell or appearance and the person you are becoming; the Moon is the person you were—or still are based on habits and memories.

Also included in the monthly forecasts is information about the planets' retrogrades. Most people have heard of "Mercury retrograde." In fact, all the planets except the Sun and Moon appear to travel backward (retrograde) in their path periodically. This appears to happen only because we on the earth are not seeing the other planets from the middle of the solar system. Rather, we are watching them from our own moving object. We are like a train that moves past cars on the freeway that are going at a slower speed. To us on the train, the cars look like they're going backward. Mercury turns retrograde about every four months for three weeks; Venus every eighteen months for six weeks; Mars every two years for two to three months. The rest of the planets each retrograde once a year for four to five months. During each retrograde, we have the opportunity to try something new, something we conceived of at the beginning of the planet's yearly cycle. The times when the planets change direction are significant, as are the beginning and midpoint (peak or culmination) of each cycle. These are noted in your forecast each month.

The "Rewarding Days" and "Challenging Days" sections indicate times when you'll feel either more centered or more out of balance. The rewarding days are not the only times you can perform well, but the times you're likely to feel better integrated! During challenging days, take extra time to center yourself by meditating or using other techniques that help you feel more objective.

The Action Table found at the end of each sign's section offers general guidelines for the best times to take particular actions. Please note, however, that your whole chart will provide more accurate guidelines for the best time to do something. Therefore, use this table with a grain of salt, and never let it stop you from taking an action you feel compelled to take.

You can use this information to gain an objective awareness about the way the current cycles are affecting you. Realize that the power of astrology is even more useful when you have a complete chart and professional guidance.

Ascendant Table

Your Sun Sign	Your Time of Birth					
	6–8 am	8–10 am	10 am–Noon	Noon–2 pm	2–4 pm	4–6 pm
Aries	Taurus	Gemini	Cancer	Leo	Virgo	Libra
Taurus	Gemini	Cancer	Leo	Virgo	Libra	Scorpio
Gemini	Cancer	Leo	Virgo	Libra	Scorpio	Sagittarius
Cancer	Leo	Virgo	Libra	Scorpio	Sagittarius	Capricorn
Leo	Virgo	Libra	Scorpio	Sagittarius	Capricorn	Aquarius
Virgo	Libra	Scorpio	Sagittarius	Capricorn	Aquarius	Pisces
Libra	Scorpio	Sagittarius	Capricorn	Aquarius	Pisces	Aries
Scorpio	Sagittarius	Capricorn	Aquarius	Pisces	Aries	Taurus
Sagittarius	Capricorn	Aquarius	Pisces	Aries	Taurus	Gemini
Capricorn	Aquarius	Pisces	Aries	Taurus	Gemini	Cancer
Aquarius	Pisces	Aries	Taurus	Gemini	Cancer	Leo
Pisces	Aries	Taurus	Gemini	Cancer	Leo	Virgo

Your Sun Sign	Your Time of Birth					
	6–8 pm	8–10 pm	10 pm–Midnight	Midnight–2 am	2–4 am	4–6 am
Aries	Scorpio	Sagittarius	Capricorn	Aquarius	Pisces	Aries
Taurus	Sagittarius	Capricorn	Aquarius	Pisces	Aries	Taurus
Gemini	Capricorn	Aquarius	Pisces	Aries	Taurus	Gemini
Cancer	Aquarius	Pisces	Aries	Taurus	Gemini	Cancer
Leo	Pisces	Aries	Taurus	Gemini	Cancer	Leo
Virgo	Aries	Taurus	Gemini	Cancer	Leo	Virgo
Libra	Taurus	Gemini	Cancer	Leo	Virgo	Libra
Scorpio	Gemini	Cancer	Leo	Virgo	Libra	Scorpio
Sagittarius	Cancer	Leo	Virgo	Libra	Scorpio	Sagittarius
Capricorn	Leo	Virgo	Libra	Scorpio	Sagittarius	Capricorn
Aquarius	Virgo	Libra	Scorpio	Sagittarius	Capricorn	Aquarius
Pisces	Libra	Scorpio	Sagittarius	Capricorn	Aquarius	Pisces

How to use this table: 1. Find your Sun sign in the left column.
2. Find your approximate birth time in a vertical column.
3. Line up your Sun sign and birth time to find your Ascendant.

This table will give you an approximation of your Ascendant. If you feel that the sign listed as your Ascendant is incorrect, try the one either before or after the listed sign. It is difficult to determine your exact Ascendant without a complete natal chart.

2015 at a Glance

Uranus in Aries, who just loves to shake things up, is still in a square aspect with determined Pluto, who's currently holding on tight to the status quo from his spot in Capricorn—and this fight isn't over just yet. So even if these two are not in the neighborhood of one of our personal planets, we should all prepare for their struggle to influence our lives in a very big way during 2015. This astrological mega-brawl has already pitted the concepts of total personal freedom (Uranus in Aries) and total accountability (Pluto in Capricorn) against each another. We'll all feel this war internally, for a variety of reasons, but on a broader level, debates over Internet privacy and cell-phone monitoring are sure to continue. Are regulations like these positive because they protect our national security or negative because they impact our privacy? Therein lies the rub.

Now, speaking of privacy, let's talk about Neptune. She's been operating invisibly and without a filter for the past few years in Pisces, her home turf. This year, she'll hone her skill at infiltration and become even better at dissolving boundaries, so privacy in many forms will be hard to come by. The social-networking sites this planet inspired during her journey through Aquarius are already routinely monitored by employers and government, and while we've all been able to find missing loved ones and reconnect with long-lost friends, choosing which personal information to casually share online will become even more of a personal responsibility. The innovative wireless technnologies we're already taking for granted are sure to take off in a very big way and become even more mind-boggling. Neptune may not rule science and technology, but her hand is certainly in the pot now.

Saturn made his way into Sagittarius late in December of 2014, and except for a brief return into Scorpio to tie up some loose ends from June 14 through September 17, he'll be devoting all his time for the next two and a half years to changing the rules we live by from the inside out, so laws will be rewritten and social mores rebuilt.

The really good news is that both Jupiter, the heavens' answer to Santa Claus, and Venus, the Goddess of Creature Comforts, will spend much of the year in Leo, a fire sign that loves to be lavish but loves to be in love even more. Jupiter will stay on duty there until

August 11, and Venus has extended her usual stay (about a month) to over three months. She'll set off for Leo on June 5, stay there until July 18, then do a return trip from July 31 through October 8. Between these two planets, we're all due to experience and provide some quality entertainment. But when they come together in late June and early July, hearing about love at first sight will become quite normal—and isn't that lovely!

2015 SUN SIGN BOOK

Forecasts by

Kim Rogers-Gallagher

Aries

The Ram
March 20 to April 19

♈

Element: Fire

Quality: Cardinal

Polarity: Yang/masculine

Planetary Ruler: Mars

Meditation: I build upon my strengths

Gemstone: Diamond

Power Stones: Bloodstone, carnelian, ruby

Key Phrase: I am

Glyph: Ram's head

Anatomy: Head, face, throat

Colors: Red, white

Animal: Ram

Myths/Legends: Artemis, Jason and the Golden Fleece

House: First

Opposite Sign: Libra

Flower: Geranium

Keyword: Initiative

The Aries Personality

Your Strengths and Challenges

You are nothing if not brave, Aries—sometimes a little too brave for your own good, in fact. You absolutely adore adrenaline, so two of your favorite hobbies include tempting fate and pushing the envelope—along with skydiving, bungee jumping, and anything else that most of us would consider far too dangerous to even consider. These things certainly do get your blood pumping (which is your ultimate goal, after all), but on a regular basis, they're also quite stressful. So, believe it or not, every now and then you might want to treat yourself to a quiet evening at home, watching a nice, relaxing action movie with lots of car chases and shootouts. You definitely don't need caffeine, but you probably brew your coffee so strong that others refer to it as "rocket fuel" and you probably think of Red Bull as the only way to get through a "normal" day. Obviously, you're the very soul of impatience, always wanting to be first in line and first to leave, well before the closing credits roll. If you had to choose a motto, it would probably be "Ready, fire, aim!" The thing is, with all that red-hot Mars energy constantly looking for an outlet, you're so darned entertaining and exciting that no one minds much if you can't sit still for more than a few minutes at a time and you just love to argue. After all, what would life be like without you astrological spark plugs?

Your Relationships

To keep up with you, Aries—well, it's no easy task. In fact, you pride yourself on being a challenge, and you prefer to spend your time with those who are also quite challenging. As such, your best bet will always be one of the other fire signs. Sagittarians seem to do best with you, since you're always game to try out one of their new ideas for an adventure, but Leos are fun, too, because they never run out of steam—or fire. Relationships between you and another Aries are definitely not boring, but you'd both better be ready for lots of passion, for better or worse. The air signs—Gemini, Libra, and Aquarius—are often good matches for you, because their brains are just as restless as yours and they're usually game to try anything at least once. Plus, remember what air does to fire. It fans those flames, which leads to all kinds of exciting possibilities. While you may seem to have quite a bit in common with the water and earth signs to start with, in the long run you could end up bored—and they could end up exhausted. In general, however, anyone who can put up with your occasional bouts of temper (which, granted, are quite refreshing, since they never last long and are wonderful for clearing the air) and give it right back to you—well, they might do just fine. What you're after isn't just the perfect mate. You also want a worthy opponent—someone you can respect because they just won't take any guff, not from you or anyone else. Heaven help anyone who does challenge or even mildly irritate your significant other, however, even if it's not intentional. You'll spring to the defense before the intruder has any idea they've just conjured up the fire of Mars—who isn't known as the "red planet" for nothing.

Your Career and Money

Anything that holds your interest needs to move fast and change often, Aries, and that certainly holds true for your work, if you're going to stay put. As long as those conditions are met, you can adapt to just about any type of job, but once you're bored—well, you're outta there. Of course, since your ruling planet, Mars, also rules steel and iron, many Aries are drawn to work that involves cutting instruments, such as surgery or florist work—which, remember, also involves a knife, even if it's for a lovely reason. Working with vehicles is fun, and welding is often a wonderful fit, too. It combines fire and metal—the best of both worlds for you—so it's fun. When it comes to spending your hard-earned paycheck, you're often a lot more careful than most of us might expect. That's not to say you won't whip out the plastic or your checkbook if there's an adventure to be had, but therein lies the rub. Objects are nice, but they quickly become boring, so you prefer to spend your money on experiences—and hopefully with companions who'll raise your blood pressure.

Your Lighter Side

What's fun for you? Well, adventure will always be first on the list, along with fire, speed, and action. What's really fun? Finding someone who's willing to do it with you, then sit down for a nice, relaxing triple espresso afterward and go over every detail—just before you head off to ride every single rollercoaster in the park. Sitting quietly by the ocean, watching the waves gently roll in and out? Not!

Affirmation for the Year

Taking a moment to think before I act is my path to success and harmony.

The Year Ahead for Aries

Romantically speaking, this will be quite the year for you, Aries. To start with, from January through August 11, Jupiter—the King of the Gods and the most excessive, extravagant planet of them all—will be in Leo, a fire-sign cousin of yours who just so happens to be known for its talent in the romance department. Add to that the fact that Jupiter will set up shop in your fifth solar house of lovers and playmates for the duration, and it's understandable how your astrological focus would most likely turn to that tender area of life for at least the first two thirds of the year. After all, Jupiter is just impossible to ignore—and why would you want to? He's a planet who just loves taking risks (one of your favorite things), who just loves adventure (yep, that's on the list too), and who never, ever did know when to quit. See? A match made in heaven.

And speaking of heavenly matches, let's not forget that loving Venus will also spend a great portion of 2015 in Leo and your solar fifth house of lovers. In fact, she'll keep Jupiter company there from June 5 through July 18, and again from July 31 through October 8. Now, this lady loves nothing more than romance, too, and in Leo, a fixed fire sign, she'll be especially determined to get it for you. Together with your own fire, Jupiter and Venus really can't help but put you on the receiving end of some lovely, lovely attention, both from your current partner, if you're already attached, and also from new fans and admirers, regardless of whether or not you're actually looking for them. In fact, you might want to be on the lookout for a flirtation or two that rubs your current partner the wrong way. A bit of attention from someone new is always fun, but at what cost? If you're happy, keep a lid on the flirting. (But no one says you can't enjoy the attention!)

If you're single, your mission will be to enjoy the buffet. Be sure to have just a taste of the company of anyone delicious the Universe tosses your way. Keep in mind, however, that you're going to need to tap into some of your considerable energy to keep up with quite a busy social schedule. Remember, the solar fifth house also pertains to playmates, so invitations to get out there and mingle will arrive in the style you love best—fast and furious!

Since this house also refers to children, if you're a parent, you'll be spending quite a bit of time with them, too, but probably for only the most delightful reasons—maybe even due to a new arrival. If you've ever had the urge to express yourself creatively in any way, such as in art, music, or entertaining, this is definitely the year to pursue it. With the help of both Venus and Jupiter—astrology's famous "benefics" (that is, the two most traditionally generous and potentially positive energies in the heavens)—it's just about guaranteed that your creative efforts in just about any field will be well received, and, as per Leo's ability to keep a crowd entertained, that you will be appreciated and applauded as well. These two are the stuff that stars are born of, the key ingredients in being at the right place at the right time. Again, you should get out as much as possible, get your name known, and be sure to strut your stuff! You could end up with a whole new way of earning your daily bread once Jupiter enters hard-working Virgo and your solar sixth house of work on August 11. Wouldn't it be delightful to love what you do for a living, and to actually look forward to getting to work every morning rather than dreading the thought of it, as many people do? Well, that and much, much more are possible for you this year, Aries.

Now, the square between Uranus and Pluto that started many, many moons ago will continue to affect us all for at least the first half of the year, Aries. This testy but often productive astrological relationship will pit your solar first house of personality and appearance against your solar tenth house of career, professional matters, and dealings with authority figures. So, just like last year, you may find that your goals seem to be a bit frustrated—at least at first. But let's go back to all that wonderful Jupiter activity, and consider the fact that you may be being pushed out of your current position because the chance to truly express yourself and follow your bliss is right around the corner.

If you're finding it tough to get along with elders, however, especially if they're asking too much of you or frowning at the path you're on, it might be time to lay down the law and let them know that this is your life and you'll live it as you see fit, with or without their approval. With Uranus on duty in your sign and your solar first house of personality and presentation, rebelliousness has become second nature to you—even more so than usual, that is—and true to your fiery nature, you will only take their criticism for so long, even if you love them. At some point, as per Uranus's love of personal freedom and independence and especially with the ongoing pressure from the square from relentless Pluto, you'll explode, and at that point, heaven help anyone who's tried to censure you or stop you from totally being you.

The good news is that the irritation of the square between these two astrological superpowers will inspire you to push your way through any roadblocks that may have hindered your progress in the past. In short, this is your year to refuse to take No for an answer—especially if you know in your heart that you are being true to yourself.

What This Year's Eclipses Mean for You

There will be four eclipses during 2015, Aries. The first pair will occur on March 20 and April 4. The Solar Eclipse (when the Sun and Moon come together in the same sign and degree) will arrive on March 20, and will plant a seed in ultra-sensitive Pisces and your solar twelfth house of secrets and private times. This might herald the beginning of a relationship that's not quite fit for public consumption at the moment, and if it does, you had better be quite careful. New Moons always hold the potential to inspire brand-new beginnings, but eclipses are supercharged New Moons, and they tend to mark major and sometimes quite sudden events. So if you start something up casually now, keep in mind that it might not remain casual—or hidden, for that matter—for long. In fact, in as little as two weeks, the entire truth might come out. This goes not just for secret relationships, but for anything you start and expect to keep hidden. Be aware of this before you do anything you might soon regret.

The second in this set of eclipses—a Lunar Eclipse—will arrive with the Full Moon of April 4. It will illuminate Libra and your solar seventh house of one-to-one relationships—so again, anything that was hidden will most definitely come to the surface now. Of course, positive news may come along, too. In fact, you might suddenly realize that the person you have been admiring from afar has been doing the same. The second set of eclipses will occur in September. On the 13th, a Solar Eclipse (supercharged New Moon) will make its presence known in your solar sixth house of work and health. Since it will also be wearing Virgo, the sign that rules work and health, you can count on some rather drastic changes in those departments. If you have been thinking of changing your occupation, there's no time like the present. You might also want to consider having a check-up, however. This is a terrific time to take stock of your physical condition. On the 27th of September, a Lunar Eclipse (Full Moon) will illuminate your sign and your solar first house of personality and appearance. Changing your wardrobe might be fun, but dig a little deeper and focus on the first impression you make on others. If it is not what you'd like it to be, figure out how to alter it in a positive way.

Saturn

Serious Saturn, the planet of career and professional matters, also rules our dealings with authority figures and elders—and if you happen to be an authority figure, this planet has an awful lot to do with your daily life. Regardless of whether you're the boss or you work for one, however, you can count on a few more intense months. From June 14 through September 17, Saturn will return to Scorpio, and remember—Scorpio is a fixed water sign that plays for keeps, much like Saturn. This is a powerful astrological combination, and since it has been on duty in your solar eighth house of endings, intimate partners, and joint resources for over a year now, you have probably experienced your share of endings—and possibly losses as well. The good news is that new growth never occurs until there is room for it to live, so whatever has left your life, while possibly quite sad, has made room for you to grow, personally as well as professionally. Finish things up in this department and move on. Saturn will spend the rest of the year in Sagittarius and your solar ninth house of new experiences, so once you've taken care of any loose ends, you'll be free to enjoy new adventures and you'll be given the chance to learn new skills. Traveling and perhaps even visiting your old stomping grounds would be a great way to make use of this thorough energy.

Uranus

Ever since 2011, Aries, this unpredictable energy has been on duty in your sign and your solar first house of personality and appearance—and to be honest, you have probably not minded Uranus's presence here, not for one single minute. Mars may be your ruling planet, but Uranus is just as much fun at times, since he also bestows the gifts of impulse and spontaneity—which, of course, are right up your alley. Uranus also rules groups, so if you have changed peer circles lately, you have probably made quite an impact on them—and they have probably made quite an impact on you as well. The personality changes you and those nearest and dearest to you have noticed in you have probably seemed quite drastic, but if you think about it, they have been brewing for many, many moons. If you were born between April 2 and April 12, you will undergo even more changes this year, however, so don't get too comfortable. You might still be in the mood to alter your physical self, take up a whole new profession, or start something up with someone you would never, ever have seen yourself with—which, of course, will be at least half the fun!

Neptune

If you were born between March 24 and March 30, Aries, you may be feeling a bit confused this year—but then, you might also begin to feel quite creatively inspired. Neptune, the planet of romance, illusion, and altered states, will form a semisextile to your Sun this year, and while this supposedly "minor" aspect is not usually known for creating large-scale events, it most certainly does get the show on the road. Of course, as with all things Neptunian, the effects will be subtle and almost unnoticeable—at first, anyway. Your mission this year is to pay attention to just how keen your antennae have suddenly become, and just how many supposed "coincidences" are coming along. If you do, you will be able to grasp the underlying pattern that has begun to occur in your life, and you will hear the message of this ultra-sensitive goddess. Your creative side will be easier to access now than it has been in a very long while, and you will see inspiration everywhere. Just be sure to keep yourself as far away as possible from negativity. Neptune dissolves boundaries and turns us into psychic sponges, and remember, sponges soak up everything around them. Pay special attention to your dreams, your intuitions, and your gut feelings, which will be quite accurate.

Pluto

Pluto is an all-or-nothing kind of energy, Aries, so he absolutely insists that we give any situation our all—or that we back away entirely and end it. If you were born from late March through April 3, you have already experienced his energy in your solar tenth house of career matters and dealings with authority figures—and some of it may not have been all that pleasant. If you were born between April 3 and April 7, you are about to get to know this planet a whole lot better. Now, since Pluto is affecting you primarily in your solar sector of professional matters, you have probably been feeling the need to make some changes in this area of life for some time now. Fortunately, this year, you will have a built-in safety net to get you through whatever Pluto tosses your way—or takes away, which is his specialty—thanks to generous Jupiter, who will enter your solar sixth house of work on August 11. In short, if you have been champing at the bit to change occupations, this is definitely the year to do it. Your mission is to resist the urge to stay with what seems safe if it means sacrificing your personal happiness.

Aries | January

Planetary Lightspots

January 13 and 14 will be great fun for you, Aries. Chatty Mercury and charming, aesthetic Venus in startling Aquarius will get together with Uranus, the most unpredictable energy in the heavens, who just so happens to be in your sign and your solar first house of personality. Pleasant surprises are due—either for you or because of you.

Relationships

Your sweetheart will necessarily take a back seat to your domestic situation around January 4, as the Full Moon in Cancer illuminates your solar fourth house of home, family matters, and dealings with children. You may need to put romance on hold for a few days, if not a few weeks—but the appreciation you'll receive will make it all worthwhile.

Money and Success

A spending spree might be in order around January 13 or 14, but since you'll probably put in some extra hours at work around January 4 or 5, why not? You deserve it. Oh, and here's a thought. Why not treat someone wonderful to an evening out? The novelty of objects wears out quickly, but good times last forever.

Planetary Hotspots

Mercury, Venus, and Mars will take turns passing through unpredictable Aquarius and your solar eleventh house of goals, friendships, and group activities during the first few weeks of the month, Aries, laying the groundwork for the New Moon there on January 20. It's the perfect time to find and begin associating with like-minded others who share your ideals.

Rewarding Days

4, 13, 14, 20, 22, 27

Challenging Days

2, 3, 15, 16, 30, 31

Aries | February

Planetary Lightspots

If you're single, the Full Moon in Leo on February 3 could bring that situation to an end. The Full Moon will occur in your solar fifth house of lovers and playmates, undoubtedly bringing along at least one new admirer who's quite passionate—and extremely determined to get to know you better. If you're attached, be careful not to make your partner jealous.

Relationships

Venus, the Goddess of Relationships, is wandering through your solar twelfth house of secrets, Aries, all done up in Pisces, which is quite the romantic sign. Clandestine affairs will be tough to resist, especially when Venus meets up with Neptune on February 1, but if you're happily settled, do your best.

Money and Success

Venus is famous for being the Goddess of Love, but she's also in charge of money and possessions. So once she arrives in your sign on February 20, Aries—and meets up with both the Moon and Mars, your very own ruling planet—well, it's easy to see how things could start turning your way, and quite quickly, too.

Planetary Hotspots

February 20 and 21 could bring some serious fireworks, Aries, as Venus and the emotional Moon make contact with red-hot Mars, your ruling planet, who's quite the astrological hothead. If you've been stewing about something, you won't be able to keep it to yourself much longer. Clear the area of unsuspecting bystanders before the battle begins.

Rewarding Days

6, 7, 8, 19, 24, 25, 26

Challenging Days

1, 5, 6, 21, 22, 23

Aries | March

Planetary Lightspots

The Sun, Venus, and Mars will all pass through your sign this month, Aries, livening things up considerably even before the Sun enters your sign on March 20, followed by chatty Mercury on March 30. Obviously, March will fly by like a fast-paced, exciting carnival ride. But then, you love nothing more than adrenaline, so you'll love every minute and probably want to go again!

Relationships

Venus attracts and Mars pursues. They're quite the team, and since they'll both be in your sign and your solar first house of personality for at least half the month, you won't have to lift a pinky to gain the attention of new admirers. Current relationships might be a bit more challenging, though. Plan to do something new and exciting together.

Money and Success

Venus will form a trine with Jupiter on March 4, Aries. You'll have champagne taste and settle for nothing but the best. With these two planets urging you to pull out your checkbook or plastic to have it all, you won't exactly be a font of willpower. If you must binge-spend, don't do it because you're trying to impress someone.

Planetary Hotspots

Be on guard around March 20, Aries, when a total Solar Eclipse will make its presence known in your solar twelfth house of secrets just a few hours before the Sun enters your sign. This could be a confusing and disorienting time, so if you need to, take a few moments alone to sit and think—before you act.

Rewarding Days

1, 3, 4, 9, 25, 26

Challenging Days

10, 11, 15, 16, 27, 28

Aries | April

Planetary Lightspots

Venus will set off for Gemini on April 11, Aries, flitting quickly through your solar third house of conversations and communications. Venus is famous for being magnetic, but right about now, she'll be adding her chatty, charming energy to your own devilishly attractive impulsiveness. Talk about totally unstoppable! Make the approach. Whether it's business or personal, no one could refuse you now.

Relationships

There really is no way for you to avoid attention this month—not with extravagant Jupiter in theatrical Leo and your solar fifth house of lovers. The thing is, you'll need to choose your new flames carefully. Leo is a fixed sign, so once you hook them, there's no throwing them back. If you're attached, it's time to rekindle the fire with your sweetheart.

Money and Success

A pack of planets in your sign will form cooperative trines with lucky Jupiter and career-oriented Saturn, Aries—a very lucky astrological break. Yes, indeed. Now's the time to sit down with higher-ups and let them know exactly how invaluable you are. Don't be shy! Oh, and it's time to open a savings account, too. April 18 through April 22 would be best.

Planetary Hotspots

A total Lunar Eclipse will occur on April 4, Aries, balancing the Sun and the emotional Moon on that celestial seesaw known as your relationship axis. Now, this is the stuff that love at first sight is made of, but sudden decisions to cut your losses and run are also possibly on the agenda. Either way, expect someone new to make a striking impression on you—and vice versa.

Rewarding Days

6, 8, 9, 10, 11, 22, 26

Challenging Days

5, 7, 15, 16, 17

Aries | May

Planetary Lightspots

Over the course of this month, the Sun, Mercury, and Mars will take turns passing through chatty, lighthearted Gemini and your solar third house of conversations and communications. In a nutshell, you have been astrologically scheduled to have some wonderful encounters with fun, interesting people. Your mission, simply, is to feed your brain. Mingle, go back to school, or plan a road trip.

Relationships

There'll be a whole lotta chattin' going on this month, Aries, so you'll have the urge—many times—to ditch your schedule and dash about, boldly exploring new and uncharted worlds. The good news is that there will be no shortage of friends or admirers who'll be eager to go along. Your motto? "The more the merrier!"

Money and Success

With Venus set to spend most of the month in your solar fourth house of home, family members, and dealings with children, Aries, you can count on doing a bit more spending than usual, all due to domestic situations. Nothing urgent, though. Think birthdays, anniversaries, and new arrivals—all terrific excuses to spoil at least one special someone.

Planetary Hotspots

You will be quite unpredictable around May 25 through May 27, Aries, so prepare yourself for just about anything. If you are angry, it will definitely emerge. If you are happy, you will go out of your way to make quite a show of it. Be sure to stay away from potentially volatile situations and negative influences.

Rewarding Days

6, 11, 16, 17, 21

Challenging Days

3, 4, 9, 14, 15, 25, 26, 27

Aries | June

Planetary Lightspots

If you've been thinking of traveling overseas, going back to school, or getting together with an old friend or loved one who lives much too far from you, Aries—well, now's the time. The Full Moon in Sagittarius on June 2 will give you all the fiery energy you need to keep you on track. Go get 'em!

Relationships

Commitments aren't easy decisions, Aries—and with so much out there to conquer and so many potential playmates/opponents, it's understandable that you'd hesitate to sign on any dotted line. Around June 6, however, when loving Venus trines commitment-loving Saturn, you might actually decide it's time to settle down. Yes, it's a shock, but when it's right, it's right. Breathe.

Money and Success

Your solar fifth house of fun and recreation will play host to Venus, the planetary ruler of love and money, and Jupiter, who expands everything he touches. Will you be spending a bit more on entertainment and evenings out? You might, but the good news is that you'll have so much fun, you won't mind seeing the bills next month.

Planetary Hotspots

Better watch that famous temper of yours around June 14, Aries. The Sun will collide with Mars—your very own red planet, by the way—right smack dab in the middle of your solar third house of communications. Yes, indeed, this might indicate an argument of epic proportions, since the contenders are the heavens' two fireballs. You're guaranteed an adrenaline rush, though, so the news isn't all bad.

Rewarding Days

2, 5, 6, 8, 9, 10, 28

Challenging Days

11, 12, 13, 15, 23, 24

Aries | July

Planetary Lightspots

Of the two Full Moons scheduled this month, Aries, the second looks to be especially beneficial for you, most especially in the department of friendships and group endeavors. You'll need to be patient until July 31, however, which won't be easy. But at that point, you'll rightfully assume the position that you know is yours.

Relationships

For much of this month, Aries, you'll feel pulled between career matters and family issues. At times, you might even feel that you're actually the center of a tug of war. The good news is that if you're smart—which you are—you'll be able to juggle both areas of life and then some, especially since you have endless energy.

Money and Success

The first Full Moon of the month will occur in your solar tenth house of career matters, Aries, and since it will make its mark in hardworking Capricorn, you will might actually, finally, be rewarded for all your hard work. Cement your relationships with authority figures and elders, too.

Planetary Hotspots

The New Moon on July 15 will help you make a new beginning in the department of home, family, and domestic matters. Up until then, you'll probably be champing at the bit to move, redecorate, or figure out a new, more positive domestic situation. Well, you can breathe easy now. Remember, help is on the way.

Rewarding Days

1, 2, 3, 5, 22, 23, 31

Challenging Days

11, 12, 14, 15, 18, 24, 25

Aries | August

Planetary Lightspots

Several planets in dramatic, theatrical Leo will spend much of the month in your solar fifth house of fun, Aries, so if you're creatively inclined and love what you do, keep creating. It doesn't matter what you create. Music, dance, art, or anything that allows you to do what you most love to do will earn you a bow.

Relationships

Leo planets are fiery, romantic critters, Aries, and with so many on duty now, convincing you to get out there and mingle won't be tough. Someone charming, entertaining, and not too hard on the eyes could be along shortly, so if you're single, keep yours open. Relationships with kids will go well, too, especially around the New Moon on August 14.

Money and Success

Until August 11, Venus will be working closely with Jupiter, who expands the energy of any planet he touches. With these two benefics joining hands in your solar fifth house of speculation, it's easy to imagine you doing just fine financially, especially if you invest your time, effort, and resources in a creative project. But hey—no gambling!

Planetary Hotspots

There's really no way to describe your August without smiling, Aries, thanks to all those Leo planets so determined to amp you up and force you to enjoy yourself. If there's any way you can arrange to take a vacation now, do it. You'll have the time of your life, especially if you leave on August 4 or 7.

Rewarding Days

2, 4, 7, 13, 14, 15, 16

Challenging Days

3, 5, 6, 21, 31

Aries | September

Planetary Lightspots

September could be a fun, exciting time for you, Aries. While it might pale in comparison to last month, if you're in the mood for a whole new beginning, you'll have plenty of astrological help on hand to get you started. Your mission will be to stay interested long enough to see the fruits of your efforts.

Relationships

On September 17, Mercury will turn retrograde in your solar seventh house of one-to-one encounters, and you'll have plenty of opportunities to retrace your steps with regard to relationship issues. If you're not happy with a recent decision you've made, undo it, but prepare yourself. This might not be the last time you rethink the matter.

Money and Success

With generous, benevolent Jupiter in your solar sixth house of work and health, Aries, money matters should go quite well—and yes, this certainly might include that raise, bonus, or promotion you've been pushing so hard for. Remember, Jupiter is like Santa Claus. Get your wish list together and sit down with a higher-up for a chat.

Planetary Hotspots

Two eclipses will occur this month, Aries, and while the first, a Solar Eclipse, will bring startling new changes to your solar sixth house of work and health, it's really the Lunar Eclipse on September 27 that will shake things up. It will cast a spotlight on your solar first house of personality and appearance, urging you to make some serious lifestyle changes.

Rewarding Days
7, 8, 21, 22, 29, 30

Challenging Days
9, 10, 16, 17, 24, 25

Aries | October

Planetary Lightspots

A lucky break will come your way around October 25 or 27. You'll be in the right place at the right time to impress all the right people and be intuitively tuned in to exactly what you need to do to get where you want to be. Don't be afraid to ask an elder or higher-up for advice.

Relationships

You'll have yet another chance for a new romance this year, Aries, thanks to the New Moon on October 12, all done up in partner-pleasing Libra and your solar seventh house of relationships. Of course, it might be that you've already started up with someone and you're now ready to commit. Yes, that is a rarity for you, but when it's right, it's right.

Money and Success

A money matter you've been working hard to solve will come to a happy conclusion on October 27, when the Full Moon in Taurus illuminates your solar second house of personal finances. Taurus just loves material possessions and is happy to work hard to have them, so plan on putting in some overtime for a special item, a trip, or a gift for a loved one.

Planetary Hotspots

If you've been thinking of making a change job-wise or even pursuing something new, you'd do well to plan it for October 8 or 17. Several planets in hardworking Virgo and your solar sixth house of work will inspire you to make the right decision. Even if it seems sudden to others, you'll know it's the right thing to do.

Rewarding Days

7, 8, 9, 12, 13, 17, 23

Challenging Days

5, 6, 10, 21, 22, 25

Aries | November

Planetary Lightspots

This month, several planets will move into Sagittarius, a fire sign you've always gotten along famously with. This merry pack will encourage you to broaden your horizons and open your mind. Whether you choose education, travel, or new experiences, you'll enjoy every moment of your "lessons." There are teachers everywhere now. Ask questions, but remember, you're a teacher too.

Relationships

Good news, Aries. Loving Venus will enter your solar seventh house of one-to-one relationships on November 8, wearing Libra, the sign that most loves to couple up. This could be the finishing touch if you're seeing someone new. If you're already attached, you two will likely discover new ways to amuse and entertain each other, and grow much closer in the process.

Money and Success

Jupiter's presence in your solar sixth house has inspired you to work really hard, and you haven't had much time to yourself. But the New Moon in your solar eighth house of joint finances and responsibilities on November 11 will inspire you to have a long chat with someone who isn't pulling their share of the weight. You might also need to deal with taxes or an inheritance.

Planetary Hotspots

Luck will definitely be on your side this month, Aries, thanks primarily to a pack of planets in generous Sagittarius. Opportunities to meet new, interesting people will abound, and at least one of your new acquaintances might tickle your fancy in far more than a simply platonic way. Your mission is to stay open to all new ideas.

Rewarding Days

8, 9, 10, 20, 22, 23, 24

Challenging Days

2, 3, 14, 21, 25, 26, 29

Aries | December

Planetary Lightspots

The New Moon on December 11 will bring you yet another chance to travel, and to make quite a trek of it. This lighthearted lunation will bring the Sun and Moon together and easily persuade you to take a bit of time off—which, at this point, you richly deserve. Even if it's just a weekend, treat yourself.

Relationships

Fiery Mars, your ruling planet, is still on duty in your solar seventh house of committed relationships, and wherever this guy goes, passion follows. Now, this might be a good thing if you have been trying to rekindle a flame, but the potential for arguments and disputes is also there. Mind your manners, but don't allow yourself to be used.

Money and Success

Keeping you focused on anything might be tough this month, Aries, with Mercury and the Sun still making their way through fun-loving Sagittarius and your solar ninth house of new experiences, but you should definitely not forget to pay attention to money matters. In particular, joint finances, credit cards, and checking accounts may need to be looked over—with a fine-tooth comb.

Planetary Hotspots

The Full Moon on December 25 will occur in Cancer, just in time for a lovely holiday season. Your focus will turn to family, children, and friends you consider extended family. What a wonderful time to open up your home to your loved ones! You might be a bit overworked, but if anyone can muster up some energy, it's you. Have the whole gang over.

Rewarding Days

1, 2, 3, 8, 24, 25, 30

Challenging Days

4, 5, 13, 14, 20, 28, 29

Aries Action Table

These dates reflect the best—but not the only—times for success and ease in these activities, according to your Sun sign.

	JAN	FEB	MAR	APR	MAY	JUN	JUL	AUG	SEP	OCT	NOV	DEC
Move	4				17							26, 29
Start a class	5, 22, 30	19		2, 9		10					20, 22, 24, 29	
Join a club	13, 14, 20, 27	2	1					4				
Ask for a raise	4, 13		17, 27, 30			6	1			15		24
Look for work	4, 5, 22	24, 25, 26			5, 6	5, 6, 8	2, 3		5, 23	8		
Get pro advice	4	24, 25		2		6, 7, 8	18, 22	6				
Get a loan					17				5	23, 25	10	
See a doctor		8					26					
Start a diet	4, 22			15					23			
End relationship	30		4	4, 15				5, 21, 31			2, 23	
Buy clothes			17					4		27		
Get a makeover		20				28		14	8	27		
New romance	19	1, 7	3, 9	22, 26	16	28	5	4, 8	22			
Vacation			3, 9			2, 22				25	10	10, 30

Taurus

The Bull
April 19 to May 20

♉

Element: Earth	Glyph: Bull's head
Quality: Fixed	Anatomy: Throat, neck
Polarity: Yin/feminine	Color: Green
Planetary Ruler: Venus	Animal: Cattle
Meditation: I trust myself and others	Myths/Legends: Isis and Osiris, Ceridwen, Bull of Minos
Gemstone: Emerald	House: Second
Power Stones: Diamond, blue lace agate, rose quartz	Opposite Sign: Scorpio
	Flower: Violet
Key Phrase: I have	Keyword: Conservation

The Taurus Personality

Your Strengths and Challenges

Your sign is composed of the earth element and the fixed quality—which basically makes you a rock, Taurus. You're impossible to move when you've decided to stay put and just as impossible to throw off track once you've decided on your course. It's like trying to dig into frozen ground or lift a shovel of earth that's soaked. This basic description, via the astrological influences that make you who you are, might sound a bit simplistic, but they certainly do explain the one thing that every Sun sign book and every astrologer will tell you, and rightly so: You're stubborn. Yep. It's true. You're really, really stubborn. Now, that's not a "bad" thing. After all, how do you get anywhere in life if you don't apply yourself and stick to a plan? Determination, focus, and hard work are all required, and you're not afraid of any of those. The thing is, you sometimes hold on too tight and for too long, even when it's obvious to others that the mission you're on should be aborted. You will, however, leave a situation or relationship behind once it becomes clear to you that what you've invested in it isn't equal to what you're getting out of it—which, again, makes you the very soul of practicality. You're slow and cautious, too, so you always have a fail-safe lined up. If Plan A doesn't work out, Plan B will. That goes for jobs and relationships, but even more so when it comes to acquiring and keeping money and possessions—and speaking of which, here's another infallible truism about your sign: What's yours is yours. And that's that.

Your Relationships

Speaking of being fixed, Taurus, and taking into consideration the alleged fact that you might possibly be just a tad stubborn, let's talk about how you behave when you're involved—which is most of the time. When you settle down, it's because you've thought it through carefully and decided that this person is and will continue to be solid and reliable—your first priority in all relationships. The good news is that when times are tough, you won't simply cut your losses and go. Without even realizing you're doing it, you'll assess the situation. If A (the time you've invested) plus B (the probability of this thing lasting a very long time, albeit with a little work) is less than X (the irritation and futility factor), then you'll dig right in and get to work repairing any damage that's been done, and there's nothing you won't do to pull that off.

Of course, if you're willing to see a relationship through the long haul, it's because you believe you've found someone who's truly worthy. To earn that rating, they need to be capable of pulling their own weight, both financially and with regard to domestic responsibilities, and of returning the physical affection your ruling planet, Venus, ensures you'll offer regularly. You only choose partners you respect, so a strong work ethic and an innate ability to buck up and weather the storm are just two of the qualities you seek out. That said, if there's a bump in the road, you'll ride over it and back up—as many times as it takes to level it out. There's no sign that more enjoys the creature comforts our lovely planet has to offer, so when you settle down, it's often with another of the physical earth signs—Virgo or Capricorn—because they, too, understand the material side of life. Most important, however, is that your partner makes all of your senses happy—no easy task, since you're such a connoisseur—so you also do well with sexy, intense Scorpio.

Your Career and Money

Your reputation for enjoying the best of what life has to offer is also well earned. You aren't afraid to pay top dollar for premium goods and first-class accommodations. Quite necessarily, however, this means not spending a single dime until you've found exactly what you're looking for. At times, this ultra-practical side of your fiscal nature can lead others to believe that you're a bit too frugal. The truth is, you don't mind opening your wallet, just as long as you're sure you're going to get the best and nothing but—and what's wrong with that? The possessive side of your nature (remember, your keywords are "I have") extends into all areas of life, but quality, not quantity, is always first and foremost on your mind. If you want it, it's The Best. Hands down. The good news is that you can afford it. Your self-assuredness and self-confidence are absolutely unshakable—a tremendous plus when you're out to negotiate a salary.

Your Lighter Side

Physical pleasure is what you crave the most, Taurus, so when it comes to enjoying yourself, you go after the richest foods, the finest wines, the best seats, and the most appealing companions. You're an expert at finding the best the five senses have to offer. It's your astrological job—so why would you even think of settling for anything less? Exactly. You wouldn't.

Affirmation for the Year
My closest relationships are my paths to transformation.

The Year Ahead for Taurus

Like all of us, Taurus, you'll be enjoying the combined attention of loving Venus, your oh-so-personable ruling planet, and outgoing, generous Jupiter, both of whom will be in Leo for much of the coming year. Jupiter will stay on duty until August 11, and Venus will make two passes through this romantic, fiery sign, from June 5 to July 18 and again from July 31 through October 8. Both planets will be showing off and turning up the drama-thermometer in your solar fourth house of home, emotions, and family matters, so expect all kinds of sudden events to come your way through those who are nearest and dearest to your heart—and lots of blessings, too.

Jupiter expands the planets he touches and the houses he affects, so it's not hard to imagine you moving long-distance, doing an expensive renovation, or even adding a room to your nest. Your family might also expand due to a wonderful new arrival. All that said, a creative pursuit you work on from home is due to turn into a nice, tidy, part-time income. If you hang on and keep at it—and the fixed nature of Leo just about guarantees that you will—that hobby turned side job could end up being your primary source of income. That's great news. After all, how many of us actually love our work? Make this a goal, because if you've ever thought about working at home, this is the year to give it a shot. Put your creations out there and pay attention to how well received they are. Take note of who's interested in them, too. Once you know your demographics, you'll be better able to produce what your audience craves the most. Of course, romantic love is also under Leo's jurisdiction, as well as Venus's, so if you're somehow still miraculously single, don't even think about turning down a family member's offer to introduce you to someone they're positive would be just perfect for you. No matter what happened last time, they may be right. Just stick to the blind-date rules and don't sign up for anything more than coffee or lunch the first time you meet. At the very least, you'll probably end up with an extremely entertaining new friend. In fact, over the course of this transit, you'll probably end up the proud owner of all kinds of interesting new acquaintances.

Even after Jupiter leaves playful Leo behind, however, don't worry about your social schedule slowing down. In fact, it will likely pick up after August 11, when Jupiter makes his way into your solar fifth house of lovers and playmates. Remember, Jupiter specializes in expansion and excess, but "lots" doesn't always mean "better." Your mission after he arrives will be to remain true to your philosophy—that quality is always better than quantity. You deserve nothing but the best, and you know it, so Jupiter in choosy Virgo will be more than happy to indulge you. Anyone thinking of approaching you with romance on their mind should have that fact memorized before they take a single step. Inform them. Nicely.

Now, let's talk about Saturn, who finally left Scorpio and your solar seventh house of one-to-one relationships late in December of 2014. This responsible guy seems to think there's something you've left undone, but he's nothing if not fair, so he'll return to Scorpio from June 14 through September 17 to give you one last try at getting everything taken care of. Marital problems that haven't been ironed out would be best tended to through the help of a professional with great references. If that doesn't work, it might be time to cut your losses and move on, which is always tough for you once you've invested your time, energy, and emotions. Any partnership that isn't positive won't stand up to Saturn's scrutiny, however.

Uranus, Neptune, and Pluto will remain where they have been for years. Uranus will continue on his trek through your solar twelfth house of Privacy, Please, but this startling guy just loves to spring surprises on us, so if you've been hiding something and you're convinced it's never, ever going to emerge, think again and prepare yourself. When Uranus unleashes something, the truth arrives suddenly and unpredictably. Safeguard those secrets. Don't trust just anyone if you never want to hear about them again. Your best bet might be to only confide in someone who's hired with the understanding that your privacy will be strictly honored.

Speaking of hired professionals, that theme holds true for the influence of Pluto in Capricorn, too, who is making his way through your solar ninth house of legal matters, insisting that you put an issue to bed with the help of a professional who knows what they're doing and isn't afraid to tell you the unvarnished truth. Pluto will continue to square off with Uranus yet again this year, however, so expect to feel pressured in many ways, most especially with regard to the timing of major life changes. Neptune's presence in your solar eleventh house of friendships and group affiliations will bring you close to spiritual and metaphysical groups, which is where you really should be. It's important that you mix and mingle with gentle, positive energy this year. Anything other than that will be positively painful.

What This Year's Eclipses Mean for You

Four eclipses are scheduled for 2015, Taurus, and even though none of them will occur in your sign, like all of us, you can still count on being affected by them. On March 20, the New Moon will turn into the first Solar Eclipse of the year. It will occur in Pisces and your solar eleventh house of friendships, and will join Neptune there to clean house. Neptune has been working on this project for quite a few years now, and her methods are gradual. Eclipses, however, are startling and striking, so if you have been trying to "do the Neptune" and ease delicately away from tough situations, you might just stop tiptoeing and start running. Friendships and groups with those who no longer share your ideals and beliefs will absolutely have to go, so resolve right now not to try to hang on. Neptune has laid the groundwork, but this eclipse will finish things up. Quickly.

The first total Lunar Eclipse will arrive on April 4, all done up in partner-oriented Libra and your solar sixth house of work and relationships with coworkers. Like last year right around this time, you might find that working alone just isn't the way to go and that you'd be far more inspired by sharing with a partner. Starting up a business is once again a possibility, but even if you work for someone else, the urge to bounce your ideas off of someone is a good one. If you're attracted to someone you work with, be careful, and be sure you can return to a working relationship if things don't work out.

The second Solar Eclipse will arrive on September 13 in Virgo and your solar fifth house of lovers, so if you haven't already signed up with that coworker or you tried it but things didn't go as planned, you might be shopping for a new flame in the fall. The good news is that this eclipse will happily bring along a number of applicants for the job, all of whom will need to bring with them the best of Virgo, including stability, practicality, and financial security. Anyone who doesn't possess those qualities will be dismissed—if you notice them at all.

The last eclipse of the year will be a Lunar Eclipse, occurring on September 27. This supercharged Full Moon will set up shop in your solar twelfth house of behind-the-scenes activities, all done up in fiery, assertive Aries. Now, Aries is too impulsive to wait, and certainly has no time to spare, so if you've been holding on to a secret and waiting for the right time to let it out, the decision may be made for you by this impetuous lunation. Just be sure not to hurt anyone who won't see this major revelation coming. Warn all parties concerned.

Saturn

Saturn left your solar seventh house of one-to-one relationships late in December of 2014, asking that you resolve all joint financial matters fairly and firmly in time for the new year—and in time to give yourself a much-needed breather. If you cooperated and made those changes, you're probably already feeling as if a huge weight has been lifted from your shoulders, especially if you were solely responsible for bringing home the bacon but now have some solid, reliable help. If you haven't yet laid down the law in that department, better get busy. You'll have three more months of Saturn's help, but you'll need to take advantage of it during his last pass through Scorpio, from June 14 through September 17.

The thing is, this issue of shared resources and responsibilities won't be going away any time soon. In fact, for the rest of the year, you'll enjoy Saturn's company in your solar eighth house, which just so happens to deal with shared income, among other things. It would be best to get finances settled as soon as possible, because one of those "other things" this house is in charge of includes intimate relationships, a far more pleasant use of Saturn's stability and reliability. If you were seeing someone casually last year, you might find that you have a lot more in common than you thought. Why, you might even be able to spend time alone without speaking, the greatest intimacy of them all. From the comfort you'll find in this grounded relationship in 2015, you'll be able to pursue your career goals without being distracted.

Uranus

If you were born between May 3 and May 13, you'll feel the full impact of this startling planet in your life this year. Fortunately, since the aspect it's making to your Sun is a semisextile, you won't be as dramatically affected as you might be—but this certainly doesn't mean Uranus's influence will go unnoticed. In particular, since this planet is working his way through your solar twelfth house of subconscious thoughts and desires, you might occasionally feel that something unbidden is surfacing, and suddenly, too. If it's memories from the past that are less than pleasant, this would be a terrific time to meet with a psychiatrist or spiritual counselor. If you're remembering times from the past that are positive—times you find yourself longing to return to—try to remain objective and think it through. You might simply be wishing for the freedom another time in your life afforded. Your personal freedom will definitely be an issue now, but it's up to you to find a way to achieve it under your present circumstances. Now, with this independent-minded planet influencing you in a relatively gentle way, even though sharing responsibilities and allowing others to step in isn't easy for you, it will be a bit easier now. Take full advantage of Uranus's energy to make seemingly minor changes that will lead to a major lightening up of restrictions, rules, responsibilities, and anything else that might be standing in your way.

Neptune

Neptune is still making her way through her favorite sign, woozy Pisces, which means she's still working her way through your solar eleventh house of groups, social acquaintances, and friendships. So you've probably already gotten used to the idea that some friends may come and go, but those who are truly kindred spirits will last forever—just like family ties. If you were born between April 25 and April 30, Neptune will make this point crystal-clear during 2015. You may learn her lesson in a less than pleasant way, but instead of focusing on those who leave your life, give thanks for those who remain. You'll be able to invest your trust in them without any worries, and they'll feel the same about you. If you're looking to replace a person or group, think about metaphysical or spiritual groups. Choose those that appeal to you because they'll eventually help you achieve your inner goals, and when you sign up to become a member, be sure it's with an open heart. This time is all about opening up, so twelve-step groups are a great idea, but any gathering of gentle, like-minded others will work just fine. Check out yoga, meditation, and metaphysical groups in particular, where smiling spiritual folks often come together.

Pluto

If you were born between May 2 and May 7, you have probably already gotten used to Pluto's presence in your solar ninth house of new experiences, long-distance travel, and education, urging you to choose a belief system and stick to it, no matter what. The intensity of this planet will pick up considerably for you this year, however, as Pluto directly contacts your Sun. The good news is that Pluto's influence will arrive via an easy trine, so the gifts he brings—stamina, perseverance, and determination—will all be readily available to you during 2015. Of course, you already own those gifts by virtue of being a fixed earth sign, but the volume will be turned up on high now. During this period, think of yourself as being temporarily endowed with superpowers, and in particular with the ability to weather any storm and come out of it feeling not exhausted, but refreshed and renewed. This house also rules politics, so if you've ever been drawn to that field, you have the astrological ammunition to begin a political career now. If you're so inclined, keep in mind that Pluto loves to dig, however, so be prepared for your past to emerge. That means all of it, for better or worse. No matter what type of transit Pluto is making or which planet he's visiting, obsessive behavior is always a possibility, so if someone you love tries to tell you that you're a bit too focused on a certain person or issue, you'd do well to pay attention. With Pluto on board, it's easy to miss that fact, and too much involvement in the lives of loved ones might drive them away.

Taurus | January

Planetary Lightspots

The Full Moon on January 4 will light up ultra-sensitive Cancer and your solar third house of communications and conversations, Taurus, and you'll find that your already soothing voice is even more reassuring. You'll be out to comfort others the best way you know how—by quieting their nerves and assuring them that all will be well.

Relationships

After January 3, you'll be dealing with Venus, the Goddess of Love, who'll be all dressed up in rebellious, quirky Aquarius. Now, Venus is your ruling planet, Taurus, so you'll definitely make do, but it would still be a good idea to prepare yourself. Odd and unusual new admirers will abound, rather than the usual well-dressed, successful suitors you usually attract.

Money and Success

Venus, the Goddess of Love and Money, will spend January 3 through January 27 in your solar tenth house of career matters and dealings with authority figures. She's an absolute money magnet, so if you're shopping for a raise or bonus, now is the time to address the issue. Be sure to let all parties concerned know exactly how hard you try to get it all right.

Planetary Hotspots

You are not usually one to make a scene, Taurus, but with fiery Mars spending most of the month in your solar eleventh house of friendships and groups, the decision may be out of your hands. This feisty guy will storm the doors of this house, demanding that you take credit where and when it's due, even if it means ruffling a few feathers.

Rewarding Days

4, 5, 12, 22, 23, 27

Challenging Days

1, 3, 15, 16, 18, 19, 30

Taurus | February

Planetary Lightspots

Between February 19 and 21, several planets will collide in red-hot Aries, the sign that never did know how to wait, pace itself, or sit tight. The spontaneity of this sign is quite appealing, and since this lively pack of planets will be in your solar twelfth house of secrets, you may find your adrenaline level being raised by someone you can't quite have at the moment. Careful!

Relationships

Until February 20, loving Venus will tiptoe through romantic Pisces, the astro-child of dreamy Neptune. This will put the Goddess of Love in cahoots with the Goddess of Fantasies and Romance—as they're both transiting your solar eleventh house of friendships. It certainly sounds like someone you think of platonically might suddenly look very, very different to you, especially around February 1.

Money and Success

Your ruling planet, Venus, rules both love and money matters, Taurus. Once she enters impetuous Aries and your solar twelfth house of secrets on February 20, she'll inspire you to spend a bit of money you don't have on something you won't be able to show off. A gift, perhaps, for someone you aren't supposed to know quite so well? Careful.

Planetary Hotspots

Don't sign anything that's legally or financially binding until at least February 11, when Mercury finally turns direct in Aquarius and your solar tenth house of career matters. You might think you have all the information you need to make an informed decision, but then again, what if you don't?

Rewarding Days
2, 7, 8, 19, 24, 25

Challenging Days
5, 6, 20, 21, 22, 23

Taurus | March

Planetary Lightspots

If you need some extra energy to put the finishing touches on a particularly challenging project, you'll have it at ready access this month. Mars and Jupiter will charge you up on March 10, and on March 30 and 31, Venus and Mars will inspire you to put your charm and smoothness to work on anyone who tries to stall you.

Relationships

The Full Moon on March 5 will set up shop in your solar fifth house of lovers and playmates, Taurus. She'll be all done up in Virgo, an earth sign like your own that knows how to choose potential partners rationally and practically. If you cross paths with someone who's well dressed and endlessly confident, don't let them escape without getting their number.

Money and Success

Oh my! Your very own ruling planet, Venus, will step seductively into your sign on March 17, followed by Mars on March 31. Now, you're already famous for being a money magnet, Taurus, but with the Goddess of Attraction working together with the God of Pursuit, there's not much you won't be able to capture. Just bide your time until the end of the month.

Planetary Hotspots

A total Solar Eclipse will occur on March 20, all done up in dreamy Pisces. This will bring the Sun and Moon together in your solar eleventh house of friendships and groups, just hours before the Sun storms off into assertive Aries. If you need to make a point, there's no better time to lay down that hoof and be sure you're heard.

Rewarding Days
2, 3, 6, 9, 17, 23, 30, 31

Challenging Days
4, 11, 12, 16, 26, 27

Taurus | April

Planetary Lightspots

Lunar Eclipses often act much like striking Uranus himself, so being prepared for what might come is critical. In this case, on April 4, the emotional Moon in partner-oriented Libra and your solar sixth house of relationships with coworkers will be on center stage, so prepare yourself. A crush or infatuation is about to be made public.

Relationships

Right up until April 11, loving Venus, your very own seductive ruling planet, will be in your very own sign. Yes, this does mean that you'll be a magnet for the attention of others, and yes, this does mean that you'll have your choice. If you're attached, however, behave yourself! Why risk what you have for a fling?

Money and Success

You're definitely magnetic, Taurus, and what you tend to attract is love and money. So with your ruling planet, Venus, on duty in your sign until April 11, you will most definitely be able to have what you want. That much is a given. Just be careful what you wish for. The career you crave may be en route, but there could be some serious strings attached.

Planetary Hotspots

Arguments over money matters could spring up around April 20 or 22, so if you're at odds with a loved one over a financial matter, keeping your distance right around this time might be best. On the other hand, if you want to clear the air and you don't mind some fireworks in the process, think again.

Rewarding Days
1, 2, 3, 6, 12, 21, 22

Challenging Days
4, 5, 7, 8, 15, 17, 20

Taurus | May

Planetary Lightspots

The Full Moon on May 3 will set up shop in your solar seventh house of one-to-one relationships, Taurus. It will be wearing sexy Scorpio at the time, and since you and Scorpio are definitely on the same page when it comes to touching, you should probably cancel all your evening appointments and indulge.

Relationships

Your ruling planet, Venus, will tiptoe into emotional Cancer on May 7. She'll be setting up shop in your solar third house of communications, asking that you bring some sympathy to all your conversations—and maybe even offer up a bit of your earthy, grounded TLC to wipe away those tears.

Money and Success

The New Moon on May 17 will occur in your sign, Taurus, and since New Moons are a terrific time for new beginnings and you just so happen to be a money magnet, you may be considering going out on your own and ditching the boss. Fine, but make your new venture part-time to start with. You need financial security, and it won't be available just yet.

Planetary Hotspots

On May 27, chatty Mercury will collide with assertive Mars in your solar second house of personal finances, Taurus, and you may feel the need to take fast action to resolve a debt. Whether it's owed to you or it's a debt you need to take care of, get it done fast and you won't have to stress about it anymore.

Rewarding Days

5, 6, 7, 11, 16, 17

Challenging Days

2, 3, 4, 9, 21, 25, 29

Taurus | June

Planetary Lightspots

The Full Moon on June 2 will be in excessive Sagittarius and your solar eighth house of intimate encounters, Taurus. Now, sex definitely fits this description, so you might be MIA from your usual group gatherings for a couple of days right around then. Remember, though, that there are many ways to be intimate. It might be that someone who worships you really needs to talk.

Relationships

Venus will spend most of the month in dramatic Leo and your solar fourth house of home, family, and domestic matters. There may be some passion coming your way, but the good news is that it might just be that the date nights you plan actually happen the way they should. Kids will draw your attention in a very big way, too.

Money and Success

If you want to earn some extra money this month, Taurus, look to June 6 and June 10. At those times, Venus will be working closely with other heavenly allies to put you in touch with at least one someone who'll admire your steadfastness and determination enough to make you a delicious offer.

Planetary Hotspots

Lucky, generous Jupiter will form a lovely, cooperative trine with startling Uranus on June 22, Taurus—and if anyone should buy a lottery ticket right around then, it's you. You might not win the entire lotto, but it's hard to imagine you walking away with nothing. Remember, though—one ticket. Not a thousand.

Rewarding Days

5, 6, 7, 8, 9, 10, 22, 28

Challenging Days

14, 15, 23, 29, 30

Taurus | July

Planetary Lightspots

The Full Moon on July 31 will join hands with Venus, your own magnetic ruling planet, to give you a shot at a whole new career, Taurus. If you've been toying with the idea but not yet made up your mind—well, what's the holdup? The Universe is ready to support you. Take the month to lay the groundwork, then get the show on the road!

Relationships

Saturn has made his way back into your solar seventh house of committed relationships, and he won't be here again for another twenty-nine and a half years, Taurus. Obviously, this time period calls for some serious thought, but if someone much older or younger than you appeals to your heart, stop doing the math and focus on the positives.

Money and Success

Mercury is the ultimate multitasker, and he'll be on duty in your solar second house of finances until July 8, Taurus. Now, you've already had some time to put him to work finding you new opportunities to work for yourself, but if he still hasn't pulled through with the right introductions, hang tough. Help is on the way.

Planetary Hotspots

The New Moon on July 15 will work together with several edgy oppositions to pit your solar third house of conversations and communications against your solar ninth house of new adventures and educational experiences. If you need to learn something new, there's no time like the present to sign up. In your personal life, expect a bit of drama.

Rewarding Days

1, 2, 5, 8, 13, 21, 22, 31

Challenging Days

6, 7, 12, 14, 15, 18, 25

Taurus | August

Planetary Lightspots

You have an excellent sense of humor, Taurus, which most folks don't often get to hear. Around August 7, however, talkative Mercury will team up with Jupiter, the original stand-up comedian, and you'll have a chance to show it off. Take it. You'll surprise a few folks who really need to be surprised!

Relationships

Oh, baby! This is what you've been waiting for, Taurus. Generous, excessive Jupiter has made his way into your solar fifth house of lovers, so you won't be spending much time alone over the coming year—at least, not unless you want to. Jupiter always travels with an entourage of interesting, fiery folks, so your list of prospective partners will become a very, very long one. Enjoy!

Money and Success

Wherever Venus goes, money follows, so now that she's at the start of her extra-long trip through dramatic Leo and your solar fourth house of home, emotions, and money matters, you should be seriously thinking about how to turn your home into at least a part-time source of income. Create a workshop, or move some fold-up chairs into the living room and host a class.

Planetary Hotspots

If you're recently separated or just now ready to begin dating again, get yourself out there around August 26, when excessive Jupiter will come together with the Sun in your solar fifth house of lovers. You'll be amazed at the lovely array of admirers who'll be there for the taking.

Rewarding Days

1, 2, 4, 11, 13, 19, 25, 26

Challenging Days

3, 5, 6, 7, 20, 21, 31

Taurus | September

Planetary Lightspots

A total Lunar Eclipse will occur in your solar twelfth house of secrets on September 27, all done up in fiery, impulsive Aries. Now, you're usually very patient, but right about now, you won't be willing to take no for an answer. If you have to lure someone behind closed doors to successfully coax them into keeping quiet, you'll do a fine job of it.

Relationships

The Sun will set off for other-oriented Libra on September 23, joining chatty Mercury there to make quite the charming splash in your solar sixth house of work, Taurus. Yes, you may still be flirting with a coworker, and yes, they are probably flirting right back. The thing is, you'll still need to work together if it doesn't work out. Are you up for that?

Money and Success

On September 17, serious Saturn will reenter Sagittarius and your solar eighth house of shared resources, where he'll stay for the next two years, at least. During this time, you may experience some very intimidating battles over money and inheritances, and you may need to get a loan. Your mission is to resist the urge to overextend your credit.

Planetary Hotspots

A Solar Eclipse will activate your solar fifth house of love affairs on September 13, Taurus, urging you to start something new in this tender department. If you're attached, your mission will be to figure out if that's how you want to be. If it is, it's time to romance your partner—seriously. If you're single, get out there. Fate is waiting for you.

Rewarding Days

4, 5, 8, 22, 23, 28

Challenging Days

9, 10, 13, 17, 24, 25, 30

Taurus | October

Planetary Lightspots

The Full Moon set to illuminate the heavens on October 27 will occur in your sign, Taurus, and since this just so happens to be your solar first house of personality and appearance, you'll probably feel quite energized and oh-so-ready to make physical changes. Go for it! It's time to be even prouder of what you see in the mirror every morning.

Relationships

On October 8, the emotional Moon will come together with loving Venus, your ruler, in your solar fifth house of lovers. When these two energies get together, there's no doubt that an attraction is possible—or probable, really. Your mission is to get out there and find someone who's delicious enough to keep you by their side for the long run.

Money and Success

Venus is your very own ruling planet, and she's the cosmic purveyor of the purse strings, Taurus, and you tend to follow where she leads. So while she's on duty in Virgo and your solar fifth house of speculation, you'll be lucky. This might be the right time to take a chance and invest in a scratch ticket, but don't get carried away or you'll defeat the purpose.

Planetary Hotspots

On October 17, fiery Mars will collide with Jupiter, who never fails to expand the energy of any planet he touches. If you were angry before that, you'll be even angrier, so beware of potentially volatile situations. If your passions have been smoldering, it won't be long before they turn into a full-fledged bonfire. Ready?

Rewarding Days
7, 8, 13, 15, 23, 30, 31

Challenging Days
5, 6, 9, 10, 17, 18, 25, 26

Taurus | November

Planetary Lightspots

If you're feeling a bit more talkative than usual this month, Taurus, it's not surprising. As of November 2, chatty Mercury will be making his merry way through your solar seventh house of personal encounters. The good news is that the Universe will see to it that there are plenty of formal and informal chat sessions to keep your mind busy—and maybe your heart, too.

Relationships

Mercury will set off for your solar seventh house of one-to-one relationships on November 2, where he'll stay until November 20. This time will be lots of fun for you, Taurus. Even if you're hanging out at home, you can expect some delightfully interesting company to keep your mind occupied. Okay, and maybe the rest of you, too...

Money and Success

If you're in love with a particular hobby or craft, Taurus, and you think you can turn it into a permanent source of at least part-time income, there's no time like the present to do a test run. On November 2, magnetic Venus and aggressive Mars will come together, determined to find you a receptive audience, no matter what.

Planetary Hotspots

The Full Moon on November 25 will occur in your solar second house of personal finances. This bright light will insist that you take a look at what you're bringing in and what you're spending. The good news is that you're ready to make some creative changes in the way you handle your money matters.

Rewarding Days
5, 6, 7, 10, 13, 14

Challenging Days
2, 3, 11, 19, 20, 24, 26, 29

Taurus | December

Planetary Lightspots

The Full Moon on December 25 will make this a particularly wonderful time for you, Taurus. It will set up shop in family-oriented Cancer, so you'll be in the mood to open up your home to your nearest and dearest. This will be an extremely loving day. Pass out lots of hugs, and be sure to linger under the mistletoe just a bit too long.

Relationships

Venus, your planetary ruler, will spend most of the month in intense Scorpio and your solar seventh house of one-to-one relationships. Now, Scorpio is a fiercely loyal sign—with a very, very long memory. Anyone who's offended you or, worse, someone you love will have to answer for that mistake this month. Be merciful! 'Tis the season.

Money and Success

The New Moon on December 11 in outgoing Sagittarius and your solar eighth house of joint money matters will give you all the inspiration you need to make major changes, Taurus. If you're not happy with your current financial situation, this will be a terrific time to lay down the law and make sure others understand that you expect them to carry their own weight.

Planetary Hotspots

On December 25, the Full Moon will light up the sky from its safe, snug place in home and family-oriented Cancer. This lunation will make it a lovely holiday season, full of warm hugs and tender glances. Having family and friends over to your place in front of the fire sounds wonderful—but you know they'll probably end up in the kitchen, anyway.

Rewarding Days
5, 8, 16, 17, 24, 25, 26

Challenging Days
1, 3, 4, 6, 10, 14, 19, 20

Taurus Action Table

These dates reflect the best—but not the only—times for success and ease in these activities, according to your Sun sign.

	JAN	FEB	MAR	APR	MAY	JUN	JUL	AUG	SEP	OCT	NOV	DEC
Move	30	3, 4			17		31	14				
Start a class		24					1		5		10	
Join a club	19, 20	7				9	8, 9					
Ask for a raise	13, 14, 22		23				30, 31				24, 25	
Look for work	3			4					13			
Get pro advice	4		30	2, 3				26		6, 13		
Get a loan	4		30							13, 14		
See a doctor		8								12	9	21
Start a diet	30			15, 16	3		18, 25		22			29
End relationship	15							5, 6			2, 3	
Buy clothes				11, 22		16			30			
Get a makeover	13			19				15, 16, 19		27, 28		
New romance		1, 7	5, 23, 27			22, 28			5, 22	16, 17		24
Vacation	30, 31		4				1, 2, 3				10, 11	24, 25, 26

Gemini

The Twins
May 20 to June 20

Ⅱ

Element: Air

Quality: Mutable

Polarity: Yang/masculine

Planetary Ruler: Mercury

Meditation: I explore my inner worlds

Gemstone: Tourmaline

Power Stones: Ametrine, citrine, emerald, spectrolite, agate

Key Phrase: I think

Glyph: Pillars of duality, the Twins

Anatomy: Shoulders, arms, hands, lungs, nervous system

Colors: Bright colors, orange, yellow, magenta

Animals: Monkeys, talking birds, flying insects

Myths/Legends: Peter Pan, Castor and Pollux

House: Third

Opposite Sign: Sagittarius

Flower: Lily of the valley

Keyword: Versatility

The Gemini Personality

Your Strengths and Challenges

You're one of the three air signs, Gemini, so you're primarily an intellectual creature. You're also mutable, or, basically, flexible and adaptable. Put it all together and you come up with a curious, witty, restless being who learns easily—and constantly, too, since you never stop asking questions and accumulating data. As a result, you're a veritable font of information, on many, many topics. Having all that information instantly available to your quick-moving brain and always right at the tip of your tongue makes you quite good at telling stories, all of which are believable because of the details you include—which may or may not be pertinent but are always entertaining.

Since Mercury, the fastest-moving planet of them all, is your astrological ruler, you're also quite quick on your feet and able to navigate through just about anything in record time. This goes for the red tape involved with many administrative processes as well as actual roadblocks, like traffic snarls, which never mean much to you. You can find a shortcut in a heartbeat, whether or not you know the area. Your specialty is speed of thought and action, which means you can juggle several projects at once and, unlike most of us, do it successfully.

Now, trying to juggle too many things at once often leads to being scattered, and on tense, stressful days, this can happen to even you. You're easily distracted at times, but it's understandable. Life provides so many interesting sensory stimulations, and you want to experience just a taste of them all.

Your Relationships

You're easily bored, Gemini, so it takes a very special person to keep your active mind occupied. See, you're not just looking for a lover. You also want a best friend and playmate—someone who'll go on every single ride at the carnival at least twice, have a taste from every food stand, and play every game. In a nutshell, if they never, ever turn down a new experience, you'll consider actually sticking around for a while. It's not that you're fickle—it's just that life is an endless parade of colors, sights, and sounds, and you mean to try out as much of it as you can. So, anyone who aspires toward being your partner had better be just as game to keep moving and keep experimenting. If they can give you a run for your money verbally, you'll be interested—in fact, it's pretty much a requirement to catch your attention. Wit and imagination are important, but if they can keep up with (and enjoy) your active social schedule and introduce you to their own friends, there's a good chance you'll be fascinated, which is the only way to hold you.

And speaking of friends, you like nothing better than to associate with a buffet of interesting, intelligent people who move fast, laugh a lot, and socialize often. You're at the top of every guest list when a party comes up—and with good reason. You keep the atmosphere lively and the conversation active.

The other air signs often make good romantic matches. You're captivated by the genius and inventiveness of Aquarius, and by Libra's ability to solve problems with their minds. Libra's unswerving focus on their partner might make you feel a bit cramped, however—and maybe even claustrophobic at times. Fiery Sagittarius is a good match, since they're just as freedom-loving and adaptable as you are, and just as curious and restless, too. Plus, they usually have at least some of the answers to your perpetual questions!

Your Career and Money

Occupations that allow you to move, chat, and learn will work just fine, Gemini. Teaching satisfies that urge, since every question you don't know the answer to gives you a reason to find one. Computers are fun, as long as the work isn't tedious. Inputting an endless string of numbers into a spreadsheet might put you to sleep, but collecting data for demographics sounds like fun. Regardless of which career you choose, it will necessarily involve a whole lot of chattin', a whole lot of change, and a whole lot of variety. You're definitely not cut out for a carpet-lined cubicle. Sales is always an option, since you can talk just about anyone into just about anything and you'll meet a constant stream of new people. When it comes to money, you're not usually very frugal, although you do tend to hold on to your cash until you can spend it on something entertaining. Might be a gadget, might be a hot new play. If you're amused, you'll pull out your wallet.

Your Lighter Side

You love games, Gemini. Intellectual games are best (and you do love your puzzles), and anyone who tries to take you on at Trivial Pursuit should prepare to have their hat handed to them. Movement is primary to your nature, too, so travel, dancing, and amusement park rides are right at the top of your list.

Affirmation for the Year
I learn most when I share my knowledge with others.

The Year Ahead for Gemini

What a year, Gemini! Venus, the Goddess of Love, has extended her stay in dramatic Leo and your solar third house of communications and conversations. Rather than passing through in under a month, she'll sashay theatrically through this house, microphone in hand, from June 5 through July 18 and again from August 1 through October 8. Now, communication is your business, and you're good at it, but while Venus is in Leo, you should probably be licensed, because your wit and ability to talk anyone into anything will be especially formidable. This is a double-edged sword, though. Before you decide to turn on the charm just to see what happens, keep in mind that Leo is a fixed sign, so you may not be able to discourage admirers as easily as you attract them. If you're not truly interested, hold your breath and direct this potent energy in another direction.

Venus will be especially powerful up until August 11, thanks to the cosmic backup of Jupiter, the God of Excess and Expansion. He'll be traveling through this same house, also wearing Leo, waving his magic wand around dramatically and turning every little move you make and every little glance you toss away into a huge gesture—and often, into an irresistible invitation to get to know you better. Again, be careful what you wish for. If you're only after attention, be sure you set this energy to work on the right kind. Romance will most definitely be in the air, but try not to get so wrapped up in it that you forget about Leo's fondness for nurturing creative talents. Your sign owns this house, so it has a lot to do with writing and speaking—which just so happen to be right at the top of your list of fun things to do. Words will feel like toys. Put some together on a computer and mail them off to the publication or e-zine of your choice. Give a talk on something you know so well you feel as if you were doing it in your last life. Doesn't matter. Just be sure to find a stage, jump up on it, and let the world know you're there.

Your conversations with children will be especially important now, too. Of all the signs, you remember best what it was like to be their age. Speak to them in that particular language.

Once Jupiter enters Virgo and your solar fourth house of home, emotions, and domestic matters on August 11, you'll turn your attention toward overhauling and perfecting your home base. Redecorating, refurbishing, and remodeling your nest will be at the top of your priority list now, and you'll tend to it all with a careful, meticulous eye. Look over documents waiting to be signed that relate to your home, children, or family. If you're not sure you're doing the right thing, call in professional counsel. Keeping an accountant or paralegal on call wouldn't be a bad idea. If you're into crafts and have been thinking about making your hobby into a business, do your homework before you quit your day job, but know that you might really have something here.

Saturn will sneak back into Scorpio and your solar sixth house from June 14 through September 17, insisting that you think back to work-oriented events from last year. If anything you've done—or haven't done—is nagging at you, there's only one way to put it to rest. Confront the individuals involved. Confess your wrongs and assert your rights, then move on. Saturn will spend the majority of this year in Sagittarius and your solar seventh house of one-to-one relationships, and you'll have better things to do than mull over the past.

Among those better things will be checking out the owner of a particularly wonderful accent or discovering that an authority figure finds you sexy, too. What you're after now is experiences, and lots of them. If you can get out there and create them anew with a partner, so much the better. If you're tied to home, you might also live them out vicariously through an exciting, fiery new Other with stories to tell. Don't worry about age differences or any other imaginary boundary. Focus in on what you share, and enjoy.

Uranus and Pluto will lock into that same square they've been pulling into and away from for years now, so your need for independence—à la Uranus—may come at a price, thanks to Pluto in commitment-oriented Capricorn and your solar eighth house of intimate partners. You've always been a bit skittish when it comes to commitments. You've often been referred to as fickle, too. Now, however, you'll understand exactly what's at stake when you sign up to be with someone exclusively, and you won't take—or make—promises lightly.

Woozy, dreamy Neptune will continue tiptoeing through Pisces and your solar tenth house of career matters and dealings with higher-ups, which might be another indication of a relationship with an authority figure. On the other hand, you might simply be willing to change careers so that what you're doing reflects who you really are. A spiritual or metaphysical calling might be the way to go, but you'll know for sure, once you're called.

What This Year's Eclipses Mean for You

Eclipses are basically supercharged meetings of the Sun and Moon. A Solar Eclipse occurs when the Sun and Moon come together at the time of the New Moon, and a Lunar Eclipse occurs with a Full Moon, when the Sun and the Moon are opposite each other. The first Solar Eclipse will arrive on March 20, all done up in gentle, sensitive Pisces, urging you on toward new beginnings from its spot in your solar tenth house of career matters. Now, the lovely lady Neptune has been here for years, whispering to you subconsciously about changing careers so that what you do for work better reflects your ideals and beliefs. If you've heard her and taken her message to heart, you'll know it when you cross paths with someone who can effect a huge change in your professional life. All you need to do is pay attention to their insights. Okay, and maybe ask for some advice, once you're comfortable.

The first Lunar Eclipse of 2015 will occur on April 4, when the emotional Moon in balance-loving Libra opposes the Sun from her spot in your solar fifth house of playmates, lovers, and recreational activities. You're a lively sign, Gemini, and you live to have fun, but during this time, you might find that you're not really having fun unless you're part of a twosome. No one's saying you have to settle down with just one companion, though. In fact, you'll have a veritable buffet of lovers and playmates to choose from. Enjoy!

On September 13, the second Solar Eclipse will plant a seed in your solar fourth house of home and family matters. You might decide to move or take drastic steps to solve an urgent family matter, even if your plans don't necessarily coincide with what your loved ones prefer. You'll be totally in charge of your domestic life, so if you want to start over, there's no better time to do it. This eclipse might also be the bearer of news regarding a brand-new family member.

The last eclipse will be Lunar Eclipse, a Full Moon in Aries. This will activate your solar axis of lovers and friends, and someone may want to switch sides. In other words, a formerly platonic relationship could suddenly become quite passionate—but a passionate affair might also fizzle out. This would be a terrific time to investigate new circles of friends. Remember, you're still trying to figure out what you want to be when you grow up, and the company you keep can either further your goals or stall them.

Saturn

The really big astrological news for you this year, Gemini, is Saturn's transit through Sagittarius and your solar seventh house of one-to-one relationships, which he started just days before 2015 arrived. With the exception of a quick retrograde back into sexy, intense Scorpio and your solar sixth house of work and work-oriented relationships from June 14 through September 17, he'll be on duty for the next two and a half years in this spot. Those three months will give you a chance to bring closure to any work-oriented projects you've left undone, intentionally or not, and you really should take advantage of them. For the rest of the year, you can expect several scenarios. For starters, since Saturn loves to challenge us, your primary relationship will endure some stress, possibly due to geographical roadblocks or a rather sizable age difference. If you have a powerful connection, forget about doing the math. Focus on what you have in common and forget about everything else. Of course, you might not be able to forget how much you miss them if this is a long-distance relationship, but fortunately, once travel-loving Jupiter enters your solar fourth house of home on August 11, one of you might decide to substantially narrow the distance between you—say, to a few inches if you have a king-size bed. In the meantime, remember that Saturn doesn't bring presents like Jupiter does, but he always sees to it that we get exactly what we deserve. If you've been faithful, honest, and committed, the Universe will help you to get together with your sweetheart.

Uranus

If you were born between June 3 and 13, Gemini, your Sun will receive a sextile this year from Uranus, who'll be making his way through your solar eleventh house of friendships and group affiliations. Now, this guy just loves surprise endings and he's still wearing impulsive Aries, a sign you've always thought of as a terrific playmate. As fond as you are of change, when Uranus brings it along, even if you only have a second to think about it, you'll dive right in and enjoy the ride—which means you'll definitely be having the time of your life. Uranus is every bit as curious as you are, and always game for a new experience. But while Uranus collects experiences much like a scientist collects data, you're after what's new and exciting strictly for the fun of it—and what's wrong with that? Life is all about change, and when Uranus in Aries comes along, there's always plenty of that, with a healthy side of adrenaline to keep you alert and interested. This planet will reopen your eyes to the colors, tastes, and sounds of the world around you. Think of his visit as a free pass to an amusement park that's open 24/7.

Neptune

During 2015, Neptune will continue on her path through her favorite sign, Pisces, and your solar tenth house of career matters and relationships with higher-ups and authority figures. If you were born at the very beginning of your sign, you are already quite familiar with her energy and have learned lots of subtle ways to get ahead in your world without appearing to climb the ladder. If you're smart—and you most certainly are—you've probably benefited more lately from tuning in to your intuition first and considering the cold, hard facts of the matter last. In this case, you're on your way to realizing that a life path that doesn't directly involve your belief system or at least get you involved in something you have faith in—well, it might not be the right path to follow. If you were born between May 26 and July 3, Neptune will form an edgy square to your Sun this year, and although she is a gentle, invisible energy, have no doubt that you will still feel pressured to change your work so that it reflects your spiritual goals. In a nutshell, it's time for you to wake up and smell the coffee, Gemini. When Joseph Campbell talked about how following our bliss inevitably leads to the one and only true personal fulfillment, he wasn't kidding. If you don't believe in what you're doing, you won't enjoy it. If you don't enjoy it, you won't do it well. Any questions?

Pluto

If you were born between June 3 and 8, Pluto will form an inconjunct aspect to your Sun this year, Gemini, and you'll need to make some major adjustments in your life. In particular, since he's still passing through your solar eighth house of intimate matters and joint resources, Pluto will demand that you reevaluate your deepest, most intense connections, both intimately and financially. Anyone who has failed you in either department will need to be tossed out. Period. The method of disposal you choose is entirely up to you, and there are several options available. You might decide to be merciful and use the energy of Neptune to slowly sidle away rather than confronting them in Plutonian style with an all-or-nothing ultimatum. If you know how they're going to deal with that ultimatum anyway, this makes sense. Why bother? On the other hand, if you're simmering over a betrayal of trust and you really want your opponent to pay for it—common feelings when Pluto is in the vicinity—you might decide to take the long way home and torture the offender slowly with words, possibly through legal confrontations. It's all up to you. Remember, though, that even if you go after revenge and achieve it, you won't be able to get back what you feel you've lost. The lesson here is to realize that even though the representatives Pluto sends along might not be nice about it, they're necessary. The whole point of Pluto's trek is to open your eyes to the fact that you too can be vulnerable, and you need to protect yourself—before, not after, a disappointing and hurtful experience.

Gemini | January

Planetary Lightspots

The New Moon in Aquarius on January 20 will activate your solar ninth house of higher education and travel, and your already fidgety mind will need some distractions. If you haven't already set out in search of long-distance adventure by then and you really can't leave right now, pick up a brochure from a college near you and check out what's available. Learning always makes you feel brand-new.

Relationships

Venus will spend most of the month in unpredictable Aquarius, skipping merrily through your solar ninth house of long-distance relationships and far-off places. You've been thinking about your roots and probably missing everyone who plays a starring role in your memories. Why not make a spontaneous trip on January 13 or 14? Bet they'll be delighted to see you.

Money and Success

The Full Moon in home-loving Cancer on January 4 will cast a bright light into your solar second house of finances, Gemini, urging you to think about using your home for a workplace. Think about that hobby—the one that friends keep saying you're good enough at to turn into a business. Why not give it shot, at least on weekends?

Planetary Hotspots

If a higher-up or elder seems to be going out of their way to make life tough for you on January 15, don't overreact, Gemini. Assertive Mars will get into a square with serious Saturn that day, demanding that you use your wits to get around roadblocks and delays. Think of it as proving yourself, and don't get frustrated.

Rewarding Days

4, 5, 13, 14, 20, 22, 27

Challenging Days

1, 2, 3, 15, 19, 29, 30

Gemini | February

Planetary Lightspots

The Full Moon on February 3 will strut off into fiery, dramatic Leo and your solar third house of communications and conversations, Gemini, and while you've always been quite the talker, you'll be especially charming now and absolutely impossible to refuse. Your mission is to use this gift to bring some magic into someone's life.

Relationships

On February 20, loving Venus will stomp her way into aggressive Aries and your solar eleventh house of friends and groups, where she'll meet up with her ancient lover, Mars, and the emotional Moon. This fiery trio will insist that you take charge of a gathering whose leader has obviously dropped the ball. Just try to do it without ruffling any feathers.

Money and Success

If you're thinking of investing, Gemini, look to February 8 to get the ball rolling. Venus, the ruler of money matters, will activate Pluto in your solar eighth house of joint finances, making this the perfect time to invest. It's also a terrific time to get in good with an authority figure. Hey, there's no shame in getting your name known.

Planetary Hotspots

A pack of Aries planets will storm the borders of your solar eleventh house of friendships and group affiliations between February 19 and 22, and suddenly your social schedule will be on fire. It might be that a new friend has entered your life and wants to introduce you around. It might be, too, that you're looking for some exciting new acquaintances.

Rewarding Days

2, 3, 19, 24, 25, 26

Challenging Days

1, 6, 20, 21, 22, 23

Gemini | March

Planetary Lightspots

Generous Jupiter in entertaining Leo will get into an easy trine with surprising Uranus on March 3, activating your solar third house of communications and your solar eleventh house of groups. Yes, it certainly does sound like you'll be doing a bit of performing, no matter where you are, but if you're at all inclined toward acting, investigate an improv troupe.

Relationships

On March 16, the time you've been spending at work might become an issue between you and your sweetheart, Gemini, so be prepared to do some compromising. Yes, you do need to put in your time, and yes, you've been extremely ambitious lately, but the home fires need tending, too. Fortunately, one heartfelt romantic gesture should make it all right.

Money and Success

Once Venus makes her way into earthy, practical Taurus on March 17, you'll feel the need to retire inward for a while, Gemini. Venus will set up camp in your solar twelfth house of Privacy, Please, asking that you devote some quality time to spoiling yourself and your loved ones. You've been working very hard for a long, long time. Relax now, just a little.

Planetary Hotspots

The total Solar Eclipse on March 20 will set up shop in your solar tenth house of career matters and dealings with authority figures, Gemini. She'll be wearing woozy Pisces, so if you're not careful to be clear, a higher-up or elder might misunderstand your motives. Be sure to say exactly what you mean. Nothing more and nothing less.

Rewarding Days

1, 2, 3, 9, 25

Challenging Days

4, 10, 11, 15, 16, 26, 27

Gemini | April

Planetary Lightspots

A total Lunar Eclipse will occur on April 4 in people-pleasing Libra and your solar fifth house of playmates and dealings with kids. You'll be feeling a bit like a tour guide, ready and willing to make every moment fun, so spending your time doing anything that's not recreational will be out of the question. You've earned this. Enjoy yourself!

Relationships

On April 11, Venus, the Goddess of Love, will set off for your sign and your solar first house of personality and appearance. For the next month, you'll be a magnet, Gemini, and you won't believe the amazing array of admirers who'll make a play for your attention. Enjoy the parade, but don't choose one until you're ready.

Money and Success

You won't just be attracting love this month, Gemini. Once Venus enters your sign on April 11, it will also be easy for you to bring money into your life. You might find a fifty dollar bill walking down the street, but putting Venus to work for you would be a much better long-term plan—and that means putting your personality to work. Sounds like fun!

Planetary Hotspots

On April 4, 8, and 9, your relationships with friends and group acquaintances could become a bit strained, Gemini, especially if you haven't been receiving the attention and appreciation you know you deserve. You might have to make a scene, but with the Sun and Mercury in red-hot Aries, that won't be a problem. Just don't make a really big scene.

Rewarding Days
1, 2, 6, 11, 21, 22, 26

Challenging Days
4, 5, 8, 9, 15, 19

Gemini | May

Planetary Lightspots

The Sun will join Mars and Mercury in your sign and your solar first house of personality and appearance on May 21, Gemini, so get ready for some serious fun. As curious and friendly as you are, there's never a shortage of invitations, but over the coming month, you might actually be overbooked. Get yourself a new day planner.

Relationships

Venus will take off for Cancer on May 7, and suddenly your home and family will become more important to you than dating—and maybe even more important than your primary partner. If you're attached, get everyone together at your place for a home-cooked meal and some late-night chitchat around the kitchen table. Your partner will join in soon enough.

Money and Success

The Full Moon on May 3 will light up your solar sixth house of work, Gemini, and probably put you on center stage for a recent accomplishment. It will be in sexy Scorpio, however, so you might also get together with a coworker to celebrate and discover you have far more in common than just your job descriptions.

Planetary Hotspots

Romance may well be in the air on May 11, but if you're not careful, you might be taken advantage of by someone who can see just how vulnerable you are at the moment. Your best bet is to spend your time with those you know and trust and who can always be counted on to see what you don't.

Rewarding Days

6, 16, 17, 21, 30

Challenging Days

3, 4, 9, 14, 15, 18, 22, 27

Gemini | June

Planetary Lightspots

The Full Moon in playful Sagittarius on June 2 will set fire to your solar relationship axis, Gemini. If you're not attached, someone who lives quite a distance from you might suddenly seem more appealing than anyone from across the street. In general, you'll be attracted to interesting accents and anyone who doesn't look and act like everyone else you know.

Relationships

Between June 6 and 8, four planets will conspire to get you introduced to an out-of-towner whom you'll be quickly convinced is worth moving for. One of those planets is Venus in Leo, who just loves a good show, so a bit of drama could be on your agenda. Keep your wits about you, even if you want to be swept off your feet.

Money and Success

Any creative pursuit does well when Venus is in Leo, but since she'll be in your solar third house of communications for most of the month, your particular skill will come in handy. Whether you're talking or writing, you'll win favor—and maybe even a new job—as long as you let your wit and intelligence show. Don't be shy!

Planetary Hotspots

On June 14, the Sun and Mars will collide in your sign, Gemini. Now, this will bring the heavens' two fireballs together in one extremely fiery blast. Needless to say, your temper might run high, so if you're bored, find something to do and work that energy off. Outdoor sports are fine outlets, but a whole lot of laughter will accomplish the same goal.

Rewarding Days
2, 5, 6, 8, 9, 10, 16, 28

Challenging Days
13, 14, 22, 23, 24

Gemini | July

Planetary Lightspots

The Full Moon on July 1 will combine talents with Venus and Jupiter, the heavens' most generous couple, to provide you with an opportunity to express yourself, in no uncertain terms. No matter what you've been waiting to say, wait no longer. The Universe will be happy to help you say it right, so no one will take it personally.

Relationships

As of July 18, when loving Venus sets off for meticulous, sometimes picky Virgo, you'll be even better armed than usual to do verbal debate with anyone who comes your way. It might be that a family member or child has pushed the envelope just a bit too far and you're ready to call them on it. You'll need to watch out for a tendency to be picky or argumentative, though.

Money and Success

The New Moon will arrive on July 15 in your solar second house of money matters, urging you to put the wheels in motion for a whole new financial start. If you've been ignoring your finances, you'll need to tend to them now, but you might be happily surprised. Consolidate some bills and you might actually be paying less.

Planetary Hotspots

On July 25, aggressive Mars will get into a testy square with shocking Uranus, creating an astrological recipe for sudden events. Not to worry, though. That same day, Venus will be stationing in earthy, practical Virgo and your solar fourth house of emotions, so you'll be well equipped to deal with any last-minute changes on the domestic scene.

Rewarding Days

1, 2, 3, 5, 22, 23

Challenging Days

6, 7, 11, 12, 14, 15, 18, 25

Gemini | August

Planetary Lightspots

If you need a change of luck, sit tight. You can expect it on August 19. Loving Venus will get into an easy trine with Uranus, who just adores change—especially the kind that happens suddenly and at the last minute. The good news is that whatever you invested your time and energy into on August 4 will begin to pan out.

Relationships

Venus, the Goddess of Love, is currently on duty in lavish, romantic Leo and your solar third house of communications, Gemini. This charming planet will influence every syllable you utter, turning it into an irresistible invitation to get to know you better. Go easy if you're not really interested, especially around August 5. This charm is much easier to turn on than off.

Money and Success

If you're after a raise, Gemini, or just wishing that someone would actually notice how much work you've done, you'll be delighted with events on August 6. Energetic Mars will team up with serious Saturn in your solar sixth house of work to see to it that your boss takes notice, and that you're properly rewarded, too.

Planetary Hotspots

The Sun, Mercury, and Jupiter will all call your solar third house home base for at least some of this month, Gemini. This powerfully communicative team will help you get your message across, big time. You won't have to shout, or even utter a word at times. Your mission is to think about the impact of your words before you let them escape your lips—which may not be easy.

Rewarding Days

2, 7, 13, 14, 15, 19, 26

Challenging Days

3, 4, 5, 6, 12, 21, 31

Gemini | September

Planetary Lightspots

The second Lunar Eclipse of the year will occur on September 27, all done up in assertive Aries. This no-nonsense lunation will charge you up and encourage you to pursue your goals through associating with others who are on the same page. If that means your current peer group needs to go on a back burner temporarily, so be it.

Relationships

Don't ignore a sibling or neighbor who wants to introduce you to someone around September 23. They may have been wrong in the past, but this time out, their instincts will probably be right on. If you're single, at least agree to coffee or lunch. If you're attached, plan an exciting date night out. No fair leaving your phones on, either!

Money and Success

On September 17, career-minded Saturn will step into your solar seventh house of one-to-one relationships. All your dealings with authority figures or bosses will be highlighted, but not to worry. You'll be able to convince them of your value to the business without even trying. You might also find one of those authorities pretty darn attractive over the next couple years.

Planetary Hotspots

A Solar Eclipse will activate Virgo on September 13, your Mercury-ruled cousin, right smack dab in the middle of your solar fourth house. Your words have been extremely well chosen lately, and it isn't over yet. If you have something to get off your chest, you'll want to do it now, and suddenly. Try to go easy on family members and on dear friends you consider family, who might not be ready for this strong a dose of reality.

Rewarding Days

4, 5, 7, 8, 22, 23

Challenging Days

9, 10, 13, 16, 24, 25, 30

Gemini | October

Planetary Lightspots

On October 12, your solar fifth house of lovers and playmates will play host to the New Moon in Libra, a partner-oriented sign that just loves to get us connected to those who'll prove to be worthy team members. Whether it's romance, work, or friendship that's involved, you'd do well to pay attention to anyone who crosses your path on that day.

Relationships

Now that serious Saturn has settled himself comfortably into your solar seventh house of one-to-one relationships, Gemini, you're probably thinking just as seriously about settling down. If you're already seeing someone casually, an elegant evening out would be a great place to start, but don't stop there. Let them know you're undoubtedly in this for the long haul.

Money and Success

The Full Moon in Taurus will arrive on October 27, Gemini. Now, this is the Moon at the peak of her energy, and Taurus is a money magnet. If you've recently started a new job or even a new business, you'll start to reap the rewards now. Just don't share the news with the world yet. Wait until you have a good, solid track record under your belt.

Planetary Hotspots

On October 30, the Sun and Neptune, the planet of illusions, will come together in an easy trine—the perfect recipe for getting into a costume and going out to a masquerade party. If you've already got one in mind, plan to wear something especially exotic. If not, how about having some coworkers and friends over to your place?

Rewarding Days

12, 13, 15, 23, 24, 30, 31

Challenging Days

5, 6, 10, 16, 17, 25

Gemini | November

Planetary Lightspots

The Full Moon in your sign will occur on November 25. It will team up with red-hot Mars and your ruling planet, Mercury, to see to it that you bring a relationship issue to an end. If you've already done that but still feel that you don't have closure, choose this day for one last heart-to-heart talk, then put it all behind you.

Relationships

On November 2, loving Venus and assertive Mars will come together, the perfect balance of feminine and masculine energies. These two planets combine attraction and pursuit to produce passion, and since they've chosen your solar fourth house of emotions for their meeting spot, it's not hard to imagine you wrapped in the delicious arms of the one you love.

Money and Success

If you're thinking about making an investment this month, Gemini, November 13 would be a terrific time to make it official. You'll have four astrological allies on duty to help you choose well, one of whom—serious Saturn himself—will also provide you with the guidance of a solid, reputable professional. Just don't risk what you don't have.

Planetary Hotspots

The New Moon will occur in intense, sexy Scorpio on November 11, Gemini, which just so happens to be your solar sixth house of work and on-the-job relationships. If you have the feeling that someone is talking behind your back, be sure they really are before you accuse them. Chances are good they're really your best ally.

Rewarding Days

5, 6, 10, 13, 14, 22, 25

Challenging Days

1, 2, 3, 16, 17, 20, 24, 29

Gemini | December

Planetary Lightspots

Your ruling planet, Mercury, will make his way through merry, funny Sagittarius and your solar seventh house of committed relationships up until December 9, Gemini, giving you every reason on earth to indulge in holiday gatherings and lighthearted social events—both of which happen to be at the very top of your "favorites" list. Enjoy yourself, but don't go overboard with rich food or heady drinks.

Relationships

From December 4 on, Venus will spend her time in sexy Scorpio. This will put all of us in the mood to snuggle up in a dimly lit place with someone special, but remember, 'tis the season, and lots of folks are counting on you to make an appearance and liven up their parties. Oh, come on! You can restrain yourselves for a few evening hours.

Money and Success

On December 9, when Mercury enters wise Capricorn and your solar eighth house of joint resources, you'll begin to see your financial picture a bit clearer. If there's anything you want to settle between you and a former partner, you'll be able to easily find the information you need to put the issue to rest. Don't let the matter ruin the holidays.

Planetary Hotspots

Venus and Jupiter will form an energetic sextile on December 24, just in time for a lovely holiday. Now, these two always bring hugs and laughter along, so don't refuse any invitations to seasonal gatherings. Perch yourself under the mistletoe. It's time to stop worrying about money and work and enjoy the good feelings.

Rewarding Days

1, 6, 7, 8, 11, 12, 24, 25

Challenging Days

3, 4, 13, 14, 19, 20, 29

Gemini Action Table

These dates reflect the best—but not the only—times for success and ease in these activities, according to your Sun sign.

	JAN	FEB	MAR	APR	MAY	JUN	JUL	AUG	SEP	OCT	NOV	DEC
Move			5			16		11	13, 16			14
Start a class	4, 5, 19	18, 19	1, 2									
Join a club	13, 14		3, 4	2, 6, 8, 18				2, 13, 19	27			1, 8, 20
Ask for a raise	27, 30	7					1	26, 27			24, 26	
Look for work				12, 22, 26	3, 6		18	26			10, 11, 13, 17	
Get pro advice	22						21, 22			11		
Get a loan			30, 31			6	21, 22			15		
See a doctor		8			27							
Start a diet			16, 17				18					
End relationship	15, 16	23		15, 16					23, 24, 25			
Buy clothes				22, 26		28						
Get a makeover					9		1, 2, 3, 5					24
New romance		21, 24				1, 2, 5, 6			23, 30	12, 13	8, 23, 24	1, 6, 12
Vacation	1, 3, 4	19, 20		6, 26				4				

Cancer

The Crab
June 20 to July 22

Element: Water

Quality: Cardinal

Polarity: Yin/feminine

Planetary Ruler: The Moon

Meditation: I have faith in the promptings of my heart

Gemstone: Pearl

Power Stones: Moonstone, Chrysocolla

Key Phrase: I feel

Glyph: Crab's claws

Anatomy: Stomach, breasts

Colors: Silver, pearl white

Animals: Crustaceans, cows, chickens

Myths/Legends: Hercules and the Crab, Asherah, Hecate

House: Fourth

Opposite Sign: Capricorn

Flower: Larkspur

Keyword: Receptivity

The Cancer Personality

Your Strengths and Challenges

A lot of people think you're a pushover for a sob story, Cancer—and to be honest, at times you are. What most people don't realize is that your instincts are the stuff that legends are made of. You can smell trouble a mile away, especially if it involves someone you love. One good, long look into the eyes of a child, friend, or lover will tell you everything they think they're hiding. You're often described as moody, and while that word has a rather negative spin attached, it's really just a description of someone who isn't afraid to experience their feelings, for better or worse, and, more importantly, to express those feelings. Of course, since most of us are trained from just about birth to do the opposite, your ease in this department is often startling to behold. But since your ruling planet is the emotional Moon herself—who experiences quite a few mood changes as she waxes, wanes, and goes through her monthly phases—it only makes sense that you'd be the perfect conduit for her energy.

Your sign is also well known for being protective about your home, which you consider not just a landing pad but also a retreat. When you finally have the chance to leave the real world behind, you're also ready to close the door behind you and shut the real world out. Anyone you don't trust implicitly will simply not be welcome, and you won't make a secret of it. Anyone you care for, however, will have the full benefits associated with your hospitality. That includes comfort food, warm hugs, and lots of TLC.

Your Relationships

When it comes down to choosing a friend or lover, you should always operate on your gut feelings, Cancer, not on anything even remotely resembling the facts of the matter. Your intuition will serve you well—at least, when you listen to it. In fact, if you think back over your life, when you have paid attention to those amazing antennae you were born with, you have probably saved yourself from getting involved in relationships that wouldn't have been positive or productive for either of you. On the other hand, a very strong part of your nature and one of your personal driving forces is to nurture and care for others, so being single doesn't suit you well. In the past, you may even have settled for someone you knew wasn't quite right for you simply to avoid being alone. Remember how much you have to offer and how much love you have to give, and you will never feel the need to settle. Just be patient. The right person will be along shortly.

Once they've arrived, of course, they'll be treated to the very best, in all departments. You'll spoil them rotten when they're well and take better care of them than their mothers did when they're not. Like Taurus, you sign up forever, and unless you're emotionally or physically abused, you'll do everything in your power to make it all work out. After all, once you've chosen a partner, they're family.

Initially, you may be drawn to the other water signs, Scorpio and Pisces. While they often make good matches for you—and good friends as well—what you're really looking for might be more easily found through the earth signs. Solid, grounded Taurus makes a good match, as well as your opposite sign, Capricorn, who'll be willing to go out and tackle the practical part of life while you tend to home and family.

Your Career and Money

Since your sign is so closely associated with kids and families, Cancer, you might initially be drawn to work that involves children—a natural match. You appreciate their innocence and candor, and they bring out the protective side in you, which is one of the qualities you are proudest of. If you decide to teach, it will likely be the little ones you prefer to work with, since they accept love and guidance so willingly. You might also be drawn toward work that brings you into the homes of others, perhaps to decorate or, if you're metaphysically inclined, to practice feng shui.

Then there's the fact that you're a water sign. You feel quite at home in, on, and around water, so getting wet—literally—might also be a daily occurrence. Many Cancers have found their calling through becoming swim instructors, pool technicians, or water conservationists. Wherever you work and whatever you do, it's an absolute given that you will be the "den mother" or "den father" to everyone around you.

Your Lighter Side

What's fun for you, Cancer? Well, nothing could possibly be better than having the whole gang over. That includes family and their kids as well as your dearest friends, whom you consider extended family. You usually love to cook, and tending to your home and garden is fun, too. Don't forget that you need an evening out every now and then. Take the kids to the movies or visit the home of a trusted loved one.

Affirmation for the Year
My financial success depends on my attitude.

The Year Ahead for Cancer

The really big astrological news this year, Cancer, involves the heavens' benefics: Venus, the Goddess of Love and Beauty, and Jupiter, everyone's favorite uncle. These two are famous all on their own for being in the vicinity when goodies are passed out, but working together, as they will be for several months—well, think of this as a very long Christmas season, full of presents of various sizes, shapes, and species. Jupiter will remain on duty in this fiery sign and your solar second house of personal finances until August 11. Now, he's been there since last July, so you're probably already quite familiar with huge credit card statements as well as wonderful windfalls out of the blue. But since Jupiter is wrapping things up here, it's the bills you should be paying attention to. With this mega-planet in lavish Leo, extravagance has likely become a way of life, but just the opposite might be true soon, if you're not careful now. You love to give, and Jupiter expands every urge, so those you love have been pretty darn spoiled lately, but once August arrives and Jupiter enters meticulous Virgo, it will be their turn to give back. Fortunately, Jupiter believes in ninefold returns on the positive energy we put out, so they probably will. Your mission is to resist the urge to ask if you really need something. You're loved by so many, all of whom would be happy to help if they only knew what to do for you. Swallow your pride and talk about it. Jupiter will continue through Virgo and your solar third house of communications and conversations for the rest of the year, giving you plenty of opportunities to show off your intelligence and wit.

Venus, of course, is in charge of money matters and possessions, so while she's in Leo, from June 5 though July 18 and July 31 through October 8, you'll be feeling especially excessive. From her spot in your solar second house of money matters, Venus will urge you to spend your hard-earned dollars on nothing but the best. Leo is a fire sign, fire signs are impulsive, and Leo likes luxury. Any questions? Jupiter's presence for the first part of her trip makes it futile to tell you to hold back on major purchases or excessive entertainment expenses, but you would be better served by tending carefully to the cherished possessions you already have and, more importantly, to the relationships you value.

Speaking of relationships, Venus in Leo will be inspiring just about all of us to be a bit more passionate in our encounters, but remember that there's a big difference between the kind of passion that leads to romance and the kind that leads to theatrical scenes. Whether you're happily attached or still searching for the right one, do your best to keep your emotions in check. No one is saying you can't experience the whole range of feelings. You're good at that. Just be careful not to bulldoze or emotionally bully anyone in the process.

Saturn will also spend much of 2015 in a fire sign, Sagittarius. This will put him in your solar sixth house of work and work-oriented encounters. Now, this planet is tough, but he's fair, so you can expect to get exactly what you deserve. That goes for wages, job security, and work relationships. He also likes to be in charge, so if you've ever thought of going into business for yourself, this is prime time to investigate those possibilities. Pick the brains of everyone you know with a bit of wisdom and experience to impart. Don't go it alone. Saturn encourages us to know our limits, and when we operate from within them, he's nothing if not helpful. From June 14 through September 17, however, while Saturn is wrapping things up in intense Scorpio and your solar fifth house of lovers, you might find you're a bit distracted from work as you mull over whether or not to make a casual relationship into something a lot deeper and more permanent. In the end, you'll be best off trusting your gut—as usual—but if someone who loves you voices some concerns, listen up. You may also be at the tail end of a tough situation with a family member or one of your kids—in which case, all you can really do is to stand by them, not live their lives for them.

Uranus, the most erratic, unpredictable planet in the heavens, will continue on his journey through fiery Aries and your solar tenth house of career matters. Now, Uranus encourages independence, so along with Saturn talking you into becoming your own boss, you might just take a shot at a whole new way of earning your daily bread. The good news is that the more offbeat and unusual the path you're considering, the more help this brilliant genius will be in getting your show on the road, so here's your celestial excuse to forget about what everyone else is doing and strike out on your own. Just be sure you have a safety net in place. Uranus is the kind of guy who might just push you to leap before you look.

Neptune will spend her time in Pisces, the sign she rules. Basically, Neptune is operating without any filter for her energies now, so her influence is even more potent. She loves un-reality, and will go to just about any length to escape anything too harsh, but she also provides us with divine inspiration and intervention. From her spot in your solar ninth house of growth-oriented experiences, including travel and higher education, she'll urge you to think about a long-distance place, possibly where The One Who Got Away is living. Seeing that person again—or seeing anyone far from you whom you haven't seen in far too long—is a fine thing, but don't get so wrapped up in the past that you forget about your goals for the future. Pluto, an all-or-nothing kind of guy, is still working his way through Capricorn and your solar seventh house of one-to-one relationships, asking that you dismiss anyone who is no longer productive or positive in your life. If you've been waiting for the right time to do so, a nudge from the Lunar Eclipse on April 4 might be all it takes to free you up from burdens you really shouldn't be dealing with alone.

What This Year's Eclipses Mean for You

Of the four eclipses that will occur this year, Cancer, none will touch your sign directly, but all will still pack the potential for bringing life-changing experiences, the first of which you'll experience on March 20. A total Solar Eclipse will arrive in Pisces and your solar ninth house of long-distance travel, education, and new experiences. If you've been thinking wistfully about the last time you went anywhere, this would be a fine time to make some plans to get yourself out of Dodge for a while. Whether you fly off or just drive away with the kids in the car for an impromptu weekend doesn't matter. Just be sure you get away from your routine long enough to stop thinking about it. Then, allow yourself to enjoy the moment.

On April 4, the first Lunar Eclipse of the year will shed its light on Libra and activate your solar axis of home versus career matters. Now, our first impulse when Libra energies influence us is to make nice, make peace, and make up—basically, to do whatever we can to avoid confrontation. In this case, however, with Pluto on duty from his spot in your solar seventh house of one-to-one relationships, you might find that you're far less willing to back down and far more willing to stand your ground, no matter who's listening.

The Solar Eclipse that energizes your solar third house of communications and conversations will be all done up in Virgo, the sign that's best at taking care of paperwork, annoying details, and tedious tasks. Yes, it's time to balance the checkbook, go over credit card statements you've been ignoring, and tackle any project you've been putting off for far too long. Your mission is simple—get organized. The good news is that Virgo is extremely patient and meticulous when there's a job to be done, but is only willing to do it once, so this lunation will inspire you to take it slow and get it right the first time.

The last eclipse of the year, on September 27, will occur in Aries, an impatient energy that likes to fire before it aims—and sometimes well before it's ready. Your solar house of personal matters will once again be at odds with your solar house of career goals, and once again, just like back in April, you'll want to juggle to make everything work out well for everyone. The thing is, you need to realize that it might not be possible to do that now. This year could be about you putting your foot down with regard to both family and work and refusing to sweep your own feelings under the carpet anymore. Think about that before you sacrifice your own needs to make someone else happy.

Saturn

This planet is very, very fond of rules and regulations and doesn't give us much wiggle room when it comes to making mistakes. He likes us to be prepared, above all else, and to touch every base before we announce we're done. That said, let's consider the passage of Saturn through your solar fifth house of lovers, which will come to a close between June 14 and September 17. Saturn will be in relentless Scorpio, so if there's anything unpleasant between you and a lover, playmate, or child that you haven't yet dealt with, better take advantage of this time period to straighten it out once and for all, because it isn't going anywhere until you do. Saturn's trip through Sagittarius will last for two and a half years, and since this planet will be in your solar sixth house of work, you should expect lots of overtime, the possibility of advancing to management, or a strong urge to branch out on your own. That hobby you've been so focused on for the past few years might make a great side business at first, but with Saturn on board, it could soon turn into the source of a stable full-time income. If you're really ready to do it, only a trusted partner will do. Otherwise, going it alone might be better.

Uranus

If you were born between July 5 and 15, your Sun will be receiving an action-oriented square from startling Uranus this year—who just loves to send us totally unexpected events and bring us the very last thing on earth we'd ever have thought possible. This can be wonderfully exhilarating, as long as you're up for the idea of complete and total change—which, fortunately, you'll be a lot more open to than you usually are, with Uranus in the neighborhood. It might be that you'll win the lottery, or maybe you'll look in the mirror one day and decide that plastic surgery is the way to go. You'll definitely want to appear different so that the world can see how different you really are now. The tough part might be getting used to this new person, who'll necessarily attract a new lifestyle, but if you stay open and look to the future, you'll be amazed at what's possible in your world. And when you wake up a new person, you'll be happy about it.

Neptune

If you were born between June 26 and July 3, you'll receive a very potent transit from dreamy, romantic, and sometimes confusing Neptune. She'll form a trine with your Sun, an easy aspect that encourages us toward spiritual, religious, and metaphysical areas of life. You could meet up with someone who'll bring you into a whole new circle of friends whose goals and ideals closely match your own. Twelve-step programs and any type of group therapy are terrific ideas now, even if you're not there for yourself. Helping others will be tremendously satisfying, too—maybe even a bit too satisfying. Be sure not to let yourself be lulled into complacency. This transit can make us feel high on life, convinced that everything is already exactly as it should be, when in fact things are rapidly dissolving around us. When in doubt, ask an earthy friend to be brutally honest with you. Your time would be best spent with supportive and gentle like-minded others, but if you have to walk among negative energies, be sure to give yourself time alone to regroup.

Pluto

Pluto is still in Capricorn and your solar seventh house of one-to-one relationships, Cancer, but if you were born between July 4 and 9, you'll really be feeling his influence in a very big way. The opposition Pluto will form with your Sun might mean a relationship is just about over, whether it's a friend, business partner, lover, or spouse. It won't be fun, but it simply must happen, and somewhere in the back of your brain, you understand that. You might even have subconsciously planted the seeds to bring it all to an end. Even if you're sure you haven't, your mission is to resist the urge to resist. Whatever leaves our lives under Pluto transits was meant to go. Just like a forest fire, however, what might be devastating at first will provide room for new life—and in your case, that means new relationships. Don't try to hold on to what's already gone, and don't despair. Pluto never fails to provide us with something better in the end. Feelings of loss are only natural, and you'll definitely need time to grieve for what's gone, but it's important that you look to the future and think of all the possibilities. Your life is fertile now, and you have a clean slate. It's like being reborn.

Cancer | January

Planetary Lightspots

A pack of planets in startling Aquarius and your solar eighth house of intimate partners and joint finances will turn those areas of life upside-down for you this month, Cancer—which may be exactly what needs to happen. If you're not happy with your love life or your shared financial situation, a total change may be necessary to get things back on track.

Relationships

The Sun will remain on duty in your solar seventh house of one-to-one relationships until January 20, Cancer, and since he will be wearing responsible, commitment-oriented Capricorn for the duration, you may be thinking of making things serious. Whoever has been a bit skittish, be it you or they, will finally come around.

Money and Success

Finances may not be all that stable this month, Cancer, so your mission is to only spend what you can comfortably afford. Set aside anything you can for a rainy day—or, should I say, a rainier day. The good news is that you'll likely find that you really don't need much to get by, and far less than you thought you did.

Planetary Hotspots

On January 4, the Full Moon will arrive in your very own sign, Cancer, and your solar first house of personality and appearance. You'll feel the need to bring closure to recent changes, so if you've been toying with the idea of starting a positive habit or quitting a bad one, it's time now to commit. Ready? Or not?

Rewarding Days

4, 5, 13, 14, 26, 27, 31

Challenging Days

2, 3, 15, 19, 29, 30

Cancer | February

Planetary Lightspots

The New Moon in unpredictable Aquarius will arrive on February 18, asking that you take a good long look at how you've been dividing domestic expenses. If you're carrying most of the weight, there's no shame in asking for help, especially from someone who clearly owes it to you. Your mission is to state your case sweetly.

Relationships

Until February 20, Venus, the Goddess of Love, will be in ultra-sensitive Pisces, a water-sign cousin of yours. She will move you to be especially compassionate, and not just to family and dear friends. Expand your comfort and support to include anyone who comes to you with a heavy burden to bear. You don't have to put them up permanently, but don't turn them away, either.

Money and Success

With Jupiter in your solar second house of personal finances, you have probably been thinking an awful lot about money lately, Cancer, and with good reason. If times are good, you may be overspending. If not— well, you're probably trying to cut back. Either way, it's important that you learn now to live within your means.

Planetary Hotspots

Several planets in assertive, impulsive Aries and your solar tenth house of authority figures will come together between February 19 and 22, Cancer, all of them urging you to break out on your own and make a name for yourself. This doesn't mean you should charge into the office of a higher-up and demand that raise to prove your mettle, but if you're forceful, polite, and firm, you might just get it anyway.

Rewarding Days

2, 5, 6, 7, 19, 24, 25

Challenging Days

1, 20, 21, 22, 23

Cancer | March

Planetary Lightspots

Several planets in assertive Aries will form easygoing trines with serious Saturn this month, Cancer. From their place in your solar tenth house of relationships with higher-ups, making your point won't be hard. Your mission is to be firm but polite—and do have your facts in order before you open your mouth!

Relationships

If you've been trying to think of a way to get yourself out of a no-win relationship, you might just come up with a solution once March 4 arrives. The thing is, you'll need to be ready to act fast, because Venus in impulsive Aries will be your astrological ally here, and she has no patience.

Money and Success

Thoughtful Mercury will stay on duty in your solar eighth house of joint finances until March 12, all done up in Aquarius, the sign of the genius. If you need to find a way out of a financial situation that is no longer profitable, all you have to do is think outside the box—or find yourself a professional who's known for those tactics.

Planetary Hotspots

The emotional Moon, your ruling planet, will chase the Sun into a total Solar Eclipse in your solar ninth house of higher education on March 20, just before the Sun dashes off into fiery Aries. Be sure you have all your certificates and employer recommendations in order, then make an appointment to meet with someone you'd really like to work for—or with. Things will happen fast, so be prepared.

Rewarding Days

2, 3, 5, 9, 17, 22, 23, 25, 30

Challenging Days

1, 4, 10, 11, 15, 16, 27

Cancer | April

Planetary Lightspots

Your solar fourth house of home, emotions, and family matters will receive a jolt on April 4 from your ruling planet, the Moon herself. She'll enter into a total Lunar Eclipse with the Sun, which ordinarily means that change will happen quickly—but it'll happen even faster now. Be sure your domestic partner is on board with changes you're ready to put in play.

Relationships

Uh oh. If you're attached, Cancer, you'll need to keep a watch on that wandering eye around April 11, when loving Venus will make her way into Gemini, a sign that, some say, can occasionally be a tad on the fickle side. If you're committed and happy about it, you'll know just what to do. If you're not, expect to be quite distracted by someone chatty, smart, and oh-so-interesting.

Money and Success

Once thoughtful Mercury enters Taurus, the astrological money-magnet sign, on April 14, you'll find it a lot easier to get by on what you have, Cancer, and to make a bit of spare cash on the side as well. This practical energy will set up shop in your solar eleventh house of groups, so talk up your hobby at a club or gathering you regularly attend.

Planetary Hotspots

The New Moon on April 18 will set up shop in your solar tenth house of professional matters and relationships with authority figures, Cancer. You are everyone's go-to gal or guy, so your boss might need you to help resolve a tough situation between two or more of your coworkers. Fortunately, they all know you're trustworthy, so it shouldn't be a problem.

Rewarding Days

1, 2, 12, 14, 19, 21

Challenging Days

4, 5, 6, 7, 8, 9, 17

Cancer | May

Planetary Lightspots

The New Moon on May 17 will bring together the Sun and your ruling planet, the Moon herself. Their astrological collision will occur in your solar eleventh house of friendships and groups, and since both planets will be wearing sensual Taurus, you might find that a formerly platonic relationship has taken a decidedly different turn.

Relationships

Your solar fifth house of lovers will play host to the Full Moon on May 3, Cancer, which means your very own ruling planet (the Moon) will be operating at full astrological speed. She'll be wearing intense, sexy Scorpio, so if you're single, expect to be approached by someone delicious who's just a bit dangerous. Before you take off with them, be sure they're not truly dangerous. Otherwise, enjoy!

Money and Success

The urge to splurge will be especially potent on May 4 and May 25, Cancer, so prepare to whip out your plastic or checkbook to pick up the tab. If you can afford it, fine. If you cannot, satisfy that urge by leaving an especially good tip. There's nothing wrong with letting others pay their own way. You do so much already!

Planetary Hotspots

Arguments with higher-ups, elders, and authority figures are quite possible on May 14, 15, and 22, Cancer, so if you have a bone to pick, try to get it out of the way through a peaceful discussion well before then. You are an emotional, instinctive creature, so you'll know the best time to sit down together. Just resolve to speak, not yell.

Rewarding Days
5, 6, 7, 16, 17

Challenging Days
3, 4, 10, 21, 22, 25, 31

Cancer | June

Planetary Lightspots

The Full Moon on June 2 will put your planet right in the middle of outgoing Sagittarius and your solar sixth house of work, Cancer, so you'll be willing to go overboard to prove to everyone that you're the person to come to when others fail to do their job. That will serve you well in the future, but be sure not to become a landing pad for projects no one else wants to tackle.

Relationships

On June 24, fiery Mars will storm the doors of your sign and your solar first house of personality, Cancer. For the next two months you'll be quite feisty, if not downright combative, especially with anyone who challenges those you love. Go to their defense, by all means, but be sure you're not endangering your own personal security.

Money and Success

With both Venus and excessive Jupiter in your solar second house of personal finances for most of the month, it's not hard to imagine you being quite free with your checkbook and credit cards. If it's for your kids, family, or home, not to worry. Otherwise, better keep a lid on your spending.

Planetary Hotspots

Once again, generous Jupiter will form an easy trine with startling Uranus, so just like back in March, you'll be able to advance your financial situation, Cancer. You might also find that you're quite attracted to someone who either works above you or for you. Be careful not to cross any lines that shouldn't be crossed.

Rewarding Days

4, 5, 6, 8, 9, 10, 28

Challenging Days

1, 13, 14, 23, 24

Cancer | July

Planetary Lightspots

The second Full Moon of the month will arrive on July 31, just in time to carry you off into August with a brand-new intimate partner. If you're single, that won't be the case much longer. Expect someone who's completely not your type to come along and sweep you off your feet. Ignore the odd hair or rebellious attitude and let your antennae decide.

Relationships

The Full Moon on July 1 will start off your month on an emotional note, Cancer. You'll need to make a very serious decision about a loved one who has been pushing the envelope for far too long. Yes, you should be understanding of their needs and their motives, but not at your own expense. Explain your feelings, and they'll be willing to cooperate.

Money and Success

Group ventures might be a bit more expensive than you'd originally planned on July 12, 15, and 25, Cancer, so if you're out and about, be sure that everyone is capable of picking up their fair share of the tab. The good news is that someone will probably offer to treat you for a change. What a concept!

Planetary Hotspots

The New Moon on July 15 will pit thoughtful Mercury and red-hot Mars against determined Pluto in your solar seventh house of one-to-one relationships. You may need to make a choice now, Cancer. Rest assured that with your ruling planet (the Moon) on board, it might not be an easy decision to make, but it will be the right one.

Rewarding Days
1, 2, 3, 5, 8, 13, 22

Challenging Days
6, 7, 11, 12, 14, 15, 16, 25

Cancer | August

Planetary Lightspots

The New Moon on August 14 will bring your ruling planet, the emotional Moon, together with the Sun himself. These astrological partners will both be wearing lavish Leo, and they have chosen your solar second house of finances for their meeting, so be prepared for a whole lot of gifts and dramatic expressions of feelings.

Relationships

If a situation between you and your current partner has come to a head recently and you have been trying to figure out exactly what to do about it, you might just be able to find a way to make it all work out on August 15. Your mission is to let them know that they are valued, supported, and protected. The rest will work itself out nicely.

Money and Success

With both generous Jupiter and Venus, the Goddess of Love and Money, on duty in your solar second house of finances right up until August 11, it's tough to imagine you having a hard time financially. You might be a bit too extravagant, but that will settle down after August 11 when Jupiter passes into practical Virgo. In the meantime, have some fun. You certainly deserve it.

Planetary Hotspots

After a year in theatrical Leo, mighty Jupiter will move off into hard-working, earthy Virgo on August 11. He'll take up residence in your solar third house of conversations and communications, so no matter what you're thinking, it will easily slip off your tongue. The good news is that you won't mince words and others will come to realize that you mean what you say.

Rewarding Days
1, 2, 7, 23, 26

Challenging Days
3, 5, 6, 12, 21, 30, 31

Cancer | September

Planetary Lightspots

All your dealings with your boss—or any other authority figure, for that matter—will go quite well on September 8 and 22. So if you need to plead your case, regardless of the reason, be sure you choose those dates to schedule your appointment. You may actually find that they need some help, too, that only you can provide.

Relationships

An argument with a higher-up that takes place on September 24 or 25 might seem like the end of your career, Cancer, but in reality, standing up for yourself is the best thing you could possibly do, in their eyes. You need and deserve respect—and you've earned it, too—so don't back down from what you know is fair.

Money and Success

After weeks of moving retrograde through your solar second house of money matters, Venus will turn direct on September 6, ready to help you straighten out any recent financial misunderstandings. You will have your choice of advisors—one of whom may actually end up being a bit more than a consultant and a lot more than a friend.

Planetary Hotspots

Two eclipses will occur this month, Cancer, so your ruling planet, the Moon, will be up in arms on September 13 and 27. On September 13, she'll lead you into battle on behalf of a sibling or neighbor who is rather helpless at the moment. On September 27, it will be an elder or authority figure you rise up to fight for. Not to worry, though. Your efforts will not go unnoticed.

Rewarding Days

4, 5, 6, 22, 23, 27, 30

Challenging Days

3, 9, 16, 24, 25

Cancer | October

Planetary Lightspots

On October 30 and 31, the Sun will get together with Neptune, who just loves playing dress-up, under any circumstances. Needless to say, this will be an especially happy Halloween, and you really should not pass up any opportunity to don an interesting disguise, get out there, and have some fun. You'll get a whole lot more treats than tricks!

Relationships

If an argument with your primary partner arises on October 6, Cancer, not to worry. In the days that follow, you'll be able to work it out and bring practical, realistic solutions into the mix. If it's not all over by October 23, just a touch of TLC accompanied by a heartfelt hug should do the trick.

Money and Success

You'll need to put your money where your mouth is this month, Cancer, both figuratively and literally, so don't make any bets you know you can't win or demands you won't stand firm on, especially around October 10. If you do get a bit overzealous, look to October 23 for the chance to pay off your debts and maintain your dignity.

Planetary Hotspots

Once Mercury turns direct in your solar fourth house of home and family matters on October 9, it will be prime time to finally have that discussion you have been putting off with a relative, child, or domestic partner. Your mission is to resist the urge to put it off any longer. Put those cards on the table!

Rewarding Days
8, 9, 13, 15, 23, 24

Challenging Days
5, 6, 10, 16, 22, 25

Cancer | November

Planetary Lightspots

There will be a whole lot of pillow talk going on after November 1, Cancer, when chatty Mercury sets off for sexy Scorpio and your solar fifth house of lovers. This passionate planet will invest all his energy into inspiring you to let someone know exactly how delicious you think they are. The good news is that they'll do the same.

Relationships

Speaking of pillow talk, it's going to be quite the passionate month. The Sun and thoughtful Mercury will spend most of it in sexy Scorpio, a water-sign cousin of yours who never was known to be shy about physical intimacy. Take advantage of this opportunity to say exactly what's on your mind—but be polite about it. Whispering is your best bet.

Money and Success

Once Venus slips into your solar fourth house of home, emotions, and family matters, you'll be able to iron out all those money-related problems with a family member. If they're not on the same page as the month begins, not to worry. After November 8, you'll find them to be extremely cooperative.

Planetary Hotspots

If an argument comes up around November 20 and it seems to be pretty darn serious, you'll have two choices. Either make nice by pointing out the humor in the situation or devote yourself to cutting things off with this person for good. Only you can make that decision, but chances are good that if you go for option number one, everything will end peacefully.

Rewarding Days
4, 5, 6, 10, 11

Challenging Days
2, 19, 20, 23, 24, 26, 29

Cancer | December

Planetary Lightspots

A bonus, raise, or promotion you've been working very hard to get will be available to you this month, Cancer, as soon as December 1. You won't see it coming, which will make it all the more exciting. If you're tempted to celebrate around December 4 or 14, go for it. Just don't spend it all in one place!

Relationships

Talk over any recent disputes with your significant other before the holiday arrives. December 19 would be a great day to begin negotiations, but you'll need to stick to your guns, no matter how determined they seem to be to have things their way. Your mission is to stay firm, refuse to buckle, and let them know you won't play games any longer.

Money and Success

If you're after a loan or trying to work out the details of a shared inheritance, Cancer, you'd do well to push matters along on December 17, when Venus and Pluto will be more than happy to help. Yes, you can do this, and yes, you can make your point and still be nice about it. Just keep your temper in check and smile pretty. 'Tis the season, after all!

Planetary Hotspots

Happy holidays! Just in time for a warm, loving gathering, your ruling planet, the emotional Moon, will become full on December 25, all done up in your warm, loving sign. This will make for lots of good feelings circulating around the dinner table and lots of long, sentimental chats in the kitchen late into the night. Enjoy!

Rewarding Days

11, 12, 15, 16, 17, 24, 25

Challenging Days

3, 4, 6, 10, 14, 20, 29

Cancer Action Table

These dates reflect the best–but not the only–times for success and ease in these activities, according to your Sun sign.

	JAN	FEB	MAR	APR	MAY	JUN	JUL	AUG	SEP	OCT	NOV	DEC
Move	4			3, 4			15, 16		9, 30	12, 13	13	
Start a class	19, 30				29, 30		1, 8, 13			30, 31		
Join a club				12, 19, 21, 22							23	
Ask for a raise	1, 19	7	3, 4	6, 22		22, 27, 28		4				1, 8
Look for work				2, 3		1, 2, 3		1, 2	23	8	24, 25	1, 8
Get pro advice	4, 5, 22		24, 25			6				13, 23		
Get a loan		17, 18, 19					20, 21, 22		23			
See a doctor			7		11, 27		26		23	23, 27	9	
Start a diet	4		27				18					
End relationship	3, 30	6			20, 21	14, 15		5			20	
Buy clothes				2, 6			22, 23	15, 19				
Get a makeover	4					24	15					
New romance		19, 21, 24, 25			2, 3		1, 2	6			10, 11	
Vacation	18, 19		23		16, 17					6, 16	6	28, 29

Leo

The Lion
July 22 to August 22

♌

Element: Fire

Quality: Fixed

Polarity: Yang/masculine

Planetary Ruler: The Sun

Meditation: I trust in the strength of my soul

Gemstone: Ruby

Power Stones: Topaz, sardonyx

Key Phrase: I will

Glyph: Lion's tail

Anatomy: Heart, upper back

Colors: Gold, scarlet

Animals: Lions, large cats

Myths/Legends: Apollo, Isis, Helios

House: Fifth

Opposite Sign: Aquarius

Flowers: Marigold, sunflower

Keyword: Magnetic

The Leo Personality

Your Strengths and Challenges

Yours is the sign of the performer, Leo, so you're perfectly happy as long as you're able to entertain and amuse the masses (which, in your mind, is anywhere people gather in groups of one or more). Entertaining comes quite easily to you, and wherever you are can quickly become a stage at a moment's notice, complete with that traveling spotlight you've always got handy and an admiring pack of fans you never fail to attract. It wouldn't be right to talk about you without mentioning the fact that you're a proud sign, and rightly so. After all, Leo has also long been known as the sign of royalty. Think of all those medieval shields and banners that featured your symbol, the lion. Lions are know for being fiercely loyal, but also playful and family-oriented. With your ruling planet being the Sun, who just so happens to be The Big Kahuna in our corner of the Universe, it would be tough not to strut a little. The Sun rules our sense of self, so your ego often comes into play in your encounters. The thing is, once that ego is bruised, intentionally or not, the offender can never totally retract their statements or actions. You do forgive, but like all the fixed signs, you never forget.

Being a lion or lioness, one of the things you enjoy the most is the thrill of victory after a hard-won battle. You're tough, aggressive, determined, and persistent, so you don't often lose, and you accept challenges quite readily. Just be sure not to put personal pride before sensibility. Even Leos are vulnerable!

Your Relationships

You're nothing if not charming, Leo, and you somehow manage to make everyone around you feel special, so it's easy to understand why you're not often alone—unless you want to be, which doesn't happen very often, and usually only when your ego is bruised or you feel unappreciated. You relish the attention and admiration of others, but the amount of thoughtfulness and energy you're willing to put out to gain it makes you a sought-after companion, a wonderfully entertaining friend, and an unbeatable partner. You know exactly how to please and delight your partner, and you're always willing to do just that. All you ask in return is a heartfelt thank-you—okay, and maybe just a bit of attention and a word or two of praise for your efforts.

Your gift for romance is world-famous, too, so anyone lucky enough to land a long-term "contract" with you knows exactly how blessed they are to have you. Just in case they can't quite believe their luck, you'll go out of your way to spoil them. It might be an elegant, expensive night out, or it might be an invitation to your place for the evening, during which time you'll cater to their every need. You'll pass out foot rubs and full massages, complete with incense, candles, and soft, sexy music—and that's just the warm-up. You make very sure that those you love never, ever need to doubt it. Making sure they know how loyal you are and what you're willing to do to protect them is a very big part of that. Just like your symbol, the lion, you fiercely protect your own, most especially your pack, which includes your family, your friends, and of course your mate.

When it comes to choosing that mate, you'll probably go through quite a few admirers but end up feeling most comfortable with Sagittarius and Aries. They'll make terrific long-term friends, but if what you're after is what you give—entertainment and loyalty—then funny, witty Gemini and partner-oriented Libra are also good bets.

Your Career and Money

You're an extremely creative soul, Leo, and perfectly capable of mastering any craft—provided you feel that you're allowed to follow your bliss and be appreciated and applauded for your efforts. Remember, you're a performer at heart, so love and admiration are primary needs, no matter which field you choose to pursue. You get along well with children, so teaching might be a good fit for you, but as long as you're "onstage" wherever you choose to earn your daily bread, all will be well in your kingdom. Since you're so fond of the spotlight, you might also choose a career that involves performing in some way. Whether it's acting, comedy, music, or art, if you use all that fixed fire, you'll make a name for yourself quickly. Money isn't always easy to manage, since you so love to spend it, especially on those you adore, most especially by providing them with fun, memorable, one-of-a-kind experiences. Remember that those who truly love you don't need to be materialistically spoiled. Just being with you is a treat.

Your Lighter Side

You're quite fiery, Leo, and very fond of adventure, which satisfies the lion in you. You love to compete, because there's nothing like an award, a medal, or a ribbon to add to your sizable collection. Most of all, though, you love performing, so if you're at all inclined, join a local theater group or get yourself to some auditions. Even if you don't get the part, the experience itself will be amazingly rewarding.

Affirmation for the Year
Whatever is dearest to my heart provides the inspiration to truly be myself.

The Year Ahead for Leo

You have quite the year ahead of you, Leo. To start with, Venus, the Goddess of Love and Money, has extended the length of her usual stay in a sign so that she can be with you for just over four months. The beauty of this is that you're the sign of the romantic and she's the planet of romance. Talk about a match made in heaven! From June 5 to July 18 and again from July 31 through October 8, this attractive, magnetic energy will hold her royal court in your solar first house of personality and appearance, easily drawing new fans your way. At least one of them might just have the right stuff to tempt you into coffee, lunch, or the ultimate prize, dinner and drinks, so this could be the beginning of a beautiful friendship. It might turn out to be much more, too, especially if you get together around July 1. Without really trying, you'll keep all your admirers enchanted, and just for fun, a few fiery, dramatic shows will probably be on the agenda, too. Expect to be extremely concerned with your physical self, and your mane to become a top priority.

Now, all that is plenty reason to imagine you happy, loved, possibly in love, and feeling more creative than you have in a long time, but once we add in the influence of extravagant, excessive Jupiter, who's signed up to travel through your sign until August 11, you'll be a force to be reckoned with. Remember, Jupiter expands the energies of any planet he's hanging out with, and since these two are the heavens' most generous, beneficial planets, there's very little you won't be able to accomplish if you put your mind to it—okay, and as long as you turn on the charm, which Venus will provide naturally.

Speaking of creativity, no matter what artform you're in love with, you'll be especially in tune with your audience this year. It's a great time to contribute to an art show, get together with an improvisational group, or just strut proudly into the boss's office and (charmingly) demand that raise. No matter where you point this pair of planets, you're just about guaranteed success. Who could possibly refuse all this positive, assertive energy? Jupiter might also prompt you to return to school for a beauty-oriented career or to help you hone a skill.

Saturn will return briefly to Scorpio to tie up a few loose ends in your solar fourth house of domestic matters from June 14 through September 17. After two and a half years of working hard to organize your home and provide support of every kind for your family, your goals will finally be in sight, if not right in your hot little hands. For the rest of the year, Saturn will spend his time in Sagittarius and your solar fifth house of playtime and creative pursuits. So while Venus and Jupiter are encouraging you to showcase your talents, Saturn will help you to maintain a respectable image. It's the perfect astrological recipe for success—provided you're doing what you really love and you're confident of your expertise.

The fifth house also includes your relationships with lovers, play-mates, and children, however, and since Saturn tends to be a rather serious, career-oriented guy, you might not have a lot of time to devote to recreation, but you'll surely make the most of it when it comes along. Saturn loves to test us, so if those closest to you seem a bit needier than usual, it might just be his not-so-subtle way of encouraging you to cut the apron strings and teach them to stand on their own two feet. His patrol this year through Sagittarius will put him in a far less critical mood, but remember, no matter what sign he's wearing, Saturn is still Saturn, the honorary authority figure. Oh, and he's also fond of bringing us relationships with a hefty age difference.

Uranus will continue his electrifying path through Aries and your solar ninth house, which rules long-distance places and people, along with higher education and new experiences. Fortunately, Aries is a fire sign as impulsive as your own, so no matter what this unpredictable planet tosses your way—and you can expect some major surprises in this department—you'll adapt. Use this energy to study computers, take off on a spontaneous trip, or get involved with a whole new political party or belief system you never, ever thought you'd even consider. You might also fall madly in love with the owner of a wonderful accent. Only one thing is for certain with Uranus: you won't be bored!

Neptune will spend yet another year in your solar eighth house, turning you into the equivalent of a psychic sponge. Your intuition will be spot on, and you'll be able to sit still, do research, and dig up clues. And speaking of research and clues, Pluto himself, the detective/analyst, will spend his time in your solar sixth house of health and work-related matters. Any position that requires you to dig up information will make you very happy now, even if you end up doing a bit more work than you'd planned on. If there's a bit of intrigue to the matter, so much the better. Also, if there's anything going on behind the scenes on the job that you need to know about, not to worry. Between Pluto and Neptune, the truth will surface. It might be that you have an ally you never knew you had, or that you find the answers yourself. Regardless, it will be very, very tough to put anything over on you. Your antennae will be operating on high, and traitors or conspirators against you will be dealt with accordingly. If that means banishment from your world, well then, that's what it means. You don't terminate relationships often, but when you decide it's over, it's definitely over.

What This Year's Eclipses Mean for You

There will be four eclipses occurring during 2015, Leo, and while none of them fall in your sign, there will still be a whole lot of astrological activity in your world due to these lunations. On March 20, a total Solar Eclipse will bring the Sun and Moon together in Pisces and your solar eighth house of intimate relationships and joint finances. Now, Pisces is a sign that's quite romantic, much like yours, so if you're seeing someone around then, expect a wonderfully romantic surprise—or to be in the mood to deliver one up yourself. If you're single and tired of what's available in your neck of the woods, a singles cruise might be just what the doctor ordered. Financial matters could be quite confusing and others may be blatantly trying to take advantage of you, so wait until the end of the month to make anything final.

On April 4, a total Lunar Eclipse will occur in Libra and your solar third house of conversations and communications. Now, you're always charming—that's just a given—but once this eclipse celestially "nukes" you with Libra's own special brand of charisma, you'll be just deadly. If you're shopping for a new lover, you should be able to land one in twenty-five words or less. If you're not interested in someone, however, take note of the date and don't flirt with them. Eclipse energy is tough to dismiss once it has a foothold. Getting in touch with someone who once lived near you or with a sibling—now, that's where you should be aiming this sweet, potent stuff.

The Solar Eclipse of September 13 will open your eyes to a financial situation that really, really needs to be reorganized, insisting that you drag out those dreaded record books and take stock of the situation. Yes, that might mean a checkbook desperately needs to be balanced or a credit card situation needs to be dealt with. Tend to your favorite possessions with loving care.

The final eclipse of the year will arrive on September 27 and will bring its high-powered Aries energy to your solar ninth house of higher education and long-distance trips. Outdoor adventures, overseas travel, and evening classes are all terrific ideas, but anything that allows you to get to know a larger world than your own will work just fine.

Saturn

Career-oriented, responsible Saturn has been rough on you lately, hasn't he? For the past two and a half years, he's been marching through intense, unyielding Scorpio and your solar fourth house of domestic matters, demanding that you manage the needs of everyone involved with both your domestic and professional lives. Oftentimes, your attention has been desperately needed by both, and you've probably developed a whole new problem-solving technique, which was exactly Pluto's point, but no one's saying it was easy. Well, help is on the way, and yes, it's almost over, but don't exhale just yet. You'll have to take care of any unfinished issues that involve your home, kids, or family members, and you'll need to do it between June 14 and September 17. It's "now or never" time, so gird your loins and get down to business.

Saturn's passage through Sagittarius this year will put him in your solar fifth house of fun times, and since he isn't much for frivolous pursuits and just loves handing out responsibility, you might need to take charge of your team, replace a leader who wasn't quite on their game, or supervise the kids in a group situation. Contrary to popular opinion, you'll be able to have fun, even with Saturn in this house. The thing is, you'll have to work for it—which will turn out to be quite gratifying. Plus, if anyone loves to lead, it's you.

Uranus

If you were born between August 4 and 14, you'll be enjoying the company of Uranus (also known as Mr. Unpredictable) for most of this year, Leo. Fortunately, he'll be forming an easy trine with your Sun, so the fireworks and surprises he'll bring along—and you can count on these, if nothing else—will, for the most part, be pleasant. Still, since he'll be in your solar ninth house of new adventures, higher education, and far-off places, you should probably get used to the whole concept of growth. You might be doing a lot more overseas or long-distance traveling, or you might actually move your home. You might suddenly decide to take up a whole new learning path or switch political parties. At first, even though you're nothing if not adventurous, so much change might be unsettling, but remember, this is your celestial chance to stretch your wings and grow on so many levels! Don't waste this opportunity. Get on that plane, sign up for those classes you've been thinking of, investigate new groups, and above all else, consider any challenge a chance to get to know what you're really made of.

Neptune

If you were born between July 28 and August 3, Neptune will form an inconjunct aspect with your Sun this year, Leo, from her spot in your solar eighth house of intense situations, joint resources, and intimate relationships. Now, remember, Neptune is a big fan of illusions. She prefers the artificial perfection of her fantasies to anything even remotely resembling reality—and above all else, she adores dimly lit places. When she visits the Sun in our charts, most of us experience an extreme case of ultra-sensitivity to anything harsh. That goes for bright lights, loud sounds, and negative people. If you're around any of that this year, take whatever steps necessary to get away, even if it means you'll need to be on your own for a bit. Avoid signing anything that will lock you into long-term payments without the advice of someone you're sure knows what they're doing. You don't need to saddle yourself with debt now, but it's a good time to get work on dissolving it. Oh, and if you're attached, remember the incense, candles, and romantic music on all of your special evenings. You're a sponge right now, and sponges soak up all sorts of things. Protect yourself. Provide yourself with nothing but the most soothing of surroundings and the most trusted of companions.

Pluto

If you were born between August 4 and 10, you'll once again be entertaining intense Pluto in your solar sixth house of health and work-related matters and relationships. Now, Pluto in this house often helps us to drive home the point that we're not just great at our job—

we're absolutely irreplaceable. This quest, to make a point of just how indispensable you are, is a major part of Pluto's mission for you right now. It's all about taking back control of your life. If you're harboring any doubts about your profession, listen to Pluto and make whatever changes are necessary. The good news is that, regardless of the reason, anything you clear out of your life over the coming year will not leave vacant space for long. In fact, this new space will be a place of new growth, and growth is a pretty common astrological theme for you this year. If you're not happy where you are or you feel that your upward movement is being stifled, look around. See what's out there. Bet you'll find something new and exciting if you dig deep enough. You'll probably be in the mood to change some health habits, and since Pluto is so fond of endings followed rapidly by new beginnings, quitting a bad habit and starting several new and healthier ones would be a stellar idea.

Leo | January

Planetary Lightspots

The New Moon on January 20 will occur in Aquarius, set and ready to get you started on a rather rebellious path. It will most likely be your significant other or an old, dear friend who inspires you to make some changes. If you're not happy or you feel some injustice has been committed, you won't stop until you've set things right.

Relationships

The Full Moon in Cancer on January 4 will cast a very bright light into your solar twelfth house of secrets, Leo. If you have been doing anything that you really do not want the rest of the world to know about, better prepare yourself. Loving Venus will make her way into startling Aquarius and your solar seventh house of one-to-one relationships on January 3, so you may need to put out some fires.

Money and Success

If you've been thinking about investing in a social cause, Leo, and you're sure it's about to take off, this is the right month to do it. On January 3, Venus, the planetary purveyor of the purse strings, will take off for Aquarius, urging you to only spend your money where it will do the most good. You'll rebel against major corporations and want to shop only with local, worthy merchants.

Planetary Hotspots

Saturn's recent arrival into your solar fifth house of lovers and playmates might initially seem to put a damper on things, Leo, especially if you have just started seeing someone. If geographical roadblocks or an age difference are tough to deal with, weigh it out. What are you willing to do to keep this thing going?

Rewarding Days
4, 5, 13, 14, 20, 22, 27

Challenging Days
2, 3, 15, 16, 19, 29, 30

Leo | February

Planetary Lightspots

You'll easily be able to have your way on February 24 and 25, Leo, when serious Saturn, the honorary authority figure, steps in to make an executive decision. No matter what battle you're trying to win, the answer is simple now: make it clear that you're in charge and you won't take no for an answer.

Relationships

For the second month in a row, a New Moon will occur in your solar seventh house of relationships, Leo, urging you to make some serious changes, not just within your personal relationships but also with regard to the way you present yourself to others when you first meet. For now, be satisfied with raising a few eyebrows.

Money and Success

Several planets will come together in impulsive Aries from February 19 through 22, Leo. One of them will be Venus, who's in charge of money matters. In this sign, and in cahoots with passionate Mars, she'll be sure to nudge you toward making some purchases that might be fun temporarily but are not necessary. How about forgetting about material things? Spend your hard-earned cash on experiences instead.

Planetary Hotspots

The Full Moon in your sign will set fire to your solar first house of personality and appearances, Leo, urging you to be true to yourself, above all else. If you need to make some physical changes, this is the perfect time. Look yourself over and decide what you like and what you don't. Map out a plan that includes ending bad habits and creating a new, more positive lifestyle.

Rewarding Days

3, 4, 7, 19, 24, 25

Challenging Days

1, 5, 6, 20, 21, 23

Leo | March

Planetary Lightspots

The big astrological news this month is the easy trine between generous Jupiter and surprising Uranus on March 3. They'll come together to inspire you to get yourself free of anything that's holding you back. If travel and education are on that list—recurring themes for most of the year—you should pay attention. Give your mind and your body an entirely new challenge.

Relationships

Chatty, sociable Mercury will leave your solar seventh house of one-to-one relationships on March 12, Leo. He's been there for two months, so getting used to life without the rollercoaster ride will be tough at first. The good news is that he'll take off for your solar eighth house of intimate partners wearing romantic Pisces, so you'll definitely have pleasant distractions to keep you occupied.

Money and Success

If you're after a loan or you're dealing with disputes over inheritances or other joint financial matters, avoid March 16, when authority figures will seem to go out of their way to stop you in your tracks. If you must handle things then, be sure you have all paperwork in order and a professional on hand to plead your case.

Planetary Hotspots

A total Solar Eclipse on March 20 will make it all too easy for you to cut your losses and run in the department of intimate partners, but before you do, be sure you're not simply acting out of anger. Is this truly what you want? Remember, eclipses play for keeps, and their effects are hard to undo.

Rewarding Days

1, 2, 3, 9, 22, 23, 25, 30

Challenging Days

5, 6, 7, 11, 16, 26, 27

Leo | April

Planetary Lightspots

The New Moon on April 18 will once again activate a rebellious urge to get out of town and distance yourself from responsibilities. A far-off loved one may contact you with regard to an urgent situation. They'll be looking for help, but sticking a band-aid on a bad situation is only a temporary solution. Get them some counseling or a seasoned advisor to help them change their ways.

Relationships

Serious Saturn is making his way through your solar fifth house of lovers, paving the way for you to get up close and personally involved with someone a lot older or younger than yourself. Before you decide to ditch the relationship before you've even taken it out for a test drive, be sure you're not just worried about what others will say—which really shouldn't matter at all.

Money and Success

Getting involved in a group project could end up being quite profitable for you this month, Leo, especially if you're going to be directly involved in how it all progresses. You're used to being in charge, and that won't change, but don't let your ego get between you and someone else's great idea just because you didn't think of it first. Stay open!

Planetary Hotspots

A total Lunar Eclipse will occur in Libra on April 4 in your solar third house of communications and conversations. Your charming people-pleasing skills will come in handy now, especially if someone asks you to mediate a dispute. Make it clear that you're willing, but you won't take sides based on your heart. It's all about making fair and unbiased decisions.

Rewarding Days

2, 6, 11, 12, 21, 22, 26, 28

Challenging Days

4, 5, 7, 15, 17, 19, 20

Leo | May

Planetary Lightspots

The Full Moon on May 3 will light up your solar fourth house of home and emotions, Leo. It will be all done up in intensely private and secretive Scorpio. Urgent situations with kids and other family members may come along, but you'll be amazed at what you can do when you're under a bit of pressure. Resolve to stay calm and avoid any drama.

Relationships

Venus will square off with shocking Uranus on May 25, pitting your solar twelfth house of secrets against your solar ninth house of long-distance lovers. If you've been trying to keep an online relationship quiet, someone may discover it now, so if you don't want that to happen, be especially discreet. Friendships will require time and energy from May 27 through May 30. All they really need is someone to talk with. Give them the benefit of your experience.

Money and Success

With Venus in Cancer, you'll probably end up spending more than you'd planned to on your home after May 7, but if it makes you happy, go for it. If you don't have time to do the housework yourself, hire a maid service for a deep cleaning. Kids may need help with expenses, or an elder may require special care you simply can't provide.

Planetary Hotspots

On May 18, talkative Mercury will stop to turn retrograde in your solar eleventh house of friendships and group activities. For the next three weeks, getting together with The Gang could be tougher than usual, so you'll need to be patient, which has never been your specialty. The good news is that if you've been performing lately, you'll be asked back for an encore.

Rewarding Days

5, 6, 7, 16, 17, 30

Challenging Days

3, 9, 15, 22, 25, 29, 31

Leo | June

Planetary Lightspots

The Full Moon in lighthearted Sagittarius will illuminate your solar fifth house of playmates and lovers on June 1, asking that you be especially generous to someone you love—which is really saying something, since you're already such a giving soul. Rather than splurging on an object, why not treat them to a fun, exciting evening out?

Relationships

Venus, the Goddess of Love, will stay on duty in your sign from June 5 on, Leo. All of us will be feeling a bit theatrical and dramatic when it comes to romance, but your mission is to resist the urge to overdo it, even if you're dreadfully in love and willing to do absolutely anything to prove it. Just be yourself. Anyone who appreciates quality will get the message.

Money and Success

Venus rules love, but also money matters, Leo. So once she enters your sign on June 5, her natural magnetism will attract all kinds of wonderful financial opportunities. Devote your time and energy to what you love. It doesn't matter whether it's art, music, performing, or teaching. Do what you do best, and success will follow.

Planetary Hotspots

Jupiter and Uranus will form an easy trine once again on June 22, Leo, bringing along the possibility of fame, fortune, and a whole lot of fans—oh, and it will happen suddenly. If you're not a contestant on *American Idol*, you should definitely apply now. No matter what you're vying for, keep your self-confidence intact and you'll easily have it.

Rewarding Days

2, 5, 6, 8, 9, 10, 22

Challenging Days

1, 13, 14, 23, 29, 30

Leo | July

Planetary Lightspots

One never knows what Uranus will bring along. He is, after all, the most unpredictable energy in the heavens. On July 2, however, he'll arrange a "coincidental" meeting for you, possibly at the convenience store on the corner or at the local dry cleaners. At some point in your day, someone who is in a position to charge you up and get you motivated will cross your path. Pay attention to small talk.

Relationships

The second Full Moon of the month, a "blue moon" in Aquarius, will storm the borders of your solar seventh house of relationships on July 31. This bright light will turn a heavenly spotlight on your relationships. For better or worse, you'll have the information you need to make the decision you've been putting off. Listen to your antennae.

Money and Success

Neptune, that dreamy, woozy planet, has been playing hide and seek in your solar eighth house for years now, Leo, so you're probably used to being a bit confused about intimate relationships and joint finances. On July 15, however, you'll need to be on your toes to guard against being taken advantage of by someone who recognizes how vulnerable you are.

Planetary Hotspots

The Sun, Mercury, and Mars in private Cancer will take turns passing through your solar twelfth house of secrets. It's easy to imagine you being ready for a little rest and relaxation—but you don't have to chill out alone. Look to July 15 for the chance to hide out together. You may have to convince them to play hooky with you, but won't that make it even more exciting?

Rewarding Days

1, 2, 3, 5, 13, 21, 22, 23

Challenging Days

6, 7, 12, 14, 15, 18, 25

Leo | August

Planetary Lightspots

On August 4, the heavens' two most generous planets will come together, Leo—in your sign. Yes, loving Venus and lucky Jupiter will collide, ready and willing to fix you up with whatever you need. Your mission is to imagine your wildest dreams becoming reality. Picture it all unfolding, and expect to see it, very soon.

Relationships

Isn't love grand, Leo? Well, it sure will be this month. Venus is on duty in your sign, and together with generous Jupiter, she'll find a way to get you connected with the person you were beginning to doubt was actually out there. The good news is that once you exchange a few words, you'll both know it was worth the wait.

Money and Success

Your financial plans may be delayed due to circumstances beyond your control on August 5, Leo, but not to worry. It's only Saturn, holding you back until the time is right. You'll be irritated by the wait, but if you can sit tight for just a few days, everything will work out and you'll understand why you shouldn't have acted sooner.

Planetary Hotspots

Jupiter, the King of Excess, will square off with frugal Saturn on August 3, Leo. Now, Jupiter is in your sign, so you will feel this celestial war more personally than most of us. The good news is that all you really have to do now is think about what's really necessary for your lifestyle and let the rest go—at least for now.

Rewarding Days

1, 2, 4, 7, 13, 15, 19, 26

Challenging Days

3, 6, 12, 21, 22, 31

Leo | September

Planetary Lightspots

The total Lunar Eclipse on September 27 will set up shop in your solar ninth house, wearing fiery, assertive Aries. If you need to make a change in your routine, you'll have the chance, and long-distance travel is a terrific way to do it. If you can't get away just yet, get involved with an educational group with members who tend to color outside the lines.

Relationships

After weeks of moving retrograde and asking that you retrace your steps and reconsider recent decisions you've made regarding a loved one, Venus will turn direct on September 6. She'll be in your sign at the time, so prepare yourself, because this will be a drastic turn-around. Ready or not, it's time to give your final answer to someone who's been more than patient.

Money and Success

If you're after financial counseling, you'd do well to seek it out around September 5, Leo, when the Sun and Pluto will come together in an easy trine. These two will see to it that you find exactly the right person you need for your particular issues. They might even be able to talk you into tightening your belt a bit.

Planetary Hotspots

Saturn will stalk off into your solar fifth house of lovers and playmates on September 17, Leo, demanding that you do whatever it takes to get your recreational activities organized. It might be that the kids need a new softball coach or a chaperone for the big dance. It doesn't matter, though. You'll have two and a half years to pull it off, but rest assured that no one will question your authority.

Rewarding Days
4, 5, 6, 8, 22, 23

Challenging Days
9, 10, 13, 16, 24, 25

Leo | October

Planetary Lightspots

'Tis the season to dress up and act out a part, Leo—which means you're due for some serious fun. The best part is that the heavens are more than willing to play along, and they'll be especially cooperative on October 30 and 31. Yes, there will be masquerade parties, and yes, you'll have a chance to perform. Talk about a good time!

Relationships

Loving Venus will square off with no-nonsense Saturn on October 10, so relationships will be challenging. An elder who lives quite a distance from you may need some support, or you might need to weigh the virtues of an assisted living facility versus bringing them home. Not an easy choice, but if you think rationally and trust your instincts, you'll know exactly what to do.

Money and Success

Venus will tiptoe into your solar second house of personal money matters on October 8, and along with her sister, the emotional Moon, she'll see to it that you don't have a thing to worry about. If you've crossed your t's and dotted your i's, all will be well. Your mission is to be sure all your paperwork is completely filled out and all your debts are paid.

Planetary Hotspots

You might need to mediate a dispute about a work-related issue on October 22, Leo, but if you stay calm and refuse to take sides, it won't be a problem. Health matters that are troubling you will work out well almost immediately. Don't let your imagination run away with you, and stay away from webmd.com.

Rewarding Days

8, 13, 14, 23, 25, 30, 31

Challenging Days

5, 6, 9, 10, 16, 17, 22

Leo | November

Planetary Lightspots

You'll be a very happy camper as of November 22, Leo. The Sun will make his way into fun, happy-go-lucky Sagittarius and your solar fifth house of lovers and playmates, asking that you spend whatever free time you have enjoying the company of those who love recreation as much as you do. It might be the kids or it might be your usual crowd. It doesn't matter. Just be sure to get your share of warm hugs and laughter.

Relationships

Once Venus makes her way into partner-pleasing Libra on November 8, you'll be more than willing to consider compromises you wouldn't have thought of a month ago, Leo. The good news is that the important people in your life will offer you the same courtesy. Obviously, it's prime time to make nice.

Money and Success

On November 2, Venus will come together with the Moon in your solar second house of personal finances. These two planets are often in the neighborhood when decisions regarding home and family come up, but not to worry. They'll be in practical Virgo, and all your choices will be based on facts, not emotions.

Planetary Hotspots

You do your level best to keep us all entertained and amused, Leo, which is no easy job. On November 20, that job might become just a bit tougher, when charming Venus gets into an edgy square with Pluto, who just loves to unearth the truth. Fortunately, you're really good at being blunt, so if someone calls you out, you'll be ready with an answer.

Rewarding Days

5, 6, 8, 10, 13, 22, 25

Challenging Days

2, 3, 17, 20, 23, 24, 26

Leo | December

Planetary Lightspots

The Sun will form an easy, cooperative trine with surprising Uranus on December 8, Leo, making it extremely easy for you to expose your secrets and make sudden announcements without needing to worry about what others might think. Your mission is to say whatever you need to say. Don't debate with yourself about the consequences. You know what needs to be left unsaid.

Relationships

As of December 4, you might need someone who's emotionally unbiased to help you sort out right from wrong on the home front, Leo. The good news is that they'll be there for you. The best news is that you'll be able to use their advice, your perceptive skills, and your knowledge of all parties involved to arrive at a fair solution.

Money and Success

Venus will spend most of the month in intense, focused Scorpio and your solar fourth house of home and domestic matters, Leo, and from that point on, you'll be dealing with at least one person who seems to be deliberately making life tough for you. They're not. Their own financial problems are so overwhelming that they can't see how their behavior is affecting you. Be merciful.

Planetary Hotspots

On December 25, just in time for a wonderful holiday, the Full Moon in warm, family-oriented Cancer will arrive, Leo, urging you to allow those who are nearest and dearest to your heart to spoil you—just a touch. Now, spoiling others is your specialty, but every now and then, you can allow the favor to be returned. Enjoy!

Rewarding Days

1, 5, 8, 10, 12, 17, 24, 25

Challenging Days

3, 4, 13, 14, 19, 29

Leo Action Table

These dates reflect the best—but not the only—times for success and ease in these activities, according to your Sun sign.

	JAN	FEB	MAR	APR	MAY	JUN	JUL	AUG	SEP	OCT	NOV	DEC
Move	13, 14, 27										10, 11, 13, 17	
Start a class		2, 19		2, 6		22, 28						10
Join a club			5, 30		27, 30	16, 17	5		7, 8			
Ask for a raise					17		31	11, 26	4, 5	25, 26, 27		17
Look for work			4, 11		5, 6		1, 6, 15			13, 14		
Get pro advice	4, 5, 22	24		2, 21, 22							13, 23	9, 25
Get a loan				12, 29, 29				29, 31		16	2, 10, 13	
See a doctor	31		5		11, 27						12	
Start a diet					4	6						
End relationship	30	5, 6						3, 4, 5	25	8, 25, 26		
Buy clothes			3, 4, 9					15		8, 16		
Get a makeover							22, 23	6, 14				
New romance	22, 23	18, 19, 20				2, 6, 7	1, 2				22, 24, 29	
Vacation	13, 14	24, 25		18					22, 23			1, 8

Virgo

The Virgin
August 22 to September 22

Element: Earth

Quality: Mutable

Polarity: Yin/feminine

Planetary Ruler: Mercury

Meditation: I can allow time for myself

Gemstone: Sapphire

Power Stones: Peridot, amazonite, rhodochrosite

Key Phrase: I analyze

Glyph: Greek symbol for containment

Anatomy: Abdomen, gallbladder, intestines

Colors: Taupe, gray, navy blue

Animals: Domesticated animals

Myths/Legends: Demeter, Astraea, Hygeia

House: Sixth

Opposite Sign: Pisces

Flower: Pansy

Keyword: Discriminating

The Virgo Personality

Your Strengths and Challenges

Every astrological description of your sign ordinarily praises you for how neat and tidy you are, Virgo, and while that's often the case, at least half of the time nothing could be further from the truth. There are definitely those among you who fall into obsessive/compulsive habits in all areas of life, who will happily stay up all night to make sure the silverware is polished and in the right slots. More often, however, you fall into category number two. That is, you meticulously organize what's dear to you, but as for the rest? Well, it really doesn't matter. You're all specialists, so you tend to focus on that one teeny little niche you've found comfortable—usually your chosen profession—and you tend to it with the careful eye of a jeweler. In the meantime, everything else can collect dust, as far as you're concerned. As long as what matters to your lifestyle is well taken care of, you're able to sleep like a baby, even if your CDs aren't alphabetized and your sock drawer is a mess. Oddly enough, what's least often written or mentioned about you is the fact that you have a terrific sense of humor. It's biting and raw, because you can see the little things that most of us miss and sum them up in ten words or less. Plus, you're witty enough to force us to recognize our universal flaws and imperfections, which makes it a lot easier to laugh about them. Like Gemini, also ruled by Mercury, you love puzzles, mainly because they put your restless mind to work, but also because they allow you to assemble all pertinent details into a project that actually works.

Your Relationships

Tired of being called "picky," Virgo? Bet you are. But you know what? It's true. As a proud member of the earth signs, however, you know quality when you see it, so a better word to describe you might be "discriminating." In all matters, including matters of the heart, you know what's worth your time and what's not. Your fast-moving mind gives you the ability to "interview" someone you're thinking about dating in roughly three and a half minutes, and to dismiss them in another thirty seconds if they don't answer your "casual" questions to your satisfaction. The thing is, you can see potential flaws and problems so well that you might actually cheat yourself out of a relationship that would succeed—if you only gave it a chance.

In most cases, however, since one of the things you're known for is a willingness to fix something, you'll be more than willing to take on what others might consider a lost cause, as long as you're sure that you two have that special, extraordinary "click" that we're all looking for. In that case, you'll work long and hard to perfect the relationship. Your mission is to refuse to choose partners whom you think need to be fixed. After all, you expect to be accepted as you are. Why shouldn't you offer the same to your partner?

Many of you are drawn to the fire signs—Sagittarius, Aries, and Leo—mostly because of their creativity and wit, but be careful while you're wading in those waters. These folks might make great friends, but as far as romance goes, you'd be better off with one of the other earth signs—Capricorn or Taurus. Being with another Virgo is truly a tough road to hoe. You're both so good at details that eventually someone will pick one hair too many off of the other's coat. The emotional water signs often work better—Scorpio in particular, who's just as fond of details as you are.

Your Career and Money

You have an eye for details and an innate ability to troubleshoot, Virgo, so you're invaluable in the workplace, as every employer and coworker you've ever worked with will honestly report. You take stock of what's really needed to get the job done, then immediately figure out how to perform that task in the quickest, most efficient way. As such, you excel in quality control, but since you pay attention to the little things and are fond of miniatures in general, the more creative side of you might enjoy building homes—on a very small scale. Creating dollhouses and models for construction businesses wouldn't even be "work" for you. When it comes to money matters, you tend to be a bit cautious—but then, that's your normal state of affairs. Plus, you were born with a calculator built into the back of your brain that automatically weighs the price you're being charged against the time you spent to earn the fee.

Your Lighter Side

You don't often take time off from work, Virgo, because what you really enjoy is being productive. When you do allow yourself to step away from the desk and let your hair down, it's because you've finally found others who are intelligent and witty enough to keep you interested—no easy task—or possibly a movie or television show that actually engages your brain.

Affirmation for the Year
My private time allows me to renew my creativity.

The Year Ahead for Virgo

Jupiter and Venus will spend a good amount of time in Leo this year, Virgo, which just so happens to be your solar twelfth house of secrets and Privacy, Please. The thing is, Leo planets aren't all that keen on privacy or secrets, so there may be a bit of an internal battle going on as you try to decide whether to let your private life become public or to hide from the spotlight until you feel the time is right. Either way, you won't be able to avoid attracting attention, so prepare for at least some of what you've been keeping under wraps to surface. The good news is that Jupiter in this house is often described as a guardian angel, so be on the lookout for earthly representatives that "coincidentally" turn up when you need them most. If you're into the performing arts, you could end up taking the lead in a production of some kind, but you'll be most comfortable running the show from behind the scenes. Love could also be on the agenda, thanks to Venus's presence in this same sign and house from June 5 through July 18 and again from July 31 through October 8. With Venus in this dimly lit place, you'll want to spend most of your time together behind closed doors, away from what you might see as the prying eyes of others. If one or both of you isn't totally available, that could make the tryst more exciting, but think hard about the consequences before you get involved. Stay away from less-than-reputable financial deals.

On August 11, Jupiter will leave Leo behind, opting to spend the coming year in your sign and your solar first house of personality and appearance. Now, Jupiter expands—it's his job, after all—and this spot shows the condition of your physical body, so yes, you might gain some weight, but not to worry. Jupiter will be more than happy to give you enough energy and stamina to work it off, and also to keep it off. You'll definitely be a bit more indulgent when it comes to what tastes and feels good. It's your job to keep it under control. If you need some distraction from a bad habit, going back to school or doing some traveling would be fine ways to find it.

Serious Saturn moved into your solar fourth house of home, emotions, and family matters late in December of 2014, where he'll stay put for the next two and half years—with one exception. From June 14 through September 17, he'll make one last trip into Scorpio and your solar third house of communications and conversations. Now, Saturn is the Cosmic Taskmaster, so wherever he happens to be, we're due for hard work, and lots of it, and he absolutely demands that we complete our tasks to the letter. If there's any paperwork of an official nature that you really want to finish up, this is your chance. Relationships that have gone past their expiration date will end now, but you'll be feeling so practical and realistic that you probably won't shed any tears.

For the rest of the year, Saturn will be sending you tests and pushing you to firm things up around the house. It might be that you're literally working on your nest or building a new one. It might also be that your domestic situation needs some work, too. In this case, you might just begin to realize how important your organizational skills and eye for detail really are to the smooth workings of your family. You'll feel some added pressure to keep performing up to par and keep everyone else on track, so be sure you have productive escape routes planned. Every now and then, even Virgos get a bit of time off.

Uranus and Pluto will once again be locked into that same square they started years ago, which will pit your solar eighth house of intimate partners and joint resources against your solar fifth house of playmates and lovers. Someone you think of as a casual acquaintance may announce they want more from you, but if you can see money matters becoming an issue, you might be better off staying away from them. Separating finances from relationships will be tough to do now, and probably problematic. Your mission is to avoid situations and relationships that will bring money problems into your life. Oh, and don't sign up for intense relationships with obviously unstable types. You might think you can "fix" them, but why should you have to?

Neptune has been working invisibly on you for some time now from her spot in your solar seventh house of one-to-one relationships. All done up in her favorite sign, watery Pisces, she's very hard to spot, but you're smart enough to notice patterns, and that's what she'll provide, in all your relationships. If you're dating and you notice that the last few admirers you've had are pretty darn similar, consider that it's not just blind luck. Yes, you might actually be sending out signals that draw this type to you. If you're happy about it, keep up the good work. Don't change a thing. If not, it might be time to reevaluate what you really want from a relationship as opposed to what's comfortable because it's familiar. You can be truly inspired by another now, but you can also easily be taken for a ride.

What This Year's Eclipses Mean for You

Four eclipses are scheduled for 2015, Virgo, and in September, one of them will land directly in your sign. In the meantime, however, starting in March, your relationships will come into question. On March 20, the first Solar Eclipse of the year will arrive in your solar seventh house of one-to-one relationships, all done up in dreamy Pisces. This may mean that the fog will lift and you'll suddenly be able to see someone as they truly are. They'll have to climb down from that pedestal you stuck them on, so you might feel disappointed and confused, but seeing others realistically is the only way to keep a relationship going. If you want to keep them around, get used to the idea that none of us are perfect, but coming close to a perfect connection is quite the accomplishment. Beware of frauds, liars, and cheats. Your gut will tell you if you're being worked, but you might need a good friend to help you admit it if you don't want to.

A total Lunar Eclipse will occur on April 4. This supercharged Full Moon will activate your solar axis of money matters, urging you to balance your own affairs so that you can charge off confidently in search of credit for a home or business soon. This lunation will be in partner-oriented Libra, however, so yet another eye-opening "aha" moment regarding your current partner may be on the agenda. This may be a time of endings, but remember, endings always come before new beginnings. If you're not happy and you want out, don't wait a moment longer than you know you should. If you're delighted with what you see, this might be the right time to turn things in a more committed direction.

On September 13, a total Solar Eclipse will plant a seed in your sign and your solar first house of personality and appearance. You'll wake up one morning with the urge to see total change in yourself, and you should pay careful attention to this astrological nudge. You've been working on yourself for several years now, but this lunation is a red flag. Get going in earnest. No more pussyfooting around. If you're going to take charge of your life and your lifestyle, you need to invest all your energy into it.

The last eclipse of the year will occur in Aries on September 27. This Lunar Eclipse will activate your solar axis of money matters, much like the Lunar Eclipse on April 4 did, so if you're feeling a touch of déjà vu, it's no wonder. The point of this meeting of the Sun and Moon is to get you into position for a new challenge that will require substantial resources to pull off. If you've been trying to get an idea off the ground for far too long and your paperwork looks good, this would be a terrific time to seek out backers and supporters who've already been where you are now.

Saturn

Saturn set off for Sagittarius and your solar fourth house of home, family matters, and emotions just before the year started, Virgo, and with the exception of a brief pass back into Scorpio from June 14 through September 17, he'll be hard at work on your domestic situation. This might mean you'll want to renovate your nest, perhaps to enlarge it for a new arrival or to accommodate the fact that you work from home. A long-distance move certainly isn't out of the question. If the opportunity arises, it will most likely be for professional reasons. Your decision is what counts, and once you make it, it will be final—but be fair. Sit the family down and discuss it with them before you commit. No matter where you're living, or with whom, security will be a priority. Adding a security system would be a fine idea, but be sure to check the structure of any new home carefully before you sign on the dotted line, and have a professional look over the cellar for potential water issues, too. If you're at all inclined to teach, holding classes in your living room might work out well. One way or the other, you'll be acting as the authority figure at home. Choose the way you'd like it to happen. Oh, and from June through September, while Saturn is finishing things up in Scorpio and your solar third house of communications and conversations, you might need to lay down some serious ground rules about life under your roof. Be sure everyone involved understands exactly what you expect.

Uranus

Uranus—Mr. Unpredictable—will continue on his trek through impulsive Aries and your solar eighth house of intimate partners and joint finances this year, Virgo. He has plans to stay pretty much locked into that ongoing square with Pluto he started years ago, too, so if you were born between September 4 and 14, you'll experience both energies in a very personal way as they work together on your Sun. The good news is they both want you to change yourself from the roots up, and you're probably already game for that. The tough part may be experiencing their entirely different methods at the same time. While Pluto urges you to transform slowly, patiently, and thoroughly, Uranus will be pushing you to do it quickly—in fact, just as soon as the urge strikes you. Uranus will keep poking until you get the message, too, by sending along last-minute changes and sudden, possibly urgent events to test you. Obviously, the process could be a bit unsettling, but keep in mind that the end result will be the same. You absolutely won't be the same person you were before these two came to visit. You might not believe it right away, but not too far down the road, you'll see that change is good. Very good.

Neptune

If you were born between August 28 and September 3, Neptune has been tiptoeing toward an opposition with your Sun over the past year or so. She'll make it official during 2015, however, from her spot in your solar seventh house of one-to-one relationships. Now, this means that several Neptunian representatives will be along shortly. Some will have a positive influence on you by guiding you into a more spiritual place and helping you to get to know who you really are. Gurus, spiritual leaders, and metaphysical mentors are all potentially on the list, but guides come in many forms, sometimes in our dreams, so if you want the full message of this subtle planet, you'll have to pay attention. Tuning in to your intuition now through yoga, meditation, or devotions will definitely help. Not-so-positive influences may also enter your life this year, however, so pay attention to them, too. You'll be able to recognize these individuals by how eager they are to help you find an escape hatch from reality, possibly through alcohol or drugs. Your mission is not to allow them access into your life—not at all, not for any reason. It will be extremely easy for others to create illusions that you'll buy into now. Make a conscious effort to protect yourself from fraud, on any level. Spend time with those you know and trust, and in all business matters, have a clear-eyed professional check out the fine print.

Pluto

If you were born between September 5 and 10, you're in the midst of some serious change right now, Virgo. Pluto has been toying with your Sun for a year or so, but his energy will peak this year, so prepare yourself. Of course, the aspect he's forming is an easy trine, so one way or the other, everything will work out just fine in the end. Still, any visit from Pluto means transformation is on the way, and humans in general aren't usually fond of that sort of thing. Trines are also notoriously lazy, so you'll have to tap into and deliberately use this energy. Hanging on to whom and what you were just won't work, but the Universe will send you lots of opportunities to come along quietly—and happily. Your best bet is to think about any parts of your personality and lifestyle that you'd dearly love to change. Chances are good the process has already begun, anyway, but if you recognize it and get involved, you'll have a say in the outcome. Now, Pluto is on duty in your solar fifth house of lovers, playmates, and relationships with children, so any of those individuals might just bring some drama into your life this year. Your mission is to help them in any way you can—without taking over. That will be the tricky part. Pluto gives us x-ray vision, so we can see what's really going on beneath the surface when others can't. Even if you know your way is best, you'll have to resolve to allow others to make their own mistakes.

Virgo | January

Planetary Lightspots

Four planets and the Moon will travel this month through your solar sixth house of work and health, Virgo, all done up in startling Aquarius. This is a great time to quit a bad habit. You'll be willing to entirely change your lifestyle and dive right into a more positive regime. You might also want to quit your job, but be sure you have other options before you do.

Relationships

You tend to look for very particular qualities in a significant other, Virgo. The person needs to be practical, well organized, and self-sufficient. This month, however, as Venus passes through eccentric Aquarius, you'll find your taste changing a bit, possibly to include a scattered coworker with an incredible brain. Just don't think of this as permanent. Aquarius planets like to move along quickly.

Money and Success

If you're thinking of changing jobs, you'll want to do it suddenly—as soon as the urge strikes you. Fortunately, you're far too realistic to jump before you know there's a net beneath you. The good news is that your safety net will arrive on January 4, 5, or 22, when Saturn, the ruler of career matters, will see fit to introduce you to someone who can help.

Planetary Hotspots

Mercury will turn retrograde on January 21, so for the next three weeks we'll all be retracing our steps in one way or another. In your case, it will likely be a work-related issue that needs to be revisited, probably because a coworker or superior didn't get it right the first time. Fix it, but don't gloat.

Rewarding Days

4, 5, 6, 13, 14, 22, 27

Challenging Days

2, 3, 12, 15, 19, 30, 31

Virgo | February

Planetary Lightspots

On February 24, an easy trine between charming Venus and grounded Saturn will help you put things right between you and a dear one you were recently at odds with. You'll be much calmer and far more willing to listen to their side of the story, and they'll be open to negotiations. Well, this is a fine time to do just that. Have no preconceived notions before you sit down.

Relationships

Your love life will turn quite passionate from February 19 through February 22, Virgo, as Venus, Mars, and the Moon collide in fiery Aries and your solar eighth house of intimate partners. Remember, though, that passion can mean anger as well as ardor. If you're simmering, talk it over rationally before this "fire department" arrives.

Money and Success

Don't go shopping without a chaperone between February 19 and February 22, Virgo. That pack of planets in impulsive Aries and your solar eighth house of joint finances will make it all too easy for you to sign up for a payment plan on a large item that you really can't afford. Try to pay cash, and think before you purchase any unnecessary warranties.

Planetary Hotspots

The New Moon on February 18 will pick up where all those planets in Aquarius left off last month, Virgo—right smack dab in the middle of your solar sixth house of work and health matters. If you haven't changed your daily regime yet, you'll definitely be game now. If you've already gotten the show on the road, you'll see positive results.

Rewarding Days

1, 2, 7, 24, 25, 26

Challenging Days

5, 6, 19, 20, 21, 22, 23

Virgo | March

Planetary Lightspots

The Full Moon on March 5 will occur in your sign, Virgo, shining a huge celestial spotlight on your solar first house of personality and appearance. You've probably been working on your health habits for months, and while you may have seen some results last month, they're nothing compared to what you'll notice now.

Relationships

Your relationship axis will be activated on March 5 by the Full Moon, Virgo. If you're with someone, the two of you will be quite wrapped up in each other, and friends may be calling to coax you out. Don't budge if you're deliriously happy now with only your sweetheart for company. If you're single, this is the perfect time to resume your hunt for someone who'll understand and appreciate you exactly as you are.

Money and Success

Any joint financial issues you've been trying unsuccessfully to settle will go along quite well if you keep your temper in check but also resolve not to be bullied or intimidated. March 3 will bring together generous Jupiter and changeable Uranus in an easy trine, so plan any negotiations as close to this day as possible.

Planetary Hotspots

The first Solar Eclipse of the year will plant a seed of new beginnings in your solar seventh house of relationships on March 20, asking that you make some drastic changes. With things going along so well lately, however, rather than ending it, you might find yourself thinking seriously about dashing off to Vegas. Careful. Eclipses aren't always good at influencing us to keep our commitments.

Rewarding Days
2, 3, 5, 9, 23, 25, 30

Challenging Days
1, 4, 10, 11, 16, 27

Virgo | April

Planetary Lightspots

The first Lunar Eclipse of the year will occur on April 4 in your solar second house, Virgo, insisting that you take a close look at your personal finances. You are usually quite detail-oriented, but recently you may have been distracted by relationship issues, so this overview is really a good idea. Don't tackle it alone, but do be sure your advisor is reliable.

Relationships

Venus will be holding court in sensual Taurus until April 11, so if you're seeing someone, your friends may have to wait just a bit longer for the honor of your company. Later this month, after Venus passes into sociable Gemini, introducing your sweetheart to The Gang would be an excellent idea. Aim for April 22 or 26.

Money and Success

By the end of April, Mars, Mercury, and the Sun will have made their way through Taurus, an earth-sign cousin of yours that's a veritable money magnet. If you're after a part-time job for additional income, be sure it's something you believe in. If you're not satisfied with your resumé, get yourself back to school to bone up on the latest happenings in your field.

Planetary Hotspots

Be careful not to say anything you might regret on April 15, Virgo. Venus in chatty Gemini will receive an opposition from Saturn that day, and it will be very tough to take anything back. No one is saying you can't speak your mind. Just be sure you know you're right before you point the finger at someone for something they may not have deliberately done.

Rewarding Days

1, 2, 14, 21, 22, 29

Challenging Days

5, 6, 7, 17, 19, 20

Virgo | May

Planetary Lightspots

The New Moon will occur in Taurus on May 17, Virgo, lighting up your solar ninth house of new experiences, travel, and higher education. If you're feeling restless, this is the perfect time to do something about it. Visiting another state, coast, or country will certainly help, but even taking a class or trying something you never thought you would do will work just fine.

Relationships

Venus will set off for nurturing Cancer and your solar eleventh house of friendships and group affiliations on May 7, Virgo, and once again, your earthy knack for calming troubled waters will come in handy. In particular, someone you've known forever might have a problem they won't want to talk about with anyone but you.

Money and Success

As of May 11, fiery Mars will be making his presence known in your solar tenth house of career matters and relationships with higher-ups. Now, this could be a good thing—if you can manage to assert yourself without any tempers flaring. If you're angry and feeling unappreciated, wait until next month to plead your case.

Planetary Hotspots

The Full Moon in intense Scorpio on May 3 will illuminate your solar third house of conversations and communications, Virgo. You may need to deal with some information that's been leaked by someone you don't quite trust. On the other hand, you may be ready to share a huge secret with the world—and, more importantly, with your partner.

Rewarding Days

5, 6, 7, 8, 16, 17

Challenging Days

2, 3, 4, 9, 15, 22, 25

Virgo | June

Planetary Lightspots

The Full Moon on June 2 will stomp off merrily into expansive Sagittarius and your solar fourth house of home and family matters, Virgo. Adding a room on to your home or preparing for a wonderful new arrival might take up a lot of your time, but you'll be more than happy to give it up. Travel or a long-distance move might also be on the horizon.

Relationships

The lovely lady Neptune has taken up residence in your solar seventh house of one-to-one relationships, Virgo, so you've probably been spending a lot of time with your significant other. If you're still single, when Neptune turns retrograde on June 12, you might be tempted to try for a second time to work things out with someone you still adore. Step carefully.

Money and Success

The New Moon on June 16 will be in chatty Gemini and your solar tenth house of career matters and dealings with higher-ups, Virgo. You'll once again have the chance to impress someone with exactly what you can and will do to make sure a job turns out right, but remember, Mars is still there, too. Don't be too aggressive.

Planetary Hotspots

As of June 5, Venus will hold court in dramatic Leo and your solar twelfth house of secrets and Privacy, Please—but before you hang that sign on the door, be sure you're with someone who's entirely available. That means no other relationships, to start with, but actually living in the same city would be helpful, too.

Rewarding Days
4, 5, 8, 10, 22, 28

Challenging Days
13, 14, 15, 23, 24

Virgo | July

Planetary Lightspots

On July 1, the Full Moon in Capricorn will set up shop in your solar fifth house of lovers and playmates, Virgo. Now, this is a very serious sign for such a playful place, but that doesn't mean you won't have fun. You might have to organize a recreational event or family celebration, but once you see it all come together, you'll absolutely want to purr with happiness and pride.

Relationships

If there's any way to avoid an all-out confrontation with a loved one around July 14, you'll do your best to find it. The thing is, with Saturn forming an action-oriented square to loving Venus, it might not be avoidable. This is the stuff that goodbyes are made of, but it's also a reason to take a hard, honest look at what you expect from others.

Money and Success

Venus and the Moon will get together on July 18 in your sign to turn you into a charming, magnetic ball of love, Virgo. Needless to say, this will do wonders for smoothing out any recent disagreements with a loved one, but it's also a great astrological recipe for charming your way into the company of helpful others. If you need financial advice, ask now.

Planetary Hotspots

The second Full Moon of the month will arrive on July 31, Virgo, all done up in surprising, unpredictable Aquarius. That same day, Venus will begin her fiery path through dramatic Leo, however, so we can all expect some fireworks. In your case, a simmering work situation could come to a rather theatrical head.

Rewarding Days

1, 2, 5, 13, 21, 22

Challenging Days

6, 12, 14, 15, 18, 24, 25, 26

Virgo | August

Planetary Lightspots

Talk about a good time! Generous, outgoing Jupiter will enter your sign and your solar first house of personality and appearance on August 11, Virgo, where he'll stay put for the coming year. Now, this guy is in charge of expansion, so be sure you use his astrological talents to grow on the inside. In other words, watch your weight!

Relationships

A romantic secret might just emerge on August 4, thanks to a collision between Venus, the Goddess of Love, and Jupiter, who never could keep quiet about anything. These two will come together in your solar twelfth house of private matters—but since they're all done up in theatrical Leo, keeping things under wraps won't be easy.

Money and Success

August 26 will likely be a day to remember, Virgo. The Sun and Jupiter will come together in your sign, an astrological recipe for luck, in a very big way. If you're looking to make a change but need a boost from someone who's already got what you're after, don't ignore any supposedly "coincidental" encounters.

Planetary Hotspots

The Sun and Venus will get together in your solar twelfth house of secrets on August 15, bringing a bit of that déjà vu feeling into your life. Yes, this is exactly what happened back on August 4, and yes, the same cast of characters is involved. This time out, however, an easy trine between Mercury and Pluto will help you to get the whole thing settled quickly—and finally.

Rewarding Days
4, 6, 10, 11, 23, 26

Challenging Days
3, 5, 12, 20, 21

Virgo | September

Planetary Lightspots

The second total Lunar Eclipse will occur on September 27, Virgo, all done up in assertive Aries. It will activate your solar axis of money matters, demanding in no uncertain terms that you reevaluate exactly what you're willing to do to earn your keep—and what you're not willing to put up with from others who aren't earning much. Be firm!

Relationships

After weeks of retracing her steps and causing just about all of us to think seriously about going back to someone we thought we'd dismissed, Venus will finally turn direct, on September 6. Yes, this means that you'll be able to actually move forward, without any regrets—and no, you won't need to feel guilty about it. Think of it as closure.

Money and Success

Powerful people who know their way around will come to your aid on September 5, Virgo—most likely when you least expect it. Venus and Pluto will get together to bring you advice, support, and possibly even the financial backing you need to make a name for yourself. Shake a lot of hands and be sure to listen carefully to every word they speak.

Planetary Hotspots

The Solar Eclipse on September 13 will bring together the Sun and the Moon in your sign, Virgo. Now, if you've been working on your health and your body all year, this lunation might just signal that you've actually achieved your goals. If you haven't gotten started on the project yet, there's really no time like the present.

Rewarding Days
4, 5, 8, 22, 23, 30

Challenging Days
9, 10, 13, 16, 24, 25

Virgo | October

Planetary Lightspots

On October 8, Venus and the emotional Moon will come together in your sign, and between the two, you're due to be on the receiving end of appreciation—not to mention a whole lot of warm hugs. If you're attached, spend the day with your sweetheart. You can fit in tending to their every need in between those lovely embraces.

Relationships

Romantic relationships will be a bit hard to read around October 16, when Venus gets into an opposition with dreamy, woozy Neptune, who always wants to see the best in others. That's a lovely quality, but occasionally, there's no good to be seen—only imagined. Be sure that's not what you're doing. You can easily be taken advantage of now.

Money and Success

Jupiter has been working overtime to get you introduced to successful others who share your particular skills, Virgo, and on October 11, you could actually find a way to make your professional dreams a reality. Nonprofit groups or spiritual causes are high on your priority list at the moment, and it looks like these worthy goals will finally be supported.

Planetary Hotspots

You may be spoiling for a fight around October 22 or 25, Virgo, and your primary partner will definitely feel the tension. The thing is, you might be causing a problem where there really isn't one, but you'll never know unless you break down and talk about what's really bothering you, honestly and openly.

Rewarding Days
8, 11, 13, 15, 23, 30

Challenging Days
6, 9, 10, 16, 17, 22, 25

Virgo | November

Planetary Lightspots

Your career and professional life has been running on track lately, and it's high time for you to see some actual monetary rewards, Virgo. Well, on November 8, Venus, the planetary purveyor of the purse strings, will amble into your solar second house of personal finances. Yes, there's likely to be much rejoicing in the kingdom.

Relationships

If you've been holding something back and you're just about ready to explode, you'll probably do just that on November 2 or 3. Venus will collide with aggressive, angry Mars, plenty of astrological reason to imagine you involved in quite the dispute. Keep in mind that clearing the air is a positive thing. Just don't let things spiral out of control.

Money and Success

On November 13, Venus will come together in an exciting sextile with hardworking, diligent Saturn, and even more good news about your financial plan for the future will come along. If you've been toiling away, Saturn will be happy to give you a pat on the back, which might mean additional financial backing. Remember, though, that Saturn only passes out rewards for what we've earned.

Planetary Hotspots

The Full Moon on November 25 will activate your solar axis of home versus career matters, Virgo, so if you feel pulled in at least two directions right around then, it's no wonder. Everyone will want a piece of you, and no one will be willing to settle for less. The good news is that this lunation will be in Gemini, a sign that's an expert at multitasking.

Rewarding Days
4, 5, 6, 10, 13, 14

Challenging Days
2, 3, 19, 20, 23, 26

Virgo | December

Planetary Lightspots

This holiday season will be astrologically wonderful for most of us, Virgo, but since the Full Moon will arrive in Cancer and your solar eleventh house of friendships on December 25, inviting a friend who has no family into your home would be a lovely idea. Don't forget about your own family members, though, especially that someone you've been feuding with.

Relationships

Between December 10 and 12, you may not be thinking practically, Virgo, so delay any relationship decisions until well after that time. Loving Venus and dreamy, nostalgic Neptune will come together in an easy trine, making it all too easy to reach out to someone familiar, even if you know they're no good for you. Distract yourself with the company of those who are.

Money and Success

On December 4, Venus will set off for Scorpio and your solar third house of communications. If you need to talk turkey with someone about your financial needs, this is the perfect time to do it. Don't wait until next year. Make financial security a high priority on your list of New Year's resolutions. As a matter of fact, put it at the very top.

Planetary Hotspots

The New Moon on December 11 will activate your solar fourth house of home, emotions, and domestic situations, Virgo. Any recent urges you've had to move or remodel will become impossible to ignore, especially if your family situation requires it. If you can, wait until after the first of the year to get started on the project, and enjoy the season.

Rewarding Days

1, 2, 12, 13, 24, 25, 30

Challenging Days

6, 7, 14, 15, 20, 29

Virgo Action Table

These dates reflect the best—but not the only—times for success and ease in these activities, according to your Sun sign.

	JAN	FEB	MAR	APR	MAY	JUN	JUL	AUG	SEP	OCT	NOV	DEC
Move				1, 2		2, 3			22, 23	13, 14	29, 30	1, 4, 8, 12
Start a class			22, 23									
Join a club					16, 17	24	13, 15		22, 23			24, 25
Ask for a raise				22, 23, 26		6, 7		25, 26, 27				
Look for work	4, 22	12, 18, 19				16	31					
Get pro advice		19				6, 7				13, 14		
Get a loan	13, 14			6, 8, 9					27		23, 24	
See a doctor			7		11, 27		19		12			
Start a diet								23, 26			2, 3	
End relationship	3	21, 23	20, 21									
Buy clothes				4				19, 31		8		
Get a makeover			5, 6				25		13	8		
New romance	18, 19	7, 8		21, 22	5, 6		1	29, 30, 31		15, 16		24, 25
Vacation			23, 27, 30								13, 29	

Libra

The Balance
September 22 to October 22

Element: Air

Quality: Cardinal

Polarity: Yang/masculine

Planetary Ruler: Venus

Meditation: I balance
conflicting desires

Gemstone: Opal

Power Stones: Tourmaline,
kunzite, blue lace agate

Key Phrase: I balance

Glyph: Scales of justice,
setting sun

Anatomy: Kidneys, lower back,
appendix

Colors: Blue, pink

Animals: Brightly plumed birds

Myths/Legends: Venus,
Cinderella, Hera

House: Seventh

Opposite Sign: Aries

Flower: Rose

Keyword: Harmony

The Libra Personality

Your Strengths and Challenges

Your strengths are easy to talk about, Libra. Your symbol is that lady with the scales—Justice herself—and you so have her gift for restoring balance. That makes you an expert negotiator, mediator, and counselor. Venus, the Goddess of Love and Attraction, is your ruling planet, so you are also quite charming and personable. Now, maintaining this reputation—as a peacemaker and a social butterfly—definitely isn't easy, and it often takes quite a bit out of you to do your astrological job. For example, at times you'll feel the need to smile sweetly and nod even when you absolutely disagree. The thing is, you're here to teach us all about tolerance and patience—or basically, about how to just get along, even when we don't really feel like it.

Of course, being so adept at knowing what others want you to say, you might feel as if you're losing yourself at times. When that happens, you need to retire to a quiet place to figure out what means more to you—people-pleasing or speaking your mind. Oddly enough, when you decide that your own opinions and viewpoints need to be recognized, you'll find a way of making your point—albeit in a very sweet, smiling manner. For this reason, you make a terrific politician. You can anticipate what's coming and in mere seconds know exactly what to say to make everyone happy—at least most of the time.

Your Relationships

Everyone thinks of you as the scales, Libra, and in the photo ops, they're always balanced. In real life, however, that's not the case, and when it comes to your relationships, you often find yourself drawn into situations and partnerships that are far from equal. The thing is, your astrological mission is really to restore balance, a skill you can't learn if everything around you is always hunky-dory and everyone around you is fair-minded. As a result, you're often involved in encounters with others who are far less than fair.

Your ability to keep things running smoothly most likely started at a very young age, when you learned to be the mediator between family members. But as you age, you will be called on again and again to help make peace between warring factions. You have a gift for seeing both sides of an issue, so your friends will likely turn to you often when they need an unbiased third party. It's tiring, but you'll always respond to their pleas. It is, after all, your job, and you know it. When you're out in a group setting, you're always "on duty," whether you realize it or not, and always determined to make everyone feel as if they're a part of the gang.

In one-to-one relationships, you are completely and totally devoted, even at the expense of friendships at times. Your partner is always your number-one priority, and no matter what happens, you will stick by their side and show the world, as well as your family and children, a united front.

Since you're such a sociable creature, the other air signs are often good matches for you. Aquarius just loves groups and knows how to keep friendships going forever—which, after all, is the key ingredient to any long-term relationship. Gemini is endlessly fascinating and is willing to charm and entice you forever. Fiery Sagittarius and Leo can also make good partners, and while Aries—your opposite—may be frustrating at times, they'll always have your back.

Your Career and Money

Since you're such an expert at making others happy, especially on a one-to-one basis, careers that involve dealing with just one person are best suited to you. For example, think of Johnny Carson and Barbara Walters, two Librans who made their living from interviewing others and were successful at it because they were able to make that all important one-to-one connection. Group situations are a bit more of a challenge, but as long as you're the honorary cruise director who's tasked with making everyone cooperate, you'll do just fine. In fact, any work situation that allows you to serve as counselor or host or hostess is where you'll feel right at home. Now, getting down to your personal finances, Libra, this area of life can often be a bit unbalanced as well. You may find that you're usually in a feast-or-famine situation. Your mission is to watch your finances regularly and keep things on an even keel.

Your Lighter Side

In your book, having fun always—and I do mean *always*—involves a partner. Going out alone, or doing anything alone, for that matter, is your idea of a nightmare. The influence of loving Venus, your ruling planet, also demands aesthetically pleasant situations for you. You learned long ago that a visit to an art gallery was far more amenable to your nature than a late-night date in a dimly lit dance bar.

Affirmation for the Year
Those I associate with will help me to realize my goals.

The Year Ahead for Libra

This year, everyone's buzzing about Jupiter and Venus, who'll spend quite a lot of time in dramatic Leo and your solar eleventh house of friendships and groups. Jupiter will stay on duty there until August 11, and Venus is so looking forward to being in this romantic sign that she's extended her stay. In fact, she'll hold her royal court in this spot from June 5 through July 18, then return for an encore appearance from July 31 through October 8. During those times, it will be terribly easy for you to charm your friends and entice group members into jumping through hoops. If you're at all involved in socially worthy causes, you might use this superpowered, magnetic combination to bring others over to your side. On the other hand, you might encounter a group of kindred spirits who actively go out of their way to bring you into the fold. Don't be afraid. You just might have stumbled onto the first circle of peers who truly accept you as is and won't expect you to be what you're not. Find them. It may take some time, but it will be time well spent.

From August 11 on, Jupiter will spend his time in Virgo and your solar twelfth house of secrets. Now, Jupiter isn't famous for being good with secrets, and Virgo is Mercury-ruled, so gossiping isn't out of the question. That said, avoid chatting behind someone's back. Yes, there may be some intrigue, and yes, it's fascinating, but there are better uses for your time. Volunteering at a homeless shelter or animal shelter will open your eyes to the suffering of those less fortunate, and since you live for equality, you might actually be able to make a difference.

Late last December, Saturn set off for Sagittarius and your solar third house of conversations and communications, and with the exception of a few summer months, he'll stay on duty there for the entire year. Now, this is an authority figure who isn't afraid to be blunt, but your usual technique is to dance merrily around any answer that might sting someone while you're working on a hundred ways to say it nicely. Prepare yourself—and more importantly, prepare anyone close to you who won't be expecting this. You won't be in the mood to just be nice. You'll see that the truth needs to come out, and you'll be happy to deliver it. You might also need to put your hand on a Bible and swear to tell the truth. Remember, Saturn often brings legal issues along. Saturn plays for keeps, however, so no matter what you say or write now, or to whom, you'll be held accountable, for better or worse. From June 14 through September 17, Saturn will reenter Scorpio for one last pass. This is your chance to clear up any nagging financial issues that you thought were resolved last year. Even if you're tired of it all, there might be one last paper to sign or one more motion to file before you're done. Stick with it if you expect any kind of reward.

Neptune will continue moving through your solar sixth house of work and health, and since this lovely lady does tend to bring dreams and fantasies as part of her entourage, you might not be seeing things clearly—unless you listen to your intuition. If a habit is beginning to take its toll on you, don't be afraid to ask for help to get that monkey off your back. If you've already accomplished that task, expect someone to come to you for guidance and support. If your work isn't fulfilling you on a spiritual level, you just might opt to make a total shift and completely change your occupation.

Uranus and Pluto will continue their astrological "war" via the square they're still locked into. These two are superpowers. They have the same agenda, but their methods are very different. While Pluto insists that you take your time and do your homework, paying detective-like attention to detail, Uranus wants you to get out of any uncomfortable situation—yesterday. You'll probably find that relationship issues will be resolved more quickly than domestic matters, but this won't be a typically easy time. Major change is coming to the most crucial areas of your life. Resistance is futile. Your best bet is to come up with a timetable.

What This Year's Eclipses Mean for You

There are four eclipses set for 2015, Libra, all of which will affect you very deeply. The first Solar Eclipse will arrive on March 20 in dreamy, romantic Pisces and your solar sixth house of work and relationships with coworkers. If you've been trading glances with someone who sits across from you, this will be the time when one of you musters up the courage to walk over and start chatting. That moment may end up being remembered as the beginning of a beautiful friendship—or, eventually, a real, live relationship. The thing is, eclipses act so suddenly that we're often not prepared for them. If you're with someone, don't start anything else until you've decided whether or not to stay put. You might also want to switch jobs, and that, too, will come about quickly. Don't worry, though. If you've been longing for a change and an offer sounds right, do your homework—then go!

The first total Lunar Eclipse of the year will be on April 4, a supercharged Full Moon in Libra. Yes, that's you, and yes, you're due to make quite the scene around that time. It's your solar first house of personality and appearance that will be affected, so a total makeover might be in order, or a day of beauty. Get a massage, and have your hair and nails done while you're at it. New clothes might be in order, too. It doesn't matter. Do whatever it takes to make you feel brand spanking new. This lunation will affect your entire relationship axis, so you might be changing your look to attract a whole new type of admirer—in which case, be sure you get it right. Ending one relationship and starting another right away is also possible, but if you can stand it, waiting a respectable amount of time would be best.

The second Solar Eclipse will pitch a tent in your solar twelfth house of secrets on September 13, and whether or not you're ready for it, something that's been buried for quite a long time might just come to the surface. Your best bet with this lunation is to cover your bases and be sure that all parties involved are made aware of what might be coming up. Obviously, this wouldn't be a terrific time to start a secret adventure, but eclipses are electric, so it will be tempting.

The last eclipse of the year will arrive on September 27, all done up in fiery, assertive Aries. This total Lunar Eclipse will bring back memories from early April, as once again an inner debate affects your relationships. The debate? Well, should you be yourself, which is becoming harder and harder to deny, or should you be the person others want and expect you to be to keep the peace? It's your decision, but the answer seems clear.

Saturn

As the year begins, Saturn in truthful Sagittarius will be setting up shop in your solar third house of communications and conversations, urging you to stop being nice and start telling others what you really think. This practical, no-nonsense energy will stay on duty for most of 2015 and for the next two years as well, so you'll have plenty of time to perfect that skill, but if you get started now, you'll never have to take anything back. This might mean that some who are used to you sugar-coating answers to their questions will raise their eyebrows, and it's a given they might not like it, but that doesn't mean you shouldn't do it anyway. Saturn is practical and realistic, but in Sagittarius, he tempers facts with humor, so you won't have to worry about hurting anyone's feelings. You might also be drawn into teaching, since Saturn does so love to instruct, and if so, it will likely be the little ones you're most interested in working with. If you're into writing, this is a terrific time to put fingers to keyboard and pound out that book you've been talking about. You'll actually have the self-discipline to sit still and do it, even if it means canceling a few of your social engagements.

From June 14 through September 17, Saturn will make his last pass through Scorpio and your solar second house of personal finances. He'll be ready to help you wrap things up in this department, but things will go best if you have a seasoned professional on hand to check the fine print on any official documents. Your value system has been tested, too, but once Saturn moves along, you'll be crystal-clear about what's dear to you. While the process might not have been much fun, the end result will be a positive and productive attitude. How much of your time are you willing to trade to be comfortable? You'll know the answer soon.

Uranus

The irritating square between startling Uranus and intense Pluto will continue for yet another year, and if you were born between October 5 and 15, you'll definitely feel it during 2015, Libra. Both planets will insist that you make drastic changes in your lifestyle in general, but while Pluto will urge you on slowly and gradually, Uranus will light a fire under you so that every time you feel repressed or stifled in any way, your first impulse will be to cut your losses and walk. Since this freedom-oriented guy is currently on duty in your solar seventh house of one-to-one relationships, letting a relationship go could be on your agenda, but it won't be easy. Your ruling planet is loving Venus herself, and your specialty is relationships, so giving up once you've invested time and emotions is tough. Your mission will be to examine whether you're staying put because you care or because you don't want to be alone. If it's the latter, stop worrying. You're charming and personable, and at the top of every guest list. You won't ever be lonely. Besides, every now and then there's nothing wrong with being alone. In fact, the point Uranus is trying to make is that you absolutely must allow yourself the same independence and freedom of expression you so easily extend to others. If you're not truly yourself, what are you really bringing to a relationship?

Neptune

If you were born between October 5 and 15, your Sun will be affected directly by Neptune this year, Libra, through an astrological relationship known as an inconjunct. Now, inconjuncts demand that adjustments be made. The thing is, they're not often clear about exactly what needs to be adjusted. This is where astrology comes in quite handy. In your case, since Neptune is working her way slowly and invisibly through your solar sixth house of work and health, you might want to rethink your attitude in general on the subject of what's good for you and what's not. The gentler methods will work best, so investigate yoga or meditation, or maybe tai chi. You need to move around, but it can't be too stressful. And since you're Venus-ruled, and Venus loves creature comforts, it's easy to imagine you having a hard time drawing any physical boundaries with Neptune on duty. That includes your health, but it might also mean that you'll be tempted to start a secret relationship with someone who's not quite available, most likely a coworker. Your mission will be to refuse these temptations, but it won't be easy. Neptune is magical and perfectly capable of casting spells that are simply impossible to resist. As far as your on-the-job performance goes, as usual, you'll do your best, but if you have the feeling that something is going on behind closed doors, you might have to do a bit of detective work to find the answers. It might be best now to pursue an occupation that more closely reflects your personal belief system and leave the intrigue behind.

Pluto

If you were born between October 6 and 11, Libra, your Sun will be receiving the full impact of a testy square from Pluto this year—and this is the most intense, focused astrological energy of all. The Sun is our sense of self—our identity. It's how we see and present ourselves, too. Squares demand action and Pluto loves transformation. In fact, when Pluto's in the neighborhood via any aspect, transformation is mandatory. All that said, cooperation with Pluto is the only way to go. Proactive tactics are best and are definitely better than waiting for Pluto to make changes for you. Get to work on any aspect of your personality or appearance that you'd like to re-create. It doesn't matter whether it's for health reasons or simply because you're in the mood to see a whole new you in the mirror.

Since you're so partner-oriented, it might also be your primary relationship that needs to transform. In that case, be fair. If you want out, be honest and end it. It would be easy to use Pluto's skill for manipulation to keep it going indefinitely, but why would you want to? If you're changing, chances are good that what you need in a partnership is changing, too. Don't deny either of you the opportunity to have it all. If you're happy together, this might be one of those years when you absolutely have to support each other through a tough time—and somehow you manage. Don't worry about being unable to cope. Perceptive, powerful Pluto will get you through it. Heaven help anyone who offends or attacks your significant other now, too. Your determination to set things right will be formidable.

Libra | January

Planetary Lightspots

The Full Moon in Cancer on January 4 will fall in your solar tenth house of higher-ups, authority figures, and elders, who'll be very much on your mind. If you're not contacted by someone you've been missing, why wait? Reach out to them first. If you've lost track of them, ask family members first, but don't forget to check out Facebook or other social media sites.

Relationships

Loving Venus will spend most of the month in your solar fifth house of lovers, Libra, so if you're somehow miraculously single, you won't be for long. This time out, however, you'll probably be surprised by how "different" you current admirers are from those who've come your way in the past, but hey—variety is the spice of life.

Money and Success

With your very own ruling planet, Venus, currently on duty in startling, unpredictable Aquarius, it's not hard to imagine you feeling a bit unsettled right about now financially, Libra. The good news is that if you've been thinking of striking out on your own or taking a part-time job to make ends meet, Venus will be happy to get you started.

Planetary Hotspots

The New Moon on January 20 will set up shop in Aquarius, joining Venus and Mercury in that same spot. This will put this pack of planets in your solar fifth house of playmates and recreational activities, so there will be some surprises on the astrological agenda. If you're bored at the moment, this lively, spontaneous gang will be much appreciated.

Rewarding Days

4, 5, 13, 14, 22, 23

Challenging Days

1, 3, 15, 16, 29, 30

Libra | February

Planetary Lightspots

Your solar fifth house of playmates and relationships with children will receive a lovely gift on February 18, Libra. The New Moon will plant a seed of new beginnings, urging you to get up close and personally involved in someone's life. Now, the lunation is going to happen in Aquarius, so it might be odd or unexpected circumstances that draw you together, but whatever the reason, enjoy the closeness.

Relationships

Venus, Mars, and the emotional Moon will invade your solar seventh house of one-to-one relationships this month. They will all come together in Aries from February 19 through 22, an aggressive, impatient pack of planets that will absolutely demand that you assert yourself. You are used to smiling and keeping the peace, but every now and then, even Libras get to vent. Vent away!

Money and Success

Now that Saturn in Scorpio has temporarily stopped squeezing your solar second house of personal finances, Libra, you should be able to guiltlessly spend just a few bucks on an evening out. You, of course, won't want to go alone, and since you're too charming to ever be alone unless you want to, your social schedule will probably pick up dramatically.

Planetary Hotspots

On February 3, the Full Moon will occur in fiery Leo. Since this means the Moon will reach her peak in your solar eleventh house of group situations wearing Leo, the most theatrical sign of all, you should expect every syllable you utter to be a bit dramatic. No matter how large or small the crowd, you'll definitely have their attention!

Rewarding Days
2, 3, 11, 18, 19, 24, 25

Challenging Days
1, 5, 6, 20, 21, 23

Libra | March

Planetary Lightspots

The Full Moon due in on March 5 will be quite an eye opener, Libra. It will occur in the middle of your solar twelfth house of Privacy, Please, a dimly lit place where secrets are stored. With this spotlight, however, keeping anything hidden will be tough. Better clear the place out before the camera crew arrives.

Relationships

On March 17, your ruling planet, Venus, will slip into Taurus—the only sign she enjoys as much as yours. She'll be a bit more focused on money than love for a few weeks, so don't be surprised if your current sweetheart is upset about all the time you're spending at work. Not to worry, though. Your undivided attention will fix everything.

Money and Success

Venus will spend the first half of the month in impulsive, impetuous Aries and your solar seventh house of one-to-one relationships, poking and prodding until you finally give in and provide your partner with an adrenaline-filled adventure. Yes, you'll need to pick up the tab, but you won't mind a bit. The memories you'll create will be worth it, many times over.

Planetary Hotspots

A total Solar Eclipse will arrive on March 20. This superpowered meeting of the Sun and Moon in dreamy Pisces will ask that you start thinking about how you can incorporate more of your belief system into your work—and wouldn't it be nice to get up every morning and look forward to your job? Your mission is to make your work important.

Rewarding Days

1, 3, 4, 24, 25, 26

Challenging Days

10, 11, 12, 16, 27, 28

Libra | April

Planetary Lightspots

The total Lunar Eclipse will storm the doors of your sign and your solar first house of personality and appearance on April 4, Libra, urging you to make whatever physical changes you see fit to ensure that everyone around you finally sees you as you really are—not as they want you to be. Don't pierce or dye anything until you're sure you aren't just acting out.

Relationships

Whatever you did to change your appearance on April 4 will attract some entirely new and different admirers this month, Libra, especially around the New Moon in Aries on April 18. This lunation will activate your solar seventh house of one-to-one relationships in a very big, enthusiastic way. If you're not seeing anyone, prepare yourself for an extremely ardent admirer who won't take no for an answer.

Money and Success

Venus holds the planetary purse strings, Libra, and since she's your ruling planet, you're in tune with her moods. So between April 22 and 26, when she bats her eyelashes at generous Jupiter and startling Uranus, it's entirely possible that you'll receive a windfall—and it won't be anything you were expecting.

Planetary Hotspots

Between April 7 and 9, things could heat up quite a bit, Libra, thanks to several planets in aggressive Aries who'll be doing their best to egg you into finding yourself a good, heated argument. If you need to clear the air, wonderful. If you're just craving an adrenaline rush, how about signing up at a gym instead?

Rewarding Days

2, 3, 4, 6, 21, 22, 26

Challenging Days

5, 7, 8, 9, 15, 17, 19, 20

Libra | May

Planetary Lightspots

The Sun, Mars, and Mercury will take turns passing through Gemini, your extremely inquisitive air-sign cousin. This pack of planets will activate your curiosity and get you wondering about how to assemble the small elements of The Big Picture into something that will be a solid five-year plan. If you don't already have one, it's time to draw up the papers.

Relationships

As of May 7, Venus will enter home and family-loving Cancer, the sign that most loves to spoil those it cares for and lives to make its home an even cozier nest. You'll have this energy on duty for the rest of the month, so if there are any authority figures you're doing battle with, have them over to your place for negotiations and mediations.

Money and Success

The New Moon on May 17 will give you a chance to start over, Libra, and from its spot in your solar eighth house of joint finances, you'll probably be quite ready to do just that. If you haven't been getting the support you need from your partner or housemates, it's time to lay down some non-negotiable ground rules.

Planetary Hotspots

Once April 11 arrives and red-hot, assertive Mars storms off into Gemini, you'll probably be in the mood to travel, Libra, and just this once, you won't worry about going off alone. You might even be eager for the chance to get out there and strut your stuff without worrying about who'll be hurt if you let loose a bit.

Rewarding Days

5, 6, 7, 16, 17, 30

Challenging Days

3, 4, 8, 9, 14, 15, 25

Libra | June

Planetary Lightspots

On June 2, a Full Moon will arrive, Libra. It will set up shop in your solar third house of communications and conversations, all done up in blunt, truth-loving Sagittarius. This lighthearted lunation will be more than happy to help you make your point, in no uncertain way. The good news is that you'll be so charming and funny about it that no one will mind.

Relationships

Venus will set off for lavish, dramatic Leo and your solar eleventh house of friendships and groups on June 5, Libra, so it's hard to imagine you not enjoying at least a touch of the spotlight this month. Venus will draw attention your way without you even trying much, so just think of what might happen if you really invest yourself.

Money and Success

If you feel the urge to shop, Libra, be sure to take someone along who's not afraid to tell you that you're overspending. Venus's presence in fiery, impulsive Leo could mean you'll be setting out to impress someone, but there's really no point in trying to do it with your wallet. What they're really after is the pleasure of your company.

Planetary Hotspots

On June 22, mighty, generous Jupiter and startling Uranus will get into a lovely, easy trine, activating your solar seventh house of one-to-one relationships in a wonderful way. At the least, you'll end up with an interesting new friend with many life lessons to impart. At best, you could cross paths with The Right One—under extremely unusual circumstances.

Rewarding Days
5, 6, 8, 9, 10, 22, 28

Challenging Days
13, 14, 23, 24, 30

Libra | July

Planetary Lightspots

There will be two Full Moons this month, Libra, the first of which will set up shop on July 1 in responsible Capricorn and your solar fourth house of home and family matters. If you've been thinking about making a move, perhaps to buy a home, this practical energy will be a huge help to you—along with a couple of solid professional opinions.

Relationships

If you've been simmering over something but not yet mentioned it, that won't last much longer, Libra. In fact, on July 12, 15, or 18 you may decide you've had it with keeping the peace, at which point you'll open up and let whomever have it. Well, good for you! It's probably about time.

Money and Success

On July 18, your ruling planet, Venus, will pass into your solar twelfth house of secrets, and you just might be tempted to stray, Libra. As partner-oriented as you are, however, you already know that one false step can often not be retraced, so before you make it, consider all the consequences. Is it really worth it?

Planetary Hotspots

The second Full Moon of the month will shine her spotlight in cerebral Aquarius and your solar fifth house of playtime and fun experiences. You might suddenly be hit by the urge to learn something new, and chances are good you'll be quite taken with your computer and your online friends. Just don't share too much with anyone you only know through an online friendship.

Rewarding Days

1, 2, 3, 5, 21, 22, 23

Challenging Days

6, 7, 12, 14, 15, 18, 24, 25

Libra | August

Planetary Lightspots

The New Moon on August 14 will get things moving in your solar eleventh house of friendships, and since she'll be all done up in fiery Leo, you can expect an equally fiery declaration of love and devotion. The thing is, before you respond, you'll need to be sure it's your heart and not your much-pleased ego talking.

Relationships

Once the New Moon makes her presence known in Leo on August 14, you'll be the star of the show, no matter where you go, Libra. The next day, however, the Sun and your own loving ruling planet, Venus, will come together, and one of your new fans may suddenly become a prospective partner who's perfectly willing to fill out all the paperwork in triplicate to apply.

Money and Success

On August 6, chatty Mercury will collide with Venus, bringing together wit and charm. In your case, while you're already quite famous for being charming, your ability to attract anyone and everyone will be absolutely lethal. If you're not sure you're interested, be careful where you aim this astrological pair. Their effect won't wear off quickly.

Planetary Hotspots

Mercury, Jupiter, and the Sun will gang up in your solar twelfth house of secrets this month, Libra—which might not ordinarily bode well if you were trying to keep something under wraps. The good news is that they'll all be wearing tactful, discreet Virgo, so your secrets may be safe for just a bit longer.

Rewarding Days
1, 2, 6, 13, 16, 19, 26

Challenging Days
3, 5, 7, 12, 21, 30, 31

Libra | September

Planetary Lightspots

On September 8, assertive Mars will get into an easy trine with surprising Uranus, and since this is the stuff that fortunate, supposedly "coincidental" encounters are made of, you single folks should get out there and look around very carefully. Regardless of your status, you'll meet up with successful others who'll help you to further your cause, and possibly your professional goals as well.

Relationships

After weeks of looking back at the past instead of into the future, loving Venus will turn direct on September 6, insisting that you do the same. Enough with the worrying about what might have been and the regrets about what you think you should have done. Enough! Let it all go and look forward. Anything is possible now. What exactly do you want?

Money and Success

Serious, career-minded Saturn will reenter Sagittarius and your solar third house of communications on September 17, Libra, so if you've been putting off a meeting with the higher-ups to discuss your raise, bonus, or promotion, wait no longer. As long as you've done your job well, you can pretty much call the shots. Set up that meeting.

Planetary Hotspots

The total Lunar Eclipse of September 27 will be in impatient Aries and your solar seventh house of one-to-one relationships, Libra. This potent lunation will give you the nudge you need to take one giant step closer toward commitment in at least one type of partnership. Just be sure to look before you leap.

Rewarding Days

4, 5, 6, 8, 22, 23

Challenging Days

9, 10, 13, 16, 24, 25, 31

Libra | October

Planetary Lightspots

An easy trine between energetic Mars and intense, unrelenting Pluto will come along on October 15, Libra, so if there's any project out there that you've been putting off, now is the time to rally your energy and put this thing to bed. The good news is that you'll be so determined to finish things off that you might even get done ahead of schedule.

Relationships

On October 8, your own ruling planet, Venus, will collide with the emotional Moon in your solar twelfth house of secrets and private matters. If you need to talk with someone about a recent clandestine event, this is the time to call the meeting to order. Refuse to be led astray by a charming new admirer who's a bit too self-effacing to be real.

Money and Success

Once the Sun sets off for Scorpio and your solar second house of finances on October 23, you'll be quite focused on money matters, Libra. Now, this might mean you're ready to bring a debt to an end, but it might also be that you're willing to forgive one. If emotions are involved, ask an unbiased professional for their opinion.

Planetary Hotspots

A minor dispute could escalate into a major problem on October 22, Libra, as talkative Mercury enters into a testy square with intense Pluto. If there's something you need to say, that doesn't mean you should hold back, however, only that you should be careful of the words you choose. Remember, Pluto has never shied away from final endings.

Rewarding Days

9, 13, 14, 15, 23, 30, 31

Challenging Days

5, 6, 10, 21, 22, 24, 25

Libra | November

Planetary Lightspots

From November 8 until December 4, Venus will hold court in your sign, Libra, which she just so happens to own. It's a lovely partnership, and will look and feel even lovelier to those fortunate folks who'll be on the receiving end of your charms for the duration. You have a way of making others feel special. Now, multiply that by ten...

Relationships

You won't be lonely this month, Libra. Your very own ruling planet, sociable Venus, will make her way into your sign and your solar first house of personality and appearance, turning up the volume on your already substantial magnetism. You'll probably have more offers than you know what to do with, but take your time and choose carefully. There's absolutely no reason to settle.

Money and Success

On or near November 5 and 10, the Sun and Mercury will bring you opportunities to finish up financial negotiations. If it's about a new home, you might have positive news on November 13. If additional paperwork is required, that would be a terrific day to file it or at least meet with an accountant or attorney who can help.

Planetary Hotspots

Mars, the red planet himself, will set off for your sign on November 12, and for the next couple of months, you'll be feeling pretty darn assertive, Libra. This will be your chance to make your voice heard, and to do it so nicely that no one will say a word. If you must do battle, kill them with kindness.

Rewarding Days

5, 6, 9, 10, 13, 24, 30

Challenging Days

2, 3, 19, 20, 26, 29

Libra | December

Planetary Lightspots

The Full Moon on December 25 will make this a perfectly delightful day, Libra, especially if you're spending it with your immediate family. The Moon will be wearing ultra-sensitive, family-oriented Cancer, a wonderful energy to have around on such a warm and wonderful occasion. Just be sure your partner is comfortable around the whole gang before you wander off to chat.

Relationships

Jealousy could enter into your relationship this month, Libra, especially if things have not gone smoothly between you two lately. Your mission is to do everything you can to let your partner know that while beauty in any form is still beauty, you are definitely quite happy where you are. If you're single, have at it. Remember, five minutes is all it takes for an "interview."

Money and Success

Venus will stay on duty in your solar second house of personal finances and money matters from December 4 though December 30, Libra, wearing all-or-nothing Scorpio. This is a wonderful energy to have around when you need a friend or you need to be a friend, but when it comes to shopping, you might be tempted to get crazy to prove your love.

Planetary Hotspots

If you're out and about shopping or celebrating on December 20, be careful while you're driving, Libra, and don't let anyone drag you into an argument you really aren't game for. If you want to say something and you've been waiting to do it, you'll let it out now, but heated arguments won't do. Smile pretty, but make your point.

Rewarding Days
1, 2, 7, 8, 14, 17, 24, 25

Challenging Days
3, 4, 6, 13, 19, 20, 29

Libra Action Table

These dates reflect the best—but not the only—times for success and ease in these activities, according to your Sun sign.

	JAN	FEB	MAR	APR	MAY	JUN	JUL	AUG	SEP	OCT	NOV	DEC
Move	3			21, 22			1, 2		5	15		
Start a class			3, 9		30	16, 17						6
Join a club		5, 6	1, 4			5, 8, 10		14, 15	22, 23			
Ask for a raise	3, 4	18, 19			3			6, 26	23	13		
Look for work		25, 26					15, 16					25
Get pro advice	30				16			26				
Get a loan			23, 30							26, 27	10, 11	
See a doctor		8	7, 8			30	19, 26				12	
Start a diet				4								
End relationship		20, 21						2, 19		10		
Buy clothes			23, 27						6		8, 13	17, 24
Get a makeover			23	4				27	23, 29	12	8, 23	
New romance	20, 27, 30			18, 26	17	22	30, 31		26, 27			
Vacation				22, 26	16, 25							

Scorpio

The Scorpion
October 22 to November 21

♏

Element: Water

Quality: Fixed

Polarity: Yin/feminine

Planetary Ruler: Pluto (Mars)

Meditation: I can surrender my feelings

Gemstone: Topaz

Power Stones: Obsidian, amber, citrine, garnet, pearl

Key Phrase: I create

Glyph: Scorpion's tail

Anatomy: Reproductive system

Colors: Burgundy, black

Animals: Reptiles, scorpions, birds of prey

Myths/Legends: The Phoenix, Hades and Persephone, Shiva

House: Eighth

Opposite Sign: Taurus

Flower: Chrysanthemum

Keyword: Intensity

The Scorpio Personality

Your Strengths and Challenges

As Pluto's child, Scorpio, you're an analyst, detective, and assassin all rolled up into one. Whichever side of you the situation calls for is the one you'll provide, but you always play for keeps and aren't afraid to permanently cut your ties and alienate others if that's what's needed. That would be the "assassin" part of your nature. The analyst in you is an expert at sizing up little things—little "tells" others give out that let you know exactly what they're planning, when, and most importantly, why. The detective knows how to sit back and watch—indirectly, at times. How often have you taken a seat in a corner with your back to the door, watching what's going on in the room via mirrors or other reflections? You can learn more about the situation looking away from it than just about anyone else who's seated right in the middle of the action. (Oops! Sorry for blowing your cover.)

You're one of the more determined signs out there, and are more than willing to stay with your mission until it's over. Born of the fixed quality and the water element, you can be as unbendable as ice when you're hurt. Of course, boiling water is just as tough to tango with, and when your passion is running high, your cup always runneth over. You need adrenaline every bit as much as Aries does. You love danger, Scorpio, and life-or-death situations are where you feel you're at your best.

Your Relationships

Very few people ever get to know you, Scorpio—at least not until you let them, and only because you've decided they're trustable. At that point, you might allow them to see the tip of the iceberg, but one false move and it's all over. Being affiliated with Pluto—that is, Mr. Invisible Processes himself—makes you quite secretive by nature, so the harder someone tries to pry you out, the more you'll shut down and withdraw into your shell, much like your water-sign Cancer cousins. When you're comfortable, however, you'll sit right down and confide all those things you don't usually share. This part of you isn't easy to coax out. It takes time, but it's definitely worth the wait. The intensity and truthfulness you bring into your personal encounters aren't easy to come by. Those qualities are invigorating and refreshing!

Pluto is also known for his quiet power. Power is pretty darn sexy, and you're Pluto's child, so you're very sexy critters—every last one of you. You're extremely sexual, and not at all ashamed or apologetic about it. In fact, you have the world's healthiest attitude toward sex. You see it as a natural instinct, so there's no reason to hide the fact that you happen to like it—a lot. The more conservative of your potential friends and lovers may be shocked, but if that's the case, they never would have lasted long anyway, so do what you do best: cut your losses and move on. If you're involved, however, your motto is "All or nothing," and you play very seriously by the rules. When you're in, you're in—till death do you part—and you expect nothing less in return. You'll firewalk for someone you love and not think twice about it. Should they deliberately betray you, however, you're outta there, and no, there's no way you'll ever go back. Since your emotions run so deep, the other water signs are often a good match for you. Cancer, who's just as protective and private, works well. Pisces also love their secrets and alone time, so you might do well with them. You're naturally drawn to Aries because of your shared love of do-or-die situations, but in the long run they often prove to be a bit too impulsive for your taste.

Your Career and Money

Thanks again to the influence of Pluto, you're naturally gifted with the ability to understand invisible processes, Scorpio, and to see the inner workings of any situation. As such, you're the perfect employee—once you've devoted yourself, that is—and after just a few weeks on the job, you're perfectly capable of running the place alone. What you don't know, you'll figure out, or you'll interview coworkers who you're sure have the info you need. For that reason, you're often promoted early in your career and tend to use your quiet power to keep your workplace under control—wherever it is or whatever you happen to be doing. When it comes to spending those hard-earned paychecks, you tend to think much like your opposite sign, Taurus. You're both willing to pay for quality, be it an object or an experience, but unless it's the best, you'll pass—and wait.

Your Lighter Side

You're a natural-born strategist, Scorpio, so you love the intricacies of politics. You probably even find following this dangerous sport fun. When you actually allow yourself to relax—which isn't often—you indulge in mysteries. It might be a mystery weekend on a train, or it might be a well-done horror movie or the latest Stephen King novel. You plot so well and pick up on subtle clues so easily that no one could possibly be better suited to poker.

Affirmation for the Year
I have the ability to be successful in any career I choose.

The Year Ahead for Scorpio

Jupiter, the King of the Gods, has been on duty in your solar tenth house of career matters since July of last year, Scorpio, bringing along his generosity and contagious optimism—not to mention a few sweet introductions to helpful and knowledgeable authority figures. He'll stay on duty here until August 11, so you can expect more of the same, but don't just sit back and wait for luck to come your way. Make it happen. If you want a raise, bonus, or promotion, continue proving you're worth it, but don't keep it a secret. If you haven't already, sit down with the higher-ups and let them know just how indispensable you are. You may also have been tossing around the idea of starting up your own business, and with independent Uranus in your solar sixth house of work, that's still very much a possibility. If that business has something to do with art, creativity, or performing, so much the better. Of course, you'll need to step into the spotlight to do it, which might take some getting used to, but you'll be able to handle it if you're doing what you love.

And speaking of love, Venus, the Goddess of Love and Money, will also spend quite a bit of time in Leo this year. She'll be charming her way through this same sixth house from June 5 through July 18 and again from July 31 through October 8. Obviously, this is the perfect time to go on interviews or meet with prospective business partners, but any type of creative work should be quite well received. Let's not forget about Venus and love, however, and her fondness for romance. A certain sexy higher-up you've been eyeing for some time might make it clear they're interested in you, too. Just be sure you can still work together comfortably if it doesn't work out.

Now, let's get down to business and talk about Saturn, who's just about done with his time in your sign. As the year begins, he'll already be in Sagittarius and your solar second house of money matters, but from June 14 through September 17, he'll be retrograding through your sign again, giving you one last chance to take care of your health, personal presentation, and appearance. If there's anything about the first impressions you make on others that you'd like to change, do it now. Once Saturn is tucked away in Sagittarius again, you'll need to focus your energy on finances, possessions, and values. You may need to cut back on expenses, but if you play your cards right—and when don't you—you'll have what you need and perhaps a bit more, provided you're willing to work hard for it. Saturn doesn't mess around in this house. You probably won't be living a life of luxury, but you'll be sure about what you're willing to do in exchange for financing your current lifestyle.

Uranus, of course, is still making his way through your solar sixth house of work. Now, this freedom-loving guy never fails to make us feel restless and even resentful about rules and regulations, so it's prime time for you to strike out on your own. If that's possible, wonderful. If it's not, that doesn't mean you can't make plans, investigate your options, and, most importantly, figure out what you can do for work that won't feel like work. In other words, you need to love what you're doing and to feel invigorated and excited about doing it on a daily basis. Once you've found it, you'll be unstoppable. Uranus will also get back into that testy long-term square with Pluto, your ruling planet, however, who's still camped out in your solar third house of communications and conversations. Now, Pluto never was very good at giving in, so along the way, there may be some power struggles or roadblocks to contend with, and with Pluto in Capricorn, authority figures may be part of it. Still, Pluto is relentless, so if you truly want something, between these two planetary Titans, you'll have it. The sixth house also rules health matters, and stress is an Aries planet's illness of choice, so be sure to find a productive physical way to vent, especially when times are hectic, and don't become so wrapped up in what you're doing that you become obsessed. Even Scorpios need a little downtime every now and then.

Woozy Neptune will continue tiptoeing through Pisces and your solar fifth house of lovers and playmates, so if you're single, you just might be in line to meet someone delightful and quite romantic. If they're also unattached, wonderful. You might have found a soul mate.

If they're not, however, don't be snowed by sob stories about a partner who doesn't understand them and how hard they're really trying to get out of the relationship. Unavailable means unavailable. Fantasies can come true with this energy on duty in this house, but there's no way you'll be alone for long, so resolve to be picky. You can afford it.

What This Year's Eclipses Mean for You

On March 20, Scorpio, the first of the four eclipses scheduled for 2015 will occur in your solar fifth house of creativity, playmates, and lovers. This one will be a Solar Eclipse in Pisces and might ordinarily feel like a tidal wave of change, but since Neptune has been gently and gradually washing everything unnecessary away from this area of your life for so long, you'll catch a break. Plus, you're nothing if not lethally perceptive, so you've seen this coming for an equally long time. Your mission is to release whatever or whoever needs to leave. Be thankful for the good memories. Paste them into your emotional scrapbook and move on.

The first Lunar Eclipse of the year will occur on April 4, all done up in partner-oriented Libra. It will influence your solar twelfth house of Privacy, Please, so you'll need to plan some time for a good old-fashioned retreat. If you're attached, it won't be hard to persuade your partner to disappear with you for a few days of complete and total peace and quiet—not to mention a whole lot of pillow talk. If you're single, some quality time alone to consider what you really want from a relationship is definitely in order. Either way, if you're not satisfied with your current situation, strategize. Come up with a battle plan, and put it in motion. Of course, this house also rules secrets, and yes, Libra rules relationships—so yes, you certainly might be tempted to take up with someone, even if one of you isn't available. The thing is, once the truth comes out, as it always does, you might be trading a few hours of pleasure for a whole lot of regret. If you're not happy, fine. Explore. But do yourself a favor and announce your decision before you do anything drastic.

The second Solar Eclipse of the year will arrive on September 13 in choosy Virgo and your solar eleventh house of friendships and peer groups. If you've been thinking about getting to know a whole new group of people, that sounds like a plan, especially if you're there for professional reasons. Just be sure not to become too involved in the politics of the organization if you're only there for fun. Your talent for understanding what's not being said will come into play in all your friendships, and you may be asked to voice an objective opinion for a dear one who knows they're not seeing things clearly. Don't hesitate. If they ask for a reality check, be a friend and give it to them.

The Lunar Eclipse on September 27, basically a superpowered Full Moon, will pit the emotional Moon in Aries against the Sun in Libra in your solar twelfth house of secrets. Yes, just like back in early April, you'll be dealing with secrets, but this time, the situation may involve a job situation or a coworker you have strong feelings for. With startling Uranus also on duty in this house and adding his electric fuel to the fire, one never knows what you might do, but chances are good it will seem drastic to others. Never mind them. Quit if you need to. Take off with a coworker if you're in love. It's time to stop hiding.

Saturn

You've been dealing with Saturn in your sign and your solar first house of personality and appearance for years now, Scorpio, so you're ready for a break, which is perfectly understandable. Wherever he is, Saturn brings added responsibility and an increased duty roster, and he's the planetary ruler of lead. Needless to say, his transits can make us feel heavy, especially since personal freedoms are restricted and roadblocks seem to pop up everywhere. Learning to live within realistic limits is one of his primary lessons, however, so if you've pulled that off over the past couple of years, you've lived up to Saturn's demands and you can expect the old taskmaster to see to it that you get exactly what you've earned. He's been influencing your solar first house of your personality and appearance, so chances are good that you've had to step in and become the authority figure several times. Learning to take charge when the need arises builds character. Learning to speak your truth without apologies does too. You've probably done a fine job of it, but if there's anything more you'd like to work out before he's gone for good, you'll have a final chance to do just that between June 14 and September 17. Before and after those dates, Saturn will be making his way through early Sagittarius and your solar second house of money matters and possessions. Saturn brings tests when he arrives, so if your finances aren't in good shape, you'll hear about it. Your best bet is to get your house in order right away. Remember, everything from bank and credit card statements to loan and insurance records are fair game. If you need to hire a professional, by all means, do. Remember, too, that this house is in charge of your value system, so you're about to become acutely aware of what's important to you—and what's not.

Uranus

If you were born between November 4 and 14, you're due for a visit from Mr. Unpredictable himself this year, the startling planet Uranus. He'll be making contact with your Sun from his spot in your solar sixth house of work, health, and relationships with coworkers via an uncomfortable inconjunct aspect. Now, the key to dealing with this tricky aspect is to know, right off the bat, that you'll need to make some adjustments. Doesn't sound that hard, but since humanity in general isn't fond of change, for many of us, even tweaking a situation that's comfortable and familiar can be traumatic. You, of course, love nothing better than tearing it all down, whatever "it" is, to start over, and your ruling planet, Pluto, will be on duty to help you through, so this time will be less stressful for you. Still, health issues could crop up, so don't ignore any nagging symptoms, even if they don't seem like cause for alarm, and if something seems off at work, be sure to find out exactly what it is. Sitting still and watching this transit go by is tempting, but using Uranus's energy to effect change immediately, wherever you sense it should happen—well, that's the name of the game.

Neptune

If you were born between October 28 and November 3, you'll be enjoying a lovely trine from Neptune this year, Scorpio. Now, Neptune is the planet of romance and fantasies, but she also specializes in illusions, and since trines make it oh-so-easy for us to fall under a spell, you'll need to be careful not to doze off for a few months and wake up married. That's an exaggeration, but the point is that you're going to feel so good now that you won't believe anything could possibly go wrong. For the most part, you'll be right, and if you channel this energy properly, a lot could go right. Your creative pursuits will be amazingly in tune with what your audience wants from you, your relationships with your children will bring you even more deeply into their lives and hearts, and yes, you just might fall in love. The tricky part will be the falling in love part. You do stand every chance of meeting someone who's truly perfect for you, but you're so longing to be in love that you might jump on the first admirer who comes along. Don't do that. This is a gradual process, and there'll likely be several false alarms before you find the right one. Your mission is to refuse to dash off to Vegas until this lovely pink fog has cleared.

Pluto

Pluto is your ruling planet, Scorpio, and it's a match made in heaven, because no other sign could handle the energy of this intense, sexual planet so well. If you were born between November 5 and 10, you'll be experiencing his potent energy this year, but not to worry. Pluto does love utter change, and sure, he's a big fan of total transformation, but he'll be forming an easy sextile with your Sun. So at the very least, you've seen this coming, as usual, and you're ready. In fact, you're probably longing for whatever he's brought along. The thing is, the Sun is charge of our sense of self, our confidence, and our ego, and Pluto tears down structures. The good news is that you'll be in charge of which structures need to go and which can stay, if they're tweaked. Enjoy this transit. The person you'll be when it's over, at least a year from now, is the person you've already visualized. The process may go unseen by others, but you'll be aware of it, every step of the way. Of course, between knowing what you know about power and control and being supercharged in those departments by Pluto, just a bit of that stuff might leak out. Even with "easy" Pluto transits, power struggles can be part of the deal. Anyone who stands up to you now— provided they're right to do so—may start out as an enemy, but could become a respected, lifelong friend, or more.

Scorpio | January

Planetary Lightspots

You don't make a move without mulling it over carefully, Scorpio, so you tend to think through important matters for quite some time. This month, however, a pack of planets in spontaneous Aquarius will urge you to toss caution to the wind. If your antennae tell you that new place is perfect—even if it happens to be hundreds or even thousands of miles away—go for it. The rest will work itself out.

Relationships

On January 12, red-hot Mars will enter your solar fifth house of lovers, Scorpio, urging you in no uncertain terms to either make a move toward permanence or step back and disappear into the woodwork. If you're pretty darn sure you have the right one within your grasp, better make a move. Trial periods are quite acceptable.

Money and Success

Once Venus sets off for your solar fifth house of recreational pursuits and hobbies on January 27, you'll be thinking seriously about turning what you love into a productive way to earn your living. The good news is that someone who has admired your work for quite a while will be happy to help. Think of them as a muse and let them do their job.

Planetary Hotspots

The New Moon on January 20 will do her best to convince you that a whole new environment would be a step in the right direction. Moving is definitely an option, but if you're set on staying where you are, how about just remodeling? Give your place a whole new look—one that reflects who you are right now.

Rewarding Days

4, 5, 22, 23, 31

Challenging Days

1, 3, 15, 18, 21, 30

Scorpio | February

Planetary Lightspots

After two years of dealing with Saturn in your sign and your solar first house of personality and appearance, Scorpio, you are probably quite done with being the honorary authority figure wherever you go, especially if you were only along for the ride and hoping to have some fun. Fortunately, Saturn has moved on, so you'll finally be able to relax and enjoy yourself.

Relationships

On February 1, Venus, the Goddess of Love, will come together with romantic Neptune in your solar fifth house of lovers, Scorpio. The two will be all done up in dreamy Pisces, so together with several planets in spontaneous Aquarius, you're definitely in line for a "love at first sight" moment. Just be sure to check out their credentials carefully before you dash off to Vegas. Or Reno.

Money and Success

On February 23, a square between the Sun and Saturn will arrive, and making ends meet—on paper, at least—may seem like a rather daunting task. Wait a day, however, and someone you work with who's a whiz with numbers will be able to come up with a plan for you to save, even as you maintain your current lifestyle.

Planetary Hotspots

Let's talk about that pack of red-hot Aries planets who'll turn up the heat in your solar sixth house from February 19 through February 22. Among the assembled planetary dignitaries will be the Moon, Venus, and Mars himself, so yes, things could get heated at work. Your mission is to sit tight until you have other options in play.

Rewarding Days

1, 7, 8, 18, 25, 26

Challenging Days

5, 6, 20, 21, 22, 23

Scorpio | March

Planetary Lightspots

The total Solar Eclipse on March 20 will plant a seed in your solar fifth house, Scorpio, which will already be a very busy place this month. Now, this house pertains to lovers and playmates, so if you've been flirting with someone but not yet actually made a date, you'll do it soon—or they'll beat you to it. Either way, it's going to be quite romantic.

Relationships

There'll be much rejoicing in your kingdom on March 17, as loving Venus sets off for your solar seventh house of one-to-one relationships. She'll be all done up in Taurus and ready to bring you several weeks of truly sensual encounters and pleasant "accidental" meetings with delicious new others. If you're single, get ready. The Universe is laying out a buffet.

Money and Success

Jupiter, the ancient king of the gods, will stay on duty in theatrical Leo and your solar tenth house of career matters for a few more months, Scorpio. You really should take advantage of his generosity, especially around March 3, when he'll come together with unpredictable Uranus in your solar tenth house of work to give you the opportunity to switch jobs and finally do what you want.

Planetary Hotspots

Be very careful on March 11, Scorpio, when your own ruling planet, intense Pluto himself, will join forces with impulsive Mars and shocking Uranus. The last thing you've ever thought possible will absolutely be on the astrological agenda, so be careful driving, avoid arguments, and direct your substantial energy in positive directions.

Rewarding Days
12, 18, 22, 23, 30

Challenging Days
2, 4, 10, 11, 16, 27

Scorpio | April

Planetary Lightspots

The New Moon will arrive on April 18, wearing Aries, the sign that just loves new beginnings. This is your solar sixth house of health, Scorpio, so if you've been thinking about changing your habits or just beginning a more energetic, healthier lifestyle, there's no time like the present to get the show on the road. Just take it easy at first. Don't push yourself to do more than you physically can.

Relationships

On April 20, the Sun will take off for sensual Taurus and your solar seventh house of one-to-one relationships, Scorpio—and then the fun begins. If you're already attached, sexy little you will find a delightful way to bring the passion back into your relationship—no doubt about it. If not, interviewing delicious candidates is a lovely way to spend the coming month, wouldn't you say?

Money and Success

No matter what type of work you do, doing it with a partner is the best way to get it done well, Scorpio, especially after April 20. You'll need someone to bounce ideas off of, and the Universe will be more than happy to provide this. On April 21 or 22, you two could come up with a great idea for a whole new way of doing business.

Planetary Hotspots

A dispute between your significant other and a family member or one of your kids could come up around April 17, and things might heat up pretty darn fast, so get ready. The good news is that if they haven't been talking about their differences, they'll be willing to do so now. There may be some shouting involved, but getting it all out on the table is the important thing.

Rewarding Days
1, 2, 6, 12, 14, 19, 21

Challenging Days
5, 7, 15, 17, 20, 22

Scorpio | May

Planetary Lightspots

The Full Moon on May 3 in your sign will demand that you take out your heaven-sent qualities and parade them around for all the world to see. You may be called on to be a detective, in which case you'll dig up subtle clues anyone else would have missed. If your talents as an analyst are needed, prepare to come up with motives. Yep. Piece of cake.

Relationships

After a long, lovely month in sensual Taurus, the Sun will move into your solar eighth house of intimate relationships on May 21, all done up in Gemini. Now, this sign has been known to be a tad on the fickle side at times, but you're steady as a rock, so even if your eye does wander, you'll be able to keep yourself in check—provided they're not simply too delicious to pass up.

Money and Success

Money matters could become a bit problematic on May 14 or 15, so if you're looking for a quick solution, get comfortable. Action-oriented Mars will face off with Saturn, who just loves to toss roadblocks in our path to stall us—until we're absolutely prepared to deal with the situation head-on. So, are you sure this is what you want?

Planetary Hotspots

If you've been trying your best to put the finishing touches on a business deal or to bring an inheritance issue to a close, if it hasn't happened by May 18, better put it off for at least three weeks, Scorpio. Mercury will turn retrograde, and all those pesky details you didn't notice could snarl things up.

Rewarding Days

5, 6, 7, 8, 16, 17

Challenging Days

4, 14, 15, 18, 21, 22, 27

Scorpio | June

Planetary Lightspots

Once again, mighty Jupiter will get together with startling Uranus on June 22, asking that you do whatever you can to further your career path by getting in good with a higher-up. All you really need to do is present yourself as you are—a hardworking, capable member of the team who is willing to do what it takes to get the job done.

Relationships

Once Neptune turns retrograde on June 12, you might begin thinking about the one who got away, Scorpio, and if that's the case, be sure you're not just remembering the good times and forgetting all about what drove you apart. Your mission is to do your best to see things clearly, no matter how much your heart insists on sugarcoating the facts—and no, it won't be easy.

Money and Success

The Full Moon will light up your solar second house of personal finances on June 2, Scorpio. If you've been a bit extravagant lately, all those bills might just end up in your mailbox. If there are notices from creditors, better tend to them shortly, or your credit will be affected in a not-so-positive way.

Planetary Hotspots

A misunderstanding between you and a lover or child on June 23 might have a long-lasting impact, Scorpio, so before you let yourself go, be sure you're not just in the mood to fight. That would be perfectly understandable, but it won't get you anywhere, and won't help you solve this tough financial dilemma. Talking it out is the only way to go.

Rewarding Days
4, 5, 9, 10, 11, 24

Challenging Days
12, 14, 15, 20, 23

Scorpio | July

Planetary Lightspots

The Full Moon on July 1 will illuminate your solar third house of communications and conversations, Scorpio, asking that you tend carefully to all those miniscule details of a situation you've been trying so hard to avoid for months now. If you haven't been practical or realistic, you'll need to be now. Call in a pro if you can't handle it alone.

Relationships

On July 13, the perfect opportunity to talk things over with a loved one will arrive. Thoughtful, chatty Mercury will form an easy trine with sentimental Neptune, and since they'll both be in emotional water signs like yours, getting to the heart of the matter won't be a problem. Bring tissues—for both of you.

Money and Success

Between now and September 17, you should get busy straightening out any financial matters that have been troublesome, Scorpio. You'd do well to use this break in the astrological action to do just that. Serious Saturn will return then, and for the next two and a half years, you'll need to answer to him for every penny.

Planetary Hotspots

Several planets will get together in emotional Cancer and your solar ninth house of long-distance relationships on July 15, Scorpio. You'll probably be bored and restless and not too happy with your current situation, but since impulsive Mars will be on duty, a way out will quickly present itself. Fasten your seat belt, though. Mars never did waste time making changes.

Rewarding Days
1, 8, 13, 17, 21, 22

Challenging Days
14, 15, 16, 18, 19, 25

Scorpio | August

Planetary Lightspots

Any conversation you've been putting off is sure to go well if you schedule it for August 1 or 2, when chatty Mercury and startling Uranus will form an easy trine, determined to bring about happy, unexpected results. Don't stall any longer. Make some coffee, hover around the kitchen, and work it out.

Relationships

Once Jupiter sets off for your solar eleventh house of friendships on August 11, anyone you've been spending a good amount of time with might suddenly take a far more prominent place in your life. Are you in love? Well, that remains to be seen, but by the Full Moon on August 29, you'll know for certain.

Money and Success

The New Moon on August 14 will activate your solar tenth house of career matters. It will occur in dramatic Leo, so making your point to an authority figure won't be a problem. If you're not equipped with all the information you need to present a solid case, however, backtracking might be an issue. Prepare, prepare, prepare.

Planetary Hotspots

Anyone who challenges your authority around August 21 had better be prepared to wake a sleeping dragon, because that's exactly what they'll be up against. You won't take no for an answer, especially if you know you're right, and you'll be willing to fight for as long as it takes to make sure you drive your point home. Be gentle on anyone who's not quite as verbally well armed.

Rewarding Days
6, 11, 13, 14, 25, 26

Challenging Days
3, 5, 7, 12, 21, 22, 31

Scorpio | September

Planetary Lightspots

On September 5, your very own ruling planet, Pluto, will form a cooperative trine with the Sun, making it especially easy for you to speak your peace, even if it's in front of a rather large group. In addition to letting your voice be heard, you'll probably also be doing a lot of good for the cause that's nearest and dearest to your heart.

Relationships

A long-distance loved one will pop into your mind around September 16, and suddenly, all your memories of the good times you two shared will be far more tangible than what you have now with an other. There is, however, such a thing as selective memory. Be sure you're not only seeing the past through rose-colored glasses before you opt to go back to it.

Money and Success

On September 17, serious, disciplined Saturn will cross the astrological state line, fully prepared to set up shop in your solar second house of money matters for the next two and a half years. Now, this guy loves preparation, so you'd do well to see to it that all your financial statements are in order, from checking to credit cards to The Books, if you're self-employed.

Planetary Hotspots

A Solar Eclipse will occur on September 13 in meticulous Virgo and your solar eleventh house of friendships. Someone you've always thought of in a strictly platonic sense may want to switch places and become a lover. If you're sure you two can still be friends if it doesn't work out, go for it.

Rewarding Days
4, 5, 6, 8, 14, 22

Challenging Days
9, 10, 16, 24, 25

Scorpio | October

Planetary Lightspots

'Tis the season to be a Scorpio. Fortunately, your ruling planet, Pluto himself, will be more than happy to help you get together with others who also adore what's scary and forbidden, especially around October 11, 15, and 23. If you haven't been invited to a masquerade party yet, why not have one at your place?

Relationships

If you're ready to say goodbye, Scorpio, you might choose October 10 to do it. Venus, the Goddess of Relationships, will square off with Saturn, who thinks in very practical, no-nonsense terms, urging you to rid yourself of any relationship that's not doing either of you any good. Be as gentle as possible, especially if you know they won't see it coming.

Money and Success

Frugal Saturn is still on duty in your solar second house of personal finances, demanding that you tighten your belt and make sure you're not spending your hard-earned money on anything—or anyone—that isn't absolutely necessary. Ready or not, Scorpio, here comes the moment of truth. What's worth it—and who's not?

Planetary Hotspots

After three long weeks, Mercury will finally turn direct on October 9 in your solar twelfth house of secrets and Privacy, Please. Any whispers you've been hearing, whether they were about you or not, will suddenly come to an end, and you'll know you were right not to feed any of your energy into spreading gossip.

Rewarding Days
7, 8, 13, 14, 15, 23, 30, 31

Challenging Days
6, 9, 10, 16, 21, 22

Scorpio | November

Planetary Lightspots

You've probably been keeping a whole lot to yourself lately, but as of November 2, that will no longer be the case. Mercury, the Messenger of the Gods, will make his way into your sign and your solar first house of personality and appearance, and with this chatty guy on duty, what you think and what you say will be only seconds apart—at least, until November 22.

Relationships

Is it love? Wait until November 10 and you'll be pretty darn sure about that answer. In fact, you might find that in addition to your own situation becoming clear, others will come to you for your advice and support right around then. Fortunately, you'll be more than able to offer them positive solutions to seemingly unsolvable problems.

Money and Success

The Full Moon in Gemini on November 25 will help you to see the details of a joint financial problem—and it's those details that have been holding you back from coming up with a final solution to your situation. It may be that you haven't wanted to acknowledge the truth, or that your heart has been in the way. Well, not to worry. All that is about to come to a rapid-fire end.

Planetary Hotspots

You may be spoiling for a fight with your significant other, and if that's the case, they'll certainly give it to you on November 20 or 23. No matter what's going on between you, your best bet is to have a good, old-fashioned chat around the kitchen table on November 13. Get it out, and move on!

Rewarding Days

1, 5, 10, 13, 17, 20, 23

Challenging Days

2, 3, 19, 24, 29

Scorpio | December

Planetary Lightspots

The Full Moon on December 25 will arrive in Cancer, an ultra-sensitive water-sign cousin of yours. This lunation will turn up the warmth in all your relationships, most especially those with family and friends you consider extended family. Yes, it's going to be a great holiday. Enjoy—and be sure to pass those good feelings around!

Relationships

If you're attracted to a complete stranger on December 10, don't write it off to the holiday season and all those warm feelings that are currently circulating. You might be right—and they might be right for you. You'll never know if you don't investigate just a bit further, so why not invite them out for an eggnog?

Money and Success

Mercury will contact impulsive Uranus from his spot in your solar second house of money matters on December 1, and your month will be off to a fun-loving but possibly also excessive start. If you're out shopping for holiday gifts, do yourself a favor and take a sensible earth-sign friend along for the ride—someone who can tell you when you're going over the top.

Planetary Hotspots

On December 30, just in time to make it a seriously fun New Year's Eve, Venus, the Goddess of Relationships, will take off for freewheeling Sagittarius, the sign that never did know when to quit. Don't hold yourself back. Just be sure to drink lots of water and take two aspirin and some electrolytes before you turn in. Happy New Year, Scorpio!

Rewarding Days
1, 7, 8, 12, 17, 19, 24, 25

Challenging Days
3, 4, 10, 14, 20, 29

Scorpio Action Table

These dates reflect the best—but not the only—times for success and ease in these activities, according to your Sun sign.

	JAN	FEB	MAR	APR	MAY	JUN	JUL	AUG	SEP	OCT	NOV	DEC
Move	19, 20		1, 2, 3				30, 31					
Start a class					21, 25		15	29				10, 11
Join a club			5, 6				18		13, 14, 16			
Ask for a raise		3, 4		2, 6				3, 15	22			1, 8
Look for work			4, 9	8, 9, 10						25, 26		
Get pro advice	3, 5, 22			2, 5			21, 22	6	23, 24	6, 23	10	
Get a loan					27, 30	16, 17			17		23, 24, 29	
See a doctor		8		28								
Start a diet		23						3, 5, 6				21, 22
End relationship			26, 27		28, 29							
Buy clothes	4					5, 6				13	13	
Get a makeover				12	2, 3						11, 12	
New romance	18, 19		20	20, 21	16, 17					26, 27, 28		
Vacation	4				16, 25	24	15, 16	30, 31			24	

Sagittarius

The Archer
November 21 to December 21

Element: Fire

Quality: Mutable

Polarity: Yang/masculine

Planetary Ruler: Jupiter

Meditation: I can take time to explore my soul

Gemstone: Turquoise

Power Stones: Lapis lazuli, azurite, sodalite

Key Phrase: I understand

Glyph: Archer's arrow

Anatomy: Hips, thighs, sciatic nerve

Colors: Royal blue, purple

Animals: Fleet-footed animals

Myths/Legends: Athena, Chiron

House: Ninth

Opposite Sign: Gemini

Flower: Narcissus

Keyword: Optimism

The Sagittarius Personality

Your Strengths and Challenges

You're ruled by Jupiter, Sagittarius, who's known not only for being the King of the Gods, but also for being the largest planet in the heavens. As such, you don't do anything "a little bit." In fact, your only real challenge is to keep your appetites restrained. Of course, with Jupiter's extravagant, excessive traits on board, that's much easier said than done. Like Liberace, you innately believe that "too much of a good thing is... WONderful," so having "just a slice" of anything simply won't work. You're as curious as Gemini and just as interested in all that life has to offer, but unlike Gemini, you won't settle for thumbnail descriptions and you won't sit still through too many details. You want The Big Picture and The Whole Story. You're willing to do your homework to get those, but that time has to involve lots of truly interesting reading or lots of long discussions with intelligent folks who are recognized experts in their field. Like Gemini, you'll ask a question, sit back and wait for the answers, and eventually be more than satisfied with all the little gems you hear in between. Of course, being generous Jupiter's favorite sign also means you're just as generous—sometimes to a fault. You're always willing to share half of what you have, but oddly enough, you tend to give your support most easily to strangers. Your thirst for whatever is new out there brings you not just to schools and varied peer groups for learning, however. You're game for just about anything that you haven't tried yet—at least once!

Your Relationships

You're extremely fond of your personal freedom, Sagittarius, so anyone who tries to tie you down or make you "behave" won't last long in your world. That goes for friends, lovers, family, and partners alike. If they try to hold you back, you'll fight fiercely to be free—and make no mistake about it, you *will* have your freedom, before all else. Once you're with someone and convinced they can keep you interested for life, you'll go out of your way to provide them with lavish thank-yous. Whether it's a gift or picking up the tab, no one who matters in your life will ever be able to doubt your generosity of spirit and your ease at providing on a material level as well.

The one thing you absolutely can't tolerate, however, is boredom. Once someone becomes predictable, you'll want to bail out—fast, just like your air-sign Aquarius cousins. You need variety and spontaneity in your life, and anyone who can't provide that is barking up the wrong tree. You believe in luck and don't believe in coincidences, which might seem rather odd to those who think they're the same thing, but you know the difference. Luck is what happens when you hear the subtle sounds of the Universe and respond, immediately. Coincidence is what others have named those times when the Universe is yelling too loudly to be ignored.

You are famously partnered with Aries, who shares your pioneering spirit and is always up for a challenge or adventure, but brave, entertaining Leo might also do the trick. The water and earth signs tend to dampen your spirit romantically, but make wonderful long-term friends. The air signs also make good matches, such as rebellious Aquarius, who is just as freedom-loving as you, and just as tough to tie down. Partnering up with Gemini also creates a nice mix of energies. They have questions, you have answers. You're both curious and restless, too, so you'll never bore each other, which would be impossible for either of you to tolerate.

Your Career and Money

Sitting in the same chair day after day in an office setting can be unbelievably tedious for you, Sagittarius—unless, of course, your mind is active. That means your career needs to be a constant challenge. You love to laugh, too, so your coworkers had better get used to that right away. If they're smart, they'll join in the fun, and absolutely everyone you work alongside will adore you for keeping the atmosphere light, even during the most stressful times. In fact, you often build your job description around your love of mingling and allowing others to see the lighter side of life. Many famous comedians are Sagittarians. Think Richard Pryor, Jon Stewart, and *Peanuts* cartoonist Charles Schulz, to name a few. When it comes to finances, you've never fancied yourself to be an expert, Sagittarius. You know you're impulsive and excessive and that you'd have a lot more money if you'd only stop treating others, but that generosity won't be going away any time soon. You should, however, do yourself a favor and find a good accountant.

Your Lighter Side

There are just a couple of things you absolutely must have in your life on a daily basis to consider it fun, Sagg. There must be laughter, and there must be learning. Lively conversations are what you love best, but you're also very fond of the company of animals—which is no surprise, considering your symbol, the Centaur, makes you half-animal yourself.

Affirmation for the Year
New experiences feed my soul.

The Year Ahead for Sagittarius

Let's start by talking about Venus and Jupiter, the heavens' most popular planets. Traditionally known astrologically as "the benefics," they do tend to be in the vicinity when "good" things happen, especially when they're operating in tandem, as they will be for a good part of 2015. They'll both be in Leo (a fire-sign cousin who gets the concept of extravagance and can be every bit as being lavish and excessive as you), and they'll be passing through your solar ninth house of long-distance adventures, far-off loved ones, and higher education. Jupiter will stay on duty the longest, straight through until August 11. During this time, you'll be able to do what you love best, with the blessings of the Universe. Classes and travel are already on that list, along with a love of different cultures, but let's not forget about laughter, your primary reason for being. If you learn something new or visit a place so different that you start to wonder if you're on another planet—well, that will definitely make you smile, but it's the people you'll run across during these adventures who'll actually make you laugh. They'll all be Jupiter's "representatives," so how could you possibly help it? If you do travel, Leo's influence will encourage you to go first-class, but don't put anything off because you can only sit in the cheap seats. It's the experience that counts, and Jupiter always brings lucky encounters with successful folks, so even if you start out in coach, you'll probably be upgraded before you know it. Besides, travel and education rejuvenate the soul and open up higher perspectives, so even if you think you're just indulging yourself now, down the road a bit you'll realize that those classes and/or that trip overseas was really a lot cheaper and a lot more helpful than therapy.

Leo loves to entertain, so you might be drawn to do a bit of performing. It doesn't matter whether it's Broadway or your kitchen table. Leo planets carry a stage with them wherever they go. It's your turn to step into that spotlight. Have fun with it!

Thanks to Venus, it might also be your turn to fall in love, but it won't be with the boy or girl next door. Between June 5 and July 18 and again from July 31 through October 8, Venus will be smiling at exotic, well-to-do types; college professors; and anyone powerful, intelligent, and entertaining enough to have the ear of the crowd. Keep an ear open for a wonderfully sexy accent all wrapped up in an exotic body, or a mentor who's a bit too sexy to think of as an authority figure. Introduce yourself. Sit down and talk to them. Bet they have a rich, interesting past, and won't be afraid to tell you all about it. Bet you won't get tired of hearing their stories for a very long time, either. If you've ever been drawn to a career in beauty, art, or acting, there's no better time to learn your trade—and with Jupiter on board, you'll pick it up quickly.

And speaking of career, with Saturn marching through your sign and your solar first house of personality and appearance for most of the year, it's going to be essential that you tend to yours, or at least learn more about the field you've chosen. Teaching looks like a strong possibility, especially with so much positive energy flowing through your solar ninth house. Of course, Saturn brings responsibilities with him wherever he goes, so expect yours to double, perhaps even to the point of making you feel physically heavy. Saturn rules lead, the heaviest metal of them all, and his visits often mean we feel overburdened. The good news is that you will be able to handle it all just fine as long as you use honesty, integrity, and a strong work ethic as your tools. Saturn will back up into Scorpio and your solar twelfth house of secrets and private time from June 14 to September 17 for one last pass, however, so before you can really step out there and make a name for yourself, you'll need just a few more months of introspection. Keep your own counsel, or share those intimate thoughts only with someone you are absolutely positive you can trust.

Now, let's talk about Uranus, Mr. Unpredictable himself. He will continue his trek through feisty Aries and your solar fifth house of lovers, playmates, and relationships with kids, asking that you act totally spontaneously in all those departments. This would be a great year to take the family on an impromptu vacation. If you're attached but have no kids, why not plan a second honeymoon or celebrate your anniversary in an odd, unusual place? You two will have stories to tell and some wonderful photos to put in your scrapbook. If you're single, forget about searching for someone who is your "type." Uranus has other ideas in mind.

Neptune's continued passage through Pisces and your solar fourth house of home, family, and emotional security might mean that you have the feeling that some of the building blocks that your life rests upon are mysteriously eroding, or that important people are slowly disappearing. These uneasy feelings may be justified, which you'll learn in time. For now, resolve not to try to hang on to anything that's flowing out of your life. It was meant to go. Release it and use your intuition to figure out what you'll need to put in its place. Pluto is still making his way through your solar second house of money matters, so power struggles are still possible, and you can just about count on old debts resurfacing, demanding to be paid. Issues you thought were solved regarding taxes, inheritances, or joint property holdings may also be a thorn in your side. As with Neptune, all you can do to keep this Pluto transit positive is to react positively—and let go.

What This Year's Eclipses Mean for You

The Solar Eclipse of March 20 is the first of four eclipses scheduled for this year, Sagittarius. This one will set up shop in your solar fourth house of home, family, and domestic issues, asking that you take a good look around and figure out what needs to change quickly. Yes, quickly. Remember, eclipses don't have time to waste and they act quite suddenly, so if you're reading this beforehand, you have a chance to decide what or whom has to change. It might not be easy to decide what, especially since this eclipse will occur in Pisces, but something will absolutely have to go. If you're honest and you trust your gut feelings, you'll come to realize it's the one something you really didn't want in your life to start with. In that case, have a party. It's over!

On April 4, a Lunar Eclipse will occur in partner-pleasing Libra and your solar eleventh house of groups and friendships. This sociable lunation is the perfect astrological recipe for getting in touch with a whole new cluster of like-minded peers. If you've been thinking about finding your tribe, go out and look for them now. Oh, and here's a tip: you'll probably find them in pairs, or in gatherings that encourage partnerships. You and your sweetheart would also do well to join a group together and extend the boundaries of your immediate circle.

The Solar Eclipse on September 13 will plant a seed in earthy Virgo and your solar tenth house of career matters, urging you to tend to every single professional detail, no matter how painful the process. You're not fond of paperwork or reports, so it will be a real effort for you to sift through bills, documents, and files and maybe even write up a new resumé, but if you're ready to move on—and you will be, once this lunation arrives—be prepared for just about anything, including an entirely new career.

Once the Lunar Eclipse of September 27 in fiery, passionate Aries gets to work, there will be little doubt about how quickly you should take action. Aries is a bullet of energy, so whatever feels right at any particular moment seems like the right thing to do. With your solar house of recreational experiences involved, sitting still and putting up with The Usual Nonsense will be out of the question. Be sure you have a safety net in place, just in case.

Saturn

Saturn has been operating from behind the scenes in your solar twelfth house for two and a half years, Sagittarius. He's been silent and just about invisible, so you probably think he hasn't done much. Not so. In Scorpio and in a spot that allows him to infiltrate your life, he's gone unnoticed, sure—but he's been extremely busy. You have a whole new attitude about the deeper side of life. Spiritual matters mean more to you now, so whether you've been doing yoga, meditating alone, or just investigating the metaphysical side of life, you've definitely deepened your character and opened yourself up to new habits that hopefully are helping you to build a solid game plan for the future. You may have spent a good part of last year alone, too, but not to worry. Except for Saturn's last pass through Scorpio, from June 14 through September 17, you're done hibernating. In fact, for most of this year, you'll be out and about and asked to take charge of many group situations you attend. This is a terrific time to return to school and beef up your resumé, or to learn a new skill that's crucial to doing what you really want to do, long-term. This doesn't mean you should quit your day job just yet, but only that you're primed and ready to perfect the skills necessary to move on to a new lifestyle. The good news is that since Saturn is the honorary principal wherever he goes, you'll feel just fine about expressing yourself as you see fit at any time. The best news is that your attitude will reflect your newfound inner authority figure, so no one will even think to question you.

Uranus

If you were born between November 27 and December 2, fasten your seat belt and put your table tray in the up position, because Uranus is on his way to shake things up—big time. Now, you're not on bad terms with this startling energy, so when he arrives with his surprises and last-minute changes of plan, you're usually just fine with that. Since Uranus is in Aries, however, you'll be even happier about the situation, and you'll be even more open to the options Uranus will bring your way from his spot in your solar fifth house of recreation and playmates. If you've been thinking about a major move, there's no time like the present to check it out. Exactly what would you have to do to switch states, or even countries? You're in the mood to dump everything and everyone who makes you feel as if you have to be a certain way. From now on, and for the next two to three years, you'll want to be yourself, totally and completely, without any excuses—and what's wrong with that? It's all about self-discovery for you now. What exactly is your particular bliss?

Neptune

If you were born between November 27 and December 3, you'll be feeling the strong effects of Neptune's square to your Sun. Among possible symptoms are an inability to tolerate noise, bright lights, and loud people. But then, no one should have to tolerate any of that, so when you object and move away from these things, as you undoubtedly will, you'll be well within your rights. In fact, those of us who've watched you wince and missed you while you've been hiding out lately will also be well within our rights to put a stop to it. The ideal atmosphere for you now is quiet and drama-free. If you don't have it yet, you might be hiding in a closet, but soon enough, the undeniable urge to simply be peaceful will take over and you'll have no choice but to find a "safe" place for yourself. If you currently live with someone, think about how nice it might be to have only yourself for a roommate, along with a few fur-people, perhaps. You might often feel confused or seek out escape hatches to get you as far away from reality as possible, but that's only because you're so ultra-sensitive. Once you emerge from your cave, you'll have the answers. All you have to do is listen to your antennae.

Pluto

There's not a lot that Pluto can't uncover during his visits, so this year, if he meets up with your Sun—even through a supposedly minor aspect like the semisextile—you should still expect some major changes. They won't necessarily be obvious in your "outer" life, but on an inner level, you'll feel something huge going on. Pluto's presence in your solar second house of personal finances means there's a major overhaul due, so get busy. Get out the files and the statements, see what happened to put you in this position to start with, and resolve to never, ever let it happen again. The need to do this will be even more compelling if you were born between December 4 and 9. Pluto will absolutely insist that you ditch everything that isn't productive and make room for new things—better things. Pluto isn't gentle, so you should be aware that the more tightly you hold on, the more determined he'll be to shake you off. Do yourself a favor. Let go of expenses that are holding you back from financial independence—and let go of any relationships that are holding you back, too. Possessions and personal values will be primary to you as you sort out what really matters and what really doesn't matter at all. Get yourself a dumpster and a confidant, and start clearing a path for new growth.

Sagittarius | January

Planetary Lightspots

You're a big fan of change, Sagittarius. You're mutable, you're a fire sign, and you get the concept of higher understanding, which would never happen if nothing ever changed. So every one of the five planets who'll make their way through unpredictable Aquarius and your solar third house of conversations this month will be quite welcome. The more the merrier—and yes, you'll want to talk about change!

Relationships

The New Moon in startling Aquarius on January 20 will plant a seed in your solar third house of communications, Sagittarius, urging you to speak your mind without any regrets. Now, that's always been the case for you, but this month, you'll be willing to cut loose even more than usual. Prepare everyone around you for an extreme case of bluntness.

Money and Success

Venus rules both love and money, Sagittarius, and she will be passing through rebellious, unpredictable Aquarius and your solar third house of communications for most of the month. If you've been thinking about getting a new computer, this is a great time to do it. If you're interested in computer programming, taking classes now will add substantially to your resumé. Your mission is to find yourself an intellectual challenge and solve it.

Planetary Hotspots

The Full Moon on January 4 will activate home-oriented Cancer, so even though you do love to travel, you'll want to hang close to your nest for a bit. You might also be considering a move—maybe even a long one—but you really shouldn't make it without talking to everyone who's involved on a domestic level.

Rewarding Days

4, 5, 13, 14, 20, 22, 31

Challenging Days

1, 3, 15, 16, 19, 21, 30

Sagittarius | February

Planetary Lightspots

Several planets will set up shop in fiery Aries this month, Sagittarius, a sign you've always loved and been eager to go out and play with. Since loving Venus and red-hot Mars are on that list, however, it might be that you're a bit too willing to take chances, especially in relationships. Be sure you're ready before you announce your plans to commit.

Relationships

From February 19 through February 22, your solar fifth house of lovers will be under the complete and utter control of several planets in red-hot Aries. Now, you're quite fond of this energy, and you do love to travel, so if you have to climb on a plane impulsively to get close to your sweetheart—well, so much the better. Whatever it takes is exactly what you'll do.

Money and Success

Seeking out the help of an advisor will be very important to you this month, Sagittarius, most especially around February 24, when you'll be able to find someone who's not just knowledgeable but also quite capable of telling you what to do about a certain financial dilemma. Listen up. After all, they're on your side.

Planetary Hotspots

Fiery Mars will set off for Aries on February 19, and just a few days later, Venus and the Moon will join him there. This creates the potential for an extremely passionate conversation, at the very least. The thing is, you should also be careful not to arouse the anger of anyone who isn't used to your particular brand of humor.

Rewarding Days
2, 3, 19, 24, 25, 26

Challenging Days
1, 6, 11, 22, 23

Sagittarius | March

Planetary Lightspots

The really big astrological news this month involves startling Uranus and your very own generous ruling planet, Jupiter. They'll get together to provide you with all the astrological tools you'll need to get out there and make a name for yourself. If you've been thinking of striking out on your own, this is a terrific time to do it. If you're already there and just need a break, try to manage it around March 3.

Relationships

These are fiery times, Sagittarius. Up until March 17, loving Venus in red-hot Aries will continue working side by side with Mars, turning up the thermostat in your solar fifth house of lovers. If you're already seeing someone, expect the relationship to take a decidedly passionate turn. If not, get out there and keep an eye open for the most impatient person in the room.

Money and Success

Once Venus enters stable, grounded Taurus on March 17, you'll find that work-oriented situations that were problematic will simmer down nicely. You might even finally land that raise, bonus, or promotion you were after. If you're thinking about the right time to plead your case, look to March 23 or 30.

Planetary Hotspots

Your solar tenth house of career opportunities and relationships with higher-ups will host this month's Full Moon in Virgo, who'll arrive on March 5. This earthy lady will bring out the more practical side of you, so if you've been thinking about making a change in your profession and a chance comes up that seems perfect, do yourself a favor and at least check it out.

Rewarding Days

2, 3, 5, 8, 9, 25, 26

Challenging Days

1, 4, 11, 15, 16, 27

Sagittarius | April

Planetary Lightspots

The total Lunar Eclipse will occur on April 4, Sagittarius, all done up in partner-pleasing Libra. Now, this is your solar eleventh house of friendships, so you might partner up with someone for a special group project and, while you're working together, discover just how much you have in common. Romantic relationships that are grounded in mutual interests tend to last. Nice!

Relationships

If you haven't already been pulled off the market by April 8 or 9, a fiery new admirer may be along. They'll spark your interest by being just bold enough to agree to your adventures at least once, but the deciding factor will be how they react if obstacles arise on April 15 or 16. Watch carefully.

Money and Success

You've never been famous for being especially frugal, but this month, you might be a bit less willing to pick up the tab every time. Venus will face off with prudent Saturn on April 15, and a great big dose of reality could be en route. No one is saying you can't treat every now and then, but consider your bank and credit card balances before you do.

Planetary Hotspots

The New Moon on April 18 will once again activate your solar fifth house of playmates and relationships with kids, Sagittarius, so if you haven't yet found time to spend with them in recreation mode, this would be a fine time to clear your schedule and make time. Your mission is to also have some fun yourself!

Rewarding Days
1, 2, 3, 6, 22, 23, 26

Challenging Days
4, 5, 7, 8, 19, 20

Sagittarius | May

Planetary Lightspots

Once May 21 comes along, the Sun will join Mars, Venus, and Mercury in your solar seventh house of one-to-one relationships. This merry pack of Gemini energies will bring along at least one person who'll actually give you a run for your money in the department of conversation, which is no easy task. Their curiosity and honestly will charm you, too.

Relationships

After just about a month in Gemini, Venus will slip into something more comfortable, Sagittarius—your dimly lit solar eighth house of intimate partners. Venus will be in privacy-loving Cancer, so you might not see much of your friends for the next few weeks—that is, unless you two come up for air and invite them over to your place.

Money and Success

The New Moon on May 17 will occur in Taurus, the sign that's a virtual money magnet. If you've been thinking about a way to make some extra cash, see about some overtime. If that's not possible, consider turning your hobby into a part-time job. If you're already enjoying it with some-one else, so much the better. You have a partner!

Planetary Hotspots

If you've been stewing over a recent offense but haven't yet let your feelings be known, watch out for May 11. Angry Mars will enter your solar house seventh of one-to-one encounters, and keeping quiet will no longer be an option. Speak your mind, but be sure not to let that situation—or any other over the next two months—turn volatile.

Rewarding Days

5, 6, 7, 16, 17, 30

Challenging Days

3, 4, 9, 14, 15, 22, 25, 27

Sagittarius | June

Planetary Lightspots

On June 2, the Full Moon will illuminate your sign and your solar first house of personality and appearance, asking that you take a good look at your body and the condition of your health. If you're not pleased with what you see, this is a great time to make changes, especially those involving weight loss or ending bad habits.

Relationships

A pack of planets in Gemini will make this quite the fun, lively month for you. If you're seeing someone, you two really should plan an adventure—something both of you have always wanted to do but have never gotten around to. If it involves a bit of adrenaline, however, stay away from April 14 or 15. You single Sagittarians should get out and strut your stuff around June 6 through 10.

Money and Success

Venus will arrive at the door of showy Leo on June 5, and suddenly, impressing someone will become quite important to you. If you can afford to do so, wonderful. Pull out all the stops. If not, remember that your company is the best gift of all, and anyone who needs more from you might not be the right choice in the long run.

Planetary Hotspots

All those curious Gemini planets will probably ignite your urge to learn, Sagittarius, which is a lifelong adventure in your book. Going back to school now would be great, but studying one on one with a mentor who knows you and your goals would be best. If you don't already know them, be specific about your needs with anyone you're considering for the post.

Rewarding Days

2, 5, 6, 8, 9, 10, 28

Challenging Days

13, 14, 23, 24, 30

Sagittarius | July

Planetary Lightspots

The second Full Moon on July 31 will activate a craving in you for conversations and communications of an extremely unusual nature. Talk with someone who's an expert on a subject you're fascinated with but know little about. Your powers of observation will be especially keen, and you'll be able to understand the motives of others, not just through their words but also through their gestures and body language.

Relationships

On July 5, Mercury and Venus will form a stimulating sextile aspect. Great conversations—which you adore—will be easy to come by. This is a terrific time for a party, but if you're only interested in a one-on-one chat, you'll know exactly whom to call. If it's been a while, make some coffee and get comfortable.

Money and Success

There will be two Full Moons this month, Sagittarius. On July 1, the first will illuminate Capricorn and your solar second house of finances. The good news is that Venus and Jupiter will come together that same day, providing you with the ability to come up with creative ideas for additional work that might actually turn out to be fun.

Planetary Hotspots

On July 15, the New Moon will combine her energy with chatty Mercury and assertive Mars to bring you very close to finding an explanation for the issues you've had recently with an intimate partner. Keep asking questions—gently, please—until you have the answers.

Rewarding Days

1, 2, 3, 5, 22, 23

Challenging Days

6, 12, 14, 15, 18, 24, 25

Sagittarius | August

Planetary Lightspots

Talk about a good time! On August 2, Mercury and Uranus will get your month off to a pleasantly surprising start. Messages crammed with long-distance affection will arrive, but you won't have to look far for a warm hug. The good you've done for others will be returned to you, when you least expect it and most need it.

Relationships

What a month! Loving Venus and your own generous ruling planet, Jupiter, will come together on August 4 to get the show on the road. If you're single, someone extremely entertaining and every bit as fiery as you are will make a rather dramatic entrance into your life that day. The romance will continue on August 6, 7, 8, 15, 19, and 31.

Money and Success

If you've been feeling stifled or held back at work, Sagittarius, help is on the way. Your own generous ruling planet, Jupiter, will enter your solar tenth house of career matters, promising you a full year of lucky breaks and fortunate encounters as of August 11. Prepare to work hard, and force yourself to tend carefully to details. Your efforts will be noticed and rewarded.

Planetary Hotspots

Generous Jupiter and frugal Saturn are astrological opposites, so when they form an irritating square on August 3, we'll all be torn between having what we want, no matter the cost, and tightening up our belts. In your case, an authority figure may limit or restrict you, and you won't take kindly to it.

Rewarding Days

1, 2, 4, 6, 7, 13, 15, 26

Challenging Days

3, 5, 21, 22, 31

Sagittarius | September

Planetary Lightspots

On September 27, a total Lunar Eclipse in red-hot Aries will set fire to your solar fifth house of playmates, lovers, and relationships with children. If you've been seeing someone casually, expect things to turn really passionate—really fast. Kids may come to you for advice or support regarding an urgent situation, but you'll be more than up to the task.

Relationships

With passionate Mars in Leo storming through your solar ninth house of travel and education for most of the month, it's tough to imagine you being bored right now, Sagittarius. Of course, with any Leo planet on duty, romance is always a possibility. Be sure to chat up that delicious stranger the Universe has seen fit to seat beside you.

Money and Success

The Full Moon last month called your attention to personal financial matters, and you probably put a good amount of time and energy—not to mention money—into straightening things out. Well, your rewards are on the way. On September 5, the Sun and Pluto will team up to help you see that whatever you let go of really had to go, and you're better off without it.

Planetary Hotspots

The Solar Eclipse in meticulous Virgo on September 13 will send a huge surge of energy into your solar tenth house of career matters. If you've done your homework and tended to the details of your work, your rewards will be right around the corner. If you haven't, better get busy. This is a very important time for you professionally.

Rewarding Days
4, 5, 6, 8, 22, 23, 30

Challenging Days
9, 10, 24, 25, 26

Sagittarius | October

Planetary Lightspots

The Full Moon on October 27 will activate your solar sixth house of work and relationships with coworkers. It will be all done up in sensual Taurus, who also happens to be the heavens' money magnet, so a lovely raise might be in order—or a wonderful new love affair with someone you see on a daily basis.

Relationships

Careful, now! Venus will be quite active as she passes through your solar tenth house of authority figures this month, and love (or at least a serious physical attraction) might just spring up in the workplace. Whether it's a higher-up or someone who works under you, be aware of possible consequences before you get too involved. If it feels totally right, though, you'll probably do it anyway.

Money and Success

You may feel that a setback on October 10 has put an end to your professional career, Sagittarius, but hang in there. A higher-up is probably only trying to test you, to see what you're made of. Rise to the challenge, prove yourself, and expect a hefty pay hike or promotion in return for your efforts.

Planetary Hotspots

Halloween looks like great fun this year. The Sun will get together with Neptune, the planet of illusions—the perfect astrological recipe for putting on a disguise and having some serious fun. This time, choose a person or character you've always wanted to be, and put your heart and soul into making the fantasy perfect.

Rewarding Days
11, 13, 14, 15, 23, 30, 31

Challenging Days
6, 9, 10, 17, 22, 25, 26

Sagittarius | November

Planetary Lightspots

On November 10, a long-term project you've put all your time and energy into will finally come to an end, Sagittarius—and what a feeling of accomplishment you'll have! Once you've put the finishing touches on it, it will be time to celebrate, and since no one has seen much of you lately, you'll be the star of the show. Enjoy!

Relationships

The Full Moon on November 25 will activate your solar relationship axis, Sagittarius—in only the loveliest of ways. Joining in the fun will be passionate Mars in partner-oriented Libra, a fiery guy who loves adrenaline, and it's easy to see you being quite attracted to someone new. If you're attached, be careful not to throw away everything you've built for an hour of excitement. If you're not attached, go for it.

Money and Success

On November 13, Venus will come together with stable Saturn, giving you the prefect opportunity to take up a project or assignment that might be tough but will ultimately give you the chance to prove yourself to your superiors. What a great time to schedule an interview or apply for a raise, bonus, or promotion!

Planetary Hotspots

The Sun and Mercury will spend much of the month in intense, sexy Scorpio and your solar twelfth house of secrets, Sagittarius, so don't even think about trying to continue hiding something from a certain someone who already seems to be on to you. Instead, reveal all, honestly and well before any details emerge.

Rewarding Days

5, 6, 9, 10, 13, 14, 25

Challenging Days

2, 3, 19, 20, 23, 24, 26

Sagittarius | December

Planetary Lightspots

Bright and early on December 25, a Full Moon in family-oriented Cancer will arrive, Sagittarius. Together with an easy trine between talkative Mercury and outgoing Jupiter—your ruling planet, by the way—the Moon will see to it that you're feeling warm and wonderful for the holidays. Hugs, laughter, and lots of sentimental stories will abound. Enjoy every minute, and don't forget about that mistletoe!

Relationships

Venus will set off for sexy, secretive Scorpio on December 4, pitching her charming tent in your solar twelfth house of Privacy, Please. You'll want to spend as much time as possible behind closed doors with your sweetheart, but try to pry yourself away long enough to indulge in the company of dear ones. On New Year's Eve, however, Venus will be in your fun-loving sign, and you'll be ready to come out and play—big time!

Money and Success

Thoughtful Mercury will enter practical Capricorn on December 9, insisting that you pay attention to financial details and money matters you might ordinarily ignore, especially with the holidays coming. Your mission now is to be creative. Find a way to give everyone exactly what they want without overspending. Be creative, and remember, your time is the greatest gift.

Planetary Hotspots

Fiery Mars will face off with shocking Uranus on December 10, turning up the thermostat on a supposedly platonic relationship. All that "subtle" flirting you've been doing? Well, prepare yourself, because someone is about to cross the line and make their intentions clear. If you're with someone, this would be the perfect time to introduce them to The Gang.

Rewarding Days

1, 8, 11, 12, 17, 24, 25, 30

Challenging Days

4, 7, 10, 14, 20, 29

Sagittarius Action Table

These dates reflect the best–but not the only–times for success and ease in these activities, according to your Sun sign.

	JAN	FEB	MAR	APR	MAY	JUN	JUL.	AUG	SEP	OCT	NOV	DEC
Move	27		20, 21		16			29, 30			24, 29, 30	
Start a class	4, 14, 20					8, 10		6, 7				
Join a club	20, 22			4			30, 31		22, 23	12, 13	12, 13, 23	
Ask for a raise	3, 30		5, 6				1			14, 15		17
Look for work			23, 24	21, 22, 29	17			25, 26		26, 27		
Get pro advice		19, 24, 25		2, 3	6			26			23, 24	24
Get a loan		7				6	15, 16					
See a doctor			6, 7		11, 12		13, 26			23, 27		
Start a diet	3, 15								17, 23		2, 3	
End relationship	30			15		14		18, 19				
Buy clothes				22, 23			1			23		12, 13, 14
Get a makeover	4					2, 3						12
New romance		24, 25		18, 19		16, 17		6, 7, 13	8, 27, 28			1, 8
Vacation			9, 10			6			8			

Capricorn

The Goat
December 21 to January 20

♑

Element: Earth

Quality: Cardinal

Polarity: Yin/feminine

Planetary Ruler: Saturn

Meditation: I know the strength of my soul

Gemstone: Garnet

Power Stones: Peridot, onyx diamond, quartz, black obsidian

Key Phrase: I use

Glyph: Head of goat

Anatomy: Skeleton, knees, skin

Colors: Black, forest green

Animals: Goats, thick-shelled animals

Myths/Legends: Chronos, Vesta, Pan

House: Tenth

Opposite Sign: Cancer

Flower: Carnation

Keyword: Ambitious

The Capricorn Personality

Your Strengths and Challenges

You're an earth sign, Capricorn, and a cardinal sign, so when you take aim at something, you squint closely at it, focus in, and refuse to be distracted until you've hit your target and the spoils of the battle are yours. That makes you quite the businessperson and quite the executive, and you seldom have a job for long without being put in a position of authority. You're pretty much an authority figure wherever you go, honestly. Your natural gifts for organization and leadership make you a shoe-in. When there's no one driving, you automatically take over the steering wheel, and no one resents it. In fact, they're usually relieved that you stepped up! The crown does weigh heavy on your head, though, especially because you so long to let go and operate under the leadership of someone you respect without needing to take on so much responsibility yourself. That's not to say that you don't enjoy leading—you do, and you're very, very good at it. Once you find a niche where others will allow you to take charge without explanation, you're in. That might involve a career, which is very important to you, but it might also be that you opt to devote your time to raising a family. Regardless of where you decide to direct your earthy aim, you're guaranteed to be successful. You'd never settle for anything less. You're nothing if not careful in all life situations, but that goes double for the way you conduct yourself in public. Your ruling planet is serious Saturn, who'd never let a sign of his go out with their shoelaces untied and strongly objects to displays of affection.

Your Relationships

Speaking of public affection, Capricorn, whoever decides to sign up with you for a mate had better get used to only seeing the tender side of you behind closed doors. You most definitely believe in love and commitment, but aren't comfortable showing off your feelings. You believe, as did at least one of your parents, that providing food and shelter for your loved ones is the best way to let them to know you care—which makes you a serious catch. Sure, you might need a bit of coaxing to forget about work and responsibilities and get down to some serious romance, but anyone who can persuade you to turn off your cell phone has the situation squarely in hand. Because of that work ethic, you're often drawn to the other earth signs. That includes practical Taurus, but most especially hardworking Virgo, who never fails to amaze you with their diligence and attention to detail. You make a terrific long-term friend or lover to any sign, as long as they're willing to invest just as much time and energy into keeping the relationship alive as you are. The thing is, you're ultra-cautious, and you occasionally take so long to decide whether or not a new romantic interest is right for you that you can lose their attention. Think of that first date as a second interview, and arrange to meet with the appealing candidate quickly—before they're snapped up by someone else. You tend to starve yourself emotionally, so accepting love and attention isn't something that comes easily. Get over that. You're worth all that and a bag of chips. Libra can often be a good match for you. They're born from the cardinal element, like you, so they're just as willing to get up and make change happen. But once they choose a mate, they tend to adopt their lifestyle, and are totally devoted, like you, for the long haul. Fixed Scorpio can also match your determination and is just as privately inclined. Cancer is also often ideal, since they'll be happy to provide you with a solid, comfortable home base to return to after you've put in your time earning your daily bread.

Your Career and Money

One way or the other, Capricorn, you always end up in charge. It might be that someone drops the ball just after you've started and you've already proven yourself to be capable of leadership, so the job naturally falls to you. Or it might be that you slowly push your way to the top, both through your thorough, tireless work and your ability to see the structure in all work-oriented groups, businesses, and organizations. It doesn't matter. Regardless of how you do it, you'll make your way to the top or die trying—and be the best darn boss anyone has ever had, never asking anyone to do anything that you wouldn't do yourself. You're definitely a hands-on learner, which makes you a great teacher, too. When someone new needs to be trained, you understand immediately what they don't know—which is far more important than what they do know. Financially speaking, you can be quite frugal, but only until you've found something that's of sufficient quality for you to put your valuable time, effort, and resources into it.

Your Lighter Side

Your idea of fun isn't often what many of us would think of, off the top of our heads. Nothing feels better to you than having things in order, so cleaning your home is fun, and when that's done, relaxing with some spreadsheets, data, and facts also clears your mind. Building or preparing anything is pleasurable, too, especially if you have to start from scratch, but in general, any structured activities will do just fine.

Affirmation for the Year

I give thanks for my ability to bring creative solutions to joint financial issues.

The Year Ahead for Capricorn

Jupiter will continue on his trip through fiery, theatrical Leo and your solar eighth house of intimate partners and joint resources straight through August 11, so you can expect the drama to last until then. Now, by "drama," I mean the fireworks that have been occurring in this intense, sexy place. On the plus side, you may have become involved in a relationship that has been physically exhausting, for only the most delightful of reasons, so the fireworks will continue to be equally delightful. (Oh, and not to worry about those flames dying down once Jupiter moves on. In fact, you two might decide to travel long-distance together or even move to a far-off place to start over.) On the difficult side, you might be tired of someone's insistence on dragging out a financial issue that really could have been settled long ago. In this case, you'll need to make a decision. What's more important: winning or having peace of mind? The good news is that just like Santa, Jupiter loves to pass out presents, so no matter when you decide to end the situation, you won't leave empty-handed.

Now, let's talk about the lovely lady Venus, who'll also spend a good part of the year in Leo and this same house. She and Jupiter are known to be positive influences, and when they're both affecting the same area of life, it's hard to imagine failure. It's also hard to imagine you spending much time alone, with magnetic Venus in this tender place—and Jupiter on hand to act as her wingman. If you're single, get out there and resume the hunt from June 5 to July 18. If you haven't found what you were looking for in a partner by then, not to worry. You'll have Venus's help again from July 31 through October 8.

Saturn will spend most of the year in your solar twelfth house of behind-the-scenes activity and secrets. The thing is, he'll be wearing outgoing, excessive Sagittarius for the duration, and Sagittarius never was very good at keeping secrets. If you're tempted to become involved in anything you wouldn't want the rest of the world to know about, keep in mind that the situation will surface eventually, and with Sagittarius energies on duty, it will make quite the splash when it does. This is a great time to plan a spiritual retreat or seek the counsel of a trusted guide or mentor. Use this transit positively and you'll learn a lot about yourself. Before Saturn commits entirely to Sagittarius, however, he will retrograde back into Scorpio and your solar eleventh house of friendships from June 14 through September 17. This will give you a chance to bring closure to any problems you've had recently with a friend, or to make things right with a circle of friends you may have become distanced from lately.

You'll need to handle a great deal of ongoing tension from Uranus and Pluto, who are still locked into that testy square. This will pit startling Uranus in your solar fourth house of home, family, and emotions against relentless Pluto in your solar first house of personality and appearance. Sounds like family matters might require some sudden attention, possibly more than once, and you'll need to bring out the authority-figure attitude to deal with it—possibly under duress. Power struggles are definitely on the agenda, and you'll want to hold on tight to those reins, but Uranus's push toward sudden change will be heightened by the eclipses of April 4 and September 27, so resistance might just prove to be futile. The good news is that any major shifts in your lifestyle that occur now really had to happen. If you feel you've lost something, take comfort in the fact that change is the only constant and that we absolutely need to cooperate with it in order to grow.

Uranus's presence in your solar fourth house of home and emotions might also leave you feeling a bit jittery and worried about the safety and security of your family and your nest. If that's the case, do what's necessary to set your mind at ease. If that means stepping up security measures, so be it. If it means a major move, that's fine too. The point is that at times you'll feel like you're on an emotional rollercoaster, so you'll need to keep your hands on the safety bar and remember that the ride won't last forever.

Mystical, magical Neptune will stay on her path through your solar third house of thoughts and communications wearing her favorite sign, Pisces. Now, this planet in this sign is operating without a filter, and she's quite the sentimental, nostalgic energy, so you might find yourself having a few regrets about the past or spending an awful lot of time with what-ifs. Don't do that. The past is the past, and the future is the future. What you've learned intuitively from both your mistakes and successes will help you make your way into your next stage of spiritual growth. Think of it as a learning curve.

It will be especially important for you to pay attention to your immediate environment around March 20 and again on September 13, when total Solar Eclipses will activate your sign and bring major changes in your solar seventh house of one-to-one relationships.

What This Year's Eclipses Mean for You

Four eclipses have been scheduled for 2015, Capricorn. None will fall in your sign, but that doesn't mean they won't affect you. For example, the total Solar Eclipse on March 20 will plant a seed of change in ultra-sensitive Pisces and your solar third house of communications and sensory experiences. Along with the steady influence of Neptune, you might feel barraged by loud sounds and bright lights at this time, and be drawn to retreat for a while. That's all well and good, but don't hide out so long that you feel awkward emerging. Everyone needs time to themselves, even a sign as hardworking as yours. The trick is to take it without making it a habit. You're far too goal-oriented to be a hermit, so stay active.

The total Lunar Eclipse in people-pleasing Libra on April 4 will pit your solar tenth house of professional matters against your solar fourth house of home, family, and domestic matters. Now, Libra knows how to juggle, so you'll probably manage to make both ends of this opposition happy—but at what cost? If you feel stuck in the middle and you are trying so hard to tend to your duties that you're no longer thinking about yourself, pick a side. Explain to family members that your career is important to you, or talk with authority figures about how to lighten your responsibilities enough so that you have more time for family. Whatever you choose, commit.

The second Solar Eclipse on September 13 will occur in Virgo and your solar ninth house of long-distance people and places, education, and new experiences. This supercharged New Moon will ask that you expand your horizons, but not in a reckless way. Part of you is bored and needs to be set free, but you will need a practical plan to make it all work out to your benefit. If work is what's become tedious, think about going back to school to improve your resumé—or to learn a whole new skill. You might also simply need a vacation to rejuvenate your attitude and open your eyes to the options available to you elsewhere.

On September 27, the second Lunar Eclipse will arrive and set up shop in your solar fourth house of home, family, and domestic issues. Sound familiar? Yes, this time period will very closely resemble what you went through back in early April, but this time out, you will need to bring closure to any problems that are still simmering. You might decide to move, take in a roommate, or cohabitate with your current sweetheart. Children and other family members may take up a good deal of your time, but if you know they need you, find that time. This lunation will bring out the assertive side in you, so don't shy away from making a change as soon as you know it's time.

Saturn

Saturn, your serious, practical ruling planet, will spend much of the year in Sagittarius, a sign that is not famous for being practical or serious. This will put Saturn in your solar twelfth house of subconscious thoughts, secret relationships, and nostalgic feelings. To start with, you'll need to watch out for a tendency to retreat inward and mull over recent losses or bad decisions just a bit too long, possibly to the point of obsession—or depression. If you feel yourself slipping into a bad place, call a lively friend who has always known exactly how to cheer you up and get you moving again. You might also become involved in a relationship that is not quite fit for public consumption—and one or both of you may already be attached. Before you dive into a no-win situation, be sure you have thought carefully about another option: making sure you are both honest with yourselves and others. We stray when our needs aren't being met. If you're really tempted, face that fact—before you do anything you might regret. The good news is that if you act with integrity at all times, what you so dearly long for could very well soon be yours, without any baggage or strings attached. Now, from June 14 through September 17, Saturn will step back into Scorpio to wrap things up in your solar eleventh house of friendships and group affiliations. You'll have a chance to bring closure to a particularly nagging dispute or disagreement, and you really should take advantage of it.

Uranus

If you were born between January 3 and 12, you're about to enjoy a square from startling Uranus this year, Capricorn. Now, this guy just loves to bring us what we least expect, and you do tend to love your schedule, so his visit might be a bit unsettling at first. But once you develop a taste for adrenaline—and you will—you might actually enjoy it. This transit feels like a rollercoaster ride. You never know what direction you'll be going in or how hard you might be jolted in the process. All you can do is hold on tight and let the ride take you. The good news is that you're primed and ready to make some drastic changes—and that's a very good thing. Uranus and Pluto are working together again this year, so just as Pluto tears down any non-working habits you think are part of you, Uranus will ready to distract you and get you interested in what might be next. Your mission is to allow yourself the amount of personal freedom you know you need, no matter what it takes. Now, if you're ready, step aboard and buckle up.

Neptune

If you were born between December 27 and January 2, your Sun will be directly contacted by Neptune this year via an easy, stimulating sextile aspect—and not a moment too soon, I'll bet. Pluto has finally left your Sun behind, and after the power struggles, intense experiences, and possible losses pass, nothing could possibly be more soothing than an easy visit from this romantic, gentle goddess in pink. She travels with incense, candles, herbal tea, and wine. It's time to be nice to yourself, to treat yourself like you would anyone you care for who's been through an ordeal. Go easy on yourself. Take lots of baths and showers, and get yourself out by the lake or the beach whenever you can. Bring a notebook, too. The inspiration Neptune provides is fleeting, like a wisp of vapor, so jot down your thoughts right away or you'll lose them. Focus on the spiritual side of life. What have you learned, and what will you do with that knowledge in the future? If you're used to exercising, you don't have to stop, but do yourself a favor and forget about doing anything strenuous for now. Yoga or tai chi might be best. It's important not to stress yourself out now. Just relax and go with the flow.

Pluto

Well, Capricorn, as good as you are at sensing upcoming trends, you've probably seen this coming for a while now, and felt it, too. If you were born in December, you've already been through it, and if you're reading this, you've lived to tell the tale. Nice. See, Pluto conjunct the Sun is never easy. Pluto is the heavens' answer to Darth Vader—a big, scary creature dressed in black—and he's been sitting right on top of you for years. Congratulations for getting through it. If you were born between January 3 and 8, he'll be having his way with you this year, so gird your loins and prepare yourself, because total change is coming. Before you run off to hide, however, think about all the areas of life that you'd really like to change. If you only checked one, that's enough reason for you to put this transit to work for you in a positive way. The trick is to direct Pluto's energy in the right direction rather than sitting still and waiting to see what will happen. If you use Pluto well, in a year or two you'll feel purged, renewed, and ready to plant seeds for the future. You're primed for new beginnings. You might not even recognize yourself when this transit is over. The thing is, Pluto has arrived. Start pruning. Anything that's no longer a positive influence needs to go. If it's broken or damaged beyond repair—and yes, that does include relationships—get rid of that, too. Think of this as your chance to be reborn.

Capricorn | January

Planetary Lightspots

If you're in the mood to break your routine, you'll be in luck, Capricorn. A pack of planets in Aquarius will give you all the excuses you need to lighten up your schedule a bit and maybe even delegate duties while you attend to the serious business of enjoying life. In particular, January 1 and 19 would be great to do a bit of spontaneous traveling, or at least make plans.

Relationships

The Full Moon on January 4 will illuminate your solar seventh house of one-to-one relationships, urging you to commit. Fortunately, once you've found what you want, that's never a problem for you, so if you have, this may be the month you decide to settle down. If not, you'll be on the prowl, interviewing prospective candidates with the careful eye of a jeweler.

Money and Success

You'll have a chance for a whole new financial start, as several planets and the New Moon in fast-acting Aquarius on January 20 activate your solar second house of personal money matters. If you've been thinking about becoming self-employed, this would be a great time to do your homework and see exactly what would be required. Speak with someone in your field who's already done it.

Planetary Hotspots

An argument on January 3 will have long-lasting repercussions, so weigh every word you say—especially if you've been simmering for a while. The angrier you are, the tougher this will be, so if you need to, excuse yourself until you've had a chance to calm down and think.

Rewarding Days

4, 5, 15, 19, 21, 30

Challenging Days

1, 3, 31

Capricorn | February

Planetary Lightspots

Mercury will turn direct on February 11, so you'll soon be able to count on your schedule once again. If you've been dealing with disorganization, cancellations, and delays, not to worry. By February 19, all should be well once again. In the meantime, use any free time you didn't know you'd have to actually relax.

Relationships

On February 24 and 25, loving Venus and passionate Mars in fiery Aries will take turns passing out easy trines to your ruling planet, serious Saturn, and between the two, they may just be able to convince you to have some fun of the romantic variety. You do love elegance, so a candlelit dinner out might be just what the doctor ordered to help you loosen up and forget about work.

Money and Success

Venus will set off for impulsive Aries on February 20. She'll be accompanied by the emotional Moon and red-hot Mars, so if you're out shopping for your home or family members, you'll be a lot more inclined to ignore your budget and splurge. Just be sure that what you're purchasing is practical and long-lasting.

Planetary Hotspots

From February 19 through February 22, things may heat up on the home front, so prepare yourself for some fireworks. If children are especially problematic, you'll need to put your foot down and make it clear that your home is your castle and you won't stand for any drama. There may be arguments on your agenda, but let them happen. It's important to clear the air every now and then.

Rewarding Days

2, 7, 8, 24, 25

Challenging Days

1, 5, 6, 19, 20, 21, 23

Capricorn | March

Planetary Lightspots

If you've been working far too hard and pulling out all the stops to impress a higher-up, then on March 5 or 30, you'll be happily surprised with their reaction to a recent project you've tackled and successfully completed—pretty much on your own. Finally, those rewards you were hoping for will arrive, complete with a well-deserved pat on the back in front of the whole crew.

Relationships

Generous Jupiter and unpredictable Uranus will form an easy trine on March 3, bringing together your solar fourth house of feelings and your solar eighth house of intimate partners. Talk about uninhibited! Prepare to raise your partner's eyebrows, and don't even try to pretend you're not enjoying the look on their face as you make a rather startling suggestion.

Money and Success

Venus will take off for your solar fifth house of recreational activities on March 17, all done up in quality-conscious Taurus. For the next month, she'll urge you to settle for nothing but the best, so dining out, traveling, and spending time with the kids may be a bit more expensive, but you'll have so much fun, you'll consider it money well spent.

Planetary Hotspots

On March 4 or 11, someone near and dear to you may seem to be deliberately testing you to see just how far they can push the envelope. This may bring up memories of last month's domestic issues, and once again, you may need to enforce your rules with regard to children or family members.

Rewarding Days
3, 5, 9, 17, 22, 23, 25, 30

Challenging Days
10, 11, 15, 16, 27

Capricorn | April

Planetary Lightspots

The total Lunar Eclipse will occur on April 4 in your solar tenth house of authority figures and dealings with higher-ups. It's definitely going to be time for a change, but you're well established enough in your field that you'll be in charge of putting it in motion. It's time to pursue a career that will make you happy, not just pay the bills.

Relationships

Several planets will spend their time this month in your solar fifth house of lovers, all done up in sensual Taurus. If you're attached, prepare to rekindle the fire in your relationship in a very big way, much to the delight of your lucky partner. If you're still looking, keep an eye out for the well-dressed, successful type tossing you meaningful glances.

Money and Success

Venus will tap at the door of your solar sixth house of work on April 11, Capricorn, so start thinking about what you'd rather do for work, if you haven't already done so. Venus will be wearing restless Gemini, so personal freedom will definitely enter into the equation, and perhaps a bit of travel as well.

Planetary Hotspots

The Sun, chatty Mercury, and unpredictable Uranus will pass through your solar fourth house of home, all done up in red-hot Aries, and the New Moon will occur there on March 18. Now, this sign acts fast and thinks later, so if you've been thinking about moving, prepare yourself to find the perfect place when you least expect it. You'll need to move fast if you really want it.

Rewarding Days
2, 4, 6, 14, 21, 22

Challenging Days
5, 7, 9, 15, 17, 19, 20

Capricorn | May

Planetary Lightspots

May 6 will bring the Sun in sensual Taurus together with intense Pluto in your sign and your solar first house of personality. You'll suddenly feel the urge to let the world how good you feel—and, more specifically, to let one particular person know just how happy you are that you've found each other.

Relationships

Venus, the Goddess of Love, will take off for your solar seventh house of relationships on May 7, wearing tenderhearted, nurturing Cancer. Your partner's needs will be especially important to you, so much so that you might even make a rare display of public affection. Remind them not to expect this sort of thing often, then feel free to gush.

Money and Success

A sudden urgent expense regarding a family member or your partner could come up around May 25, Capricorn, so be prepared to tap into your savings to take care of it. If it's justified, resolve not to lecture them. On the other hand, both kinds of financial unpredictability are possible now, so buying a lottery ticket wouldn't be a bad idea—but just one.

Planetary Hotspots

If you have the feeling an authority figure or elder is working against you from behind the scenes around May 14 or 15, be sure not to rush to any judgments. They may be discussing you in private, but chances are good that they're talking you up, not undermining you. Sit down and have a serious chat. You might be pleasantly surprised.

Rewarding Days

5, 6, 7, 8, 16, 17

Challenging Days

4, 9, 14, 15, 21, 22, 25

Capricorn | June

Planetary Lightspots

The Full Moon on June 2 in optimistic Sagittarius will get your month off to a merry start, especially if you've been keeping a pleasant secret under wraps to surprise someone close to you. They may figure it out, but they won't know when it's due, so you'll still be able to spring it on them when they least expect it. Cover your tracks!

Relationships

Prepare yourself, Capricorn. On June 21, the Sun himself will set off for your solar seventh house of one-to-one relationships, followed by passionate Mars on June 24. This means that the heavens' two most fiery ambassadors will be storming through all your encounters, personal and casual. Remember, you get to call the shots now—and that means all of them!

Money and Success

On June 5, Venus will set off for dramatic Leo and your solar eighth house of joint money matters. It's time to settle up and make your peace with those who owe you, which goes for any kind of debt, be it emotional or financial. Your mission is to refuse to contribute to any theatrics the debtor wants to bring along.

Planetary Hotspots

Serious Saturn, your sign's ruling planet, will turn retrograde on June 14, asking that you—and especially you—begin a very careful review period. No matter what you've been up to over the past six months, if it was at all secret, it might fall under the scrutiny of higher-ups or authority figures. At some point soon, be prepared to divulge all.

Rewarding Days
6, 7, 8, 9, 10, 22

Challenging Days
11, 12, 13, 14, 23, 24

Capricorn | July

Planetary Lightspots

The first Full Moon for the month will arrive on July 1 in your sign, casting its bright light into your solar first house of personality and appearance. Now, you're usually quite fond of keeping things exactly as they are, since your motto is "If it's not broken, don't fix it," but right about now you might be thinking about how much better you could be with just a little effort. Go for it!

Relationships

The New Moon in tender Cancer will arrive on July 15, urging you to see to it that everyone you care for has absolutely everything they need. The thing is, on that day, intense Pluto won't make it easy for you. He's on duty in your sign and your solar first house of personality, demanding that you act like the honorary principal, even when your heart is involved.

Money and Success

A second Full Moon on July 31 will activate your solar second house of personal money matters. This lunation will occur in rebellious Aquarius, so anyone who regularly needs a loan will definitely be shown the door. The good news is that once you've done it, they won't come back for another shot at the title. End it. Now.

Planetary Hotspots

If you've recently committed to someone new, Capricorn, you might find that there's a bit of tension between this new partner and your family members, who might be a tad resistant to even meeting someone new, much less accepting them into their lives. Push your way through this and don't be deterred. You've certainly earned the right to be happy.

Rewarding Days

1, 8, 9, 17, 21, 22

Challenging Days

6, 7, 11, 12, 14, 15, 18

Capricorn | August

Planetary Lightspots

The Full Moon on August 29 will work together with the lovely lady Neptune to turn up the volume on your antennae, Capricorn. Regardless of what's going on around that time, you'll need to tap into your intuition and do the hardest thing of all. That is, forget about rules and regulations and anything else you've been taught and let your feelings guide you.

Relationships

Whatever it is that you've been used to getting on an intimate level from your partner will need to shift as of August 14, Capricorn, so prepare yourself to talk about those personal issues you're not usually comfortable with. The good news is that whatever you reveal now will do far more good than harm, so open up and let it all out.

Money and Success

On August 8, assertive Mars will stomp off into your solar eighth house of joint finances—and wherever this fiery guy goes, fireworks are sure to follow. You don't like scenes, under any circumstances, but just this once, if you're challenged about taxes, inheritances, or who owes what, you'll be willing to provide one for whoever happens to be in the vicinity.

Planetary Hotspots

On August 3, 5, 6, and 21, a pack of planets in determined Leo will take turns forming testy squares with serious Saturn, who just so happens to be your ruling planet. Since you're so susceptible to his moods, you'll probably feel a bit uneasy and restless. Put those feelings to work for you. Finish up any project you've left undone, quickly.

Rewarding Days
2, 4, 7, 11, 13, 19, 26

Challenging Days
3, 5, 6, 21, 22, 31

Capricorn | September

Planetary Lightspots

The Sun in hardworking Virgo will form an easy trine with Pluto on September 5, creating an earthy, practical astrological recipe that makes for the easy realization of goals, especially when all dues are paid. You're very good at taking care of your debts, so this meeting of the minds will likely mean that the solution to a work-related decision will now become quite clear and you'll be free to move on.

Relationships

Venus will turn direct on September 6 in Leo and your solar eighth house of intimate partnerships. This puts the Goddess of Love in the mood to show off for others, which is definitely not your style—but for now, you might actually enjoy the attention your sweetheart gains. Your mission is to stop holding back, whether in public or in private. If this is The One, let them have it all.

Money and Success

Now that Jupiter has taken up residence in your solar ninth house of long-distance relationships and dealings with far-off places, you might want to reconsider a recent offer involving a raise, bonus, or promotion, even if it does involve relocating. If the money is right, think about it seriously and imagine how your life might be in a few years.

Planetary Hotspots

An argument with a higher-up, elder, or authority figure might arise on September 9, Capricorn, and even though you are the very soul of practicality and reason, you could be moved by the Mercury-Pluto square that day to say things you won't be able to take back. Now that you know, be warned. Your career is at stake. Isn't that more important than winning a battle?

Rewarding Days

4, 5, 6, 8, 23, 30

Challenging Days

9, 12, 13, 16, 17, 24, 25

Capricorn | October

Planetary Lightspots

Halloween will be great fun! You don't ordinarily get dressed up in anything other than what's practical for what you're doing, but let go of all that and play dress-up. The Sun and Neptune will get together to help you find your way into a costume, and if worse comes to worse, wear a suit, kiss some babies, and tell everyone you're pretending to be a politician.

Relationships

On October 8, the emotional Moon and Venus will come together in Virgo, an earth-sign cousin, urging you to get down to the serious business of establishing a relationship. Yes, really. Even if you're quite a distance apart at the moment, you'll be able to make practical decisions about the future based on what you already know about each other.

Money and Success

Anyone who tries to entice you into investing on October 10 will be met with a brick wall of resistance, as well they should be. On October 16, however, you'll need to be on your toes, when a smooth operator could talk even you into taking a financial risk.

Planetary Hotspots

Talkative Mercury and rebellious Uranus will face off on October 25, demanding that you make an effort to compromise between the time that you spend at work and the hours your loved ones really need you to put in to let them know you're invested in them. Venus and Jupiter will be on duty, so it's a foregone conclusion that love will win out over business—especially since lots of coworkers owe you one.

Rewarding Days
7, 8, 13, 15, 23, 30, 31

Challenging Days
5, 6, 10, 16, 17, 21, 22

Capricorn | November

Planetary Lightspots

Playful Mercury will make his way into your solar eleventh house of friendships and group affiliations on November 2, so you'll be doing quite a bit of chitchatting about the rules of the game you're currently playing. Mercury will be in intense Scorpio, however, so that game could turn quite serious, and once again, you may find yourself at the helm. Are you up for that?

Relationships

Venus will tiptoe off into Libra on November 8. She'll set up shop in your solar tenth house of career-oriented relationships, so someone you've only thought of as a higher-up may suddenly appeal to you for far more than their business skills. Your mission now is to ignore what you don't have in common and focus on what has ignited that lovely spark.

Money and Success

On November 13 and 23, Venus and Mars will form easy, stimulating sextiles with Saturn, your ruling planet, who just so happens to be an expert at business matters. If you've been waiting for the right time to present your case to the boss, wait no longer. This is it. Just be sure you have all the right paperwork in hand before you get to their office.

Planetary Hotspots

By the time November comes to a close, your solar twelfth house of secrets will be playing host to three planets in outgoing Sagittarius—a sign that was never, ever any good at keeping quiet about anything. The good news is that Sagittarius is very good at being totally blunt and honest, which will be required, no matter what surfaces—or how.

Rewarding Days

4, 5, 6, 10, 13, 24

Challenging Days

2, 19, 20, 26, 27, 29

Capricorn | December

Planetary Lightspots

A Full Moon will come along on December 25, teaming up with a warm, loving trine between thoughtful Mercury and generous Jupiter to turn this into a truly wonderful holiday season. Hugs, gifts, and long-lost loved ones will be everywhere, so there's really no way you won't enjoy yourself. Be sure your dearest loved ones are close at hand.

Relationships

If you've been seeing a lot of someone casually lately, Capricorn, you can expect the holidays to bring you much, much closer. On December 24 or 25, a trine between thoughtful Mercury and optimistic Jupiter might even convince you that it's time to introduce them to your friends and family—which, of course, will be especially easy now, and can't help but go well.

Money and Success

Once Venus enters Scorpio on December 4, you'll be concerned with joint financial matters, Capricorn, but also with shared possessions. If this means you're ending something, you can count on some wonderful astrological allies to help you get through it—not to mention the human allies who'll be ready to circle the wagons.

Planetary Hotspots

On December 20, an argument may start between you and a family member, possibly about your plans for the holidays. If they're not happy about the celebration you've chosen, take time to talk to them about what they'd like to see. 'Tis the season to compromise. Be open to ideas and you'll all have a lovely time.

Rewarding Days
1, 8, 11, 12, 17, 19, 24, 25

Challenging Days
4, 5, 6, 20, 28, 29

Capricorn Action Table

These dates reflect the best—but not the only—times for success and ease in these activities, according to your Sun sign.

	JAN	FEB	MAR	APR	MAY	JUN	JUL	AUG	SEP	OCT	NOV	DEC
Move	13, 14	21, 24	1, 9, 11	18		9, 10		2, 13, 19	26, 27			
Start a class					17, 18		18, 19			25, 26	13	
Join a club					3				23		10, 11	16, 17, 18
Ask for a raise	4, 5	18, 19	9, 11			7, 8	30, 31		29, 30	5, 6		
Look for work				3, 4	27, 30					12	24, 25	
Get pro advice			30, 31						23			
Get a loan		3, 4	1, 2			8, 10		14, 15			10	
See a doctor	31			28								
Start a diet	30							26				
End relationship				15, 16	21, 22		14, 15, 16					
Buy clothes						6						
Get a makeover							1, 2					
New romance	4, 5		29, 30	22, 23	5, 6					26, 27, 28		24, 25, 26
Vacation		23					17, 18		12, 13	11	10	

Aquarius

The Water Bearer
January 20 to February 19

Element: Air

Quality: Fixed

Polarity: Yang/masculine

Planetary Ruler: Uranus

Meditation: I am a wellspring
of creativity

Gemstone: Amethyst

Power Stones: Aquamarine,
black pearl, chrysocolla

Key Phrase: I know

Glyph: Currents of energy

Anatomy: Ankles,
circulatory system

Colors: Iridescent blues, violet

Animals: Exotic birds

Myths/Legends: Ninhursag,
John the Baptist, Deucalion

House: Eleventh

Opposite Sign: Leo

Flower: Orchid

Keyword: Unconventional

The Aquarius Personality

Your Strengths and Challenges

You just love bumper stickers, don't you, Aquarius? They're a terrific way to get humans thinking, which is what you love best. You're famous for being the sign of the rebel and for being absolutely hell-bent on total freedom of expression—for everyone, mind you—and you never disappoint. You might have odd piercings or strikingly unusual hair, or maybe it's the tattoos. However, you might also be one of those Aquarians who dresses in conservative business suits, holds down a day job very tightly, and prefers to hold just as tightly to your views until your personal input on the subject will actually help a worthy cause. In that case, you'll yank your opinions right out and march down the street with them. Proudly.

Between protests and making your point on a smaller scale, you stick to your astrological job description, which also includes observing others. You readily admit to often feeling like you're an alien on this planet. Sure, you walk among us and mingle well enough, but you've never felt that you fit in. Fortunately, watching humans as we go about our daily affairs is quite enlightening and entertaining. As an added bonus, the more you watch, the more insights you gain about how to get along with such an odd species. The thing is, it's the fact that you don't fit in that makes us love you most, so please, please don't ever change. You're interesting and unpredictable. Talk about a good time! You also make sure to let everyone know how wonderful it is to be unique. You make us feel good about being whoever we are and give us the inspiration to follow in your footsteps, chin held high. What a tremendous gift—to encourage others to be true to themselves simply by living your life exactly the way you want to. Many thanks from all of us!

Your Relationships

Your insistence that we should all be totally and completely ourselves often attracts kindred spirits—that is, those who choose to live their lives by coloring outside of the lines. Once you find them, you'll put aside your quest for independence and devote yourself to the care and (intellectual) feeding of a unique and fascinating human who will be equally devoted to you—and why not? It's a treat to be involved with someone open-minded enough to actually encourage you to share yourself. Your love of individuality and your fondness for those with a touch of the rebel in them will follow you into all your relationships.

See, when you take an interest in someone—anyone—it's a tremendous compliment. You're picky about both friends and lovers, but not because you're critical. It's all about being amused and entertained by someone who shares your views and ideals. That's what builds friendship and camaraderie, two prerequisites for anyone who wants to keep you—well, along with instinctively understanding that trying to hold on to you in any way is an exercise in futility and that any such behavior will lead to the beginning of the end. Immediately. The good news is that if someone can adapt to your mandatory "open hands" policy, you'll guarantee them total freedom in return—which is quite a perk.

So who's best suited to you? Well, the first sign that comes to mind is Sagittarius. They're every bit as freedom-oriented, and they're perpetually interested in The Big Picture. They'll help you make changes from the ground up without batting an eyelash and applaud your ultra-cerebral, occasionally detached take on the world. Geminis are also good matches, since they're endlessly curious and game to gobble up your latest set of data with gusto. You might initially be attracted to other Aquarians, but be careful. If you're on opposite sides, you'll end up doing battle to decide who's right.

Your Career and Money

When it comes to work, you're not at all pleased with the concept in general. First of all, it really puts a cramp in your social schedule, and second, it's all about trading oh-so-precious hours of your life to continue living. Doesn't that defeat the purpose? Since life here does require us to work, however, what you really need to do on a daily basis absolutely must be whatever it is you really feel the need to do. Most likely, it will involve getting some kind of message out to the masses or encouraging the exchange of positive intellectual energy. In that case, you'll work tirelessly. You're always be mindful of how much time you've traded for the money in your wallet, however, so when you spend, it's because you want to, not because you feel pressured.

Your Lighter Side

What's fun for you, Aquarius? Well, if you're not in the midst of kindred spirits, good times are tough to come by, so you do tend to gravitate toward like-minded others. You love to keep abreast of the news, so the Internet often affords you comfort when you're alone—especially since you think of computers as friends. (Yours might even have a name.)

Affirmation for the Year
I can retain my independence even if I share myself with another.

The Year Ahead for Aquarius

Venus will spend a total of four months in your solar seventh house of one-to-one relationships during 2015, from June 5 through July 18 and then again from July 31 through October 8. Now, this is the Goddess of Love and Money we're talking about, and this is a very long stay for her, and while she's in the neighborhood, she'll be all done up in fiery, dramatic Leo. Yes, this certainly does mean that all your one-to-one encounters will be equally passionate and possibly quite theatrical as well—but no, it doesn't mean that you'll eventually end up in an argument. If you do, however, at the least, you'll be very, very well equipped, astrologically speaking, to handle it. Just be sure to steer clear of any potentially volatile situations. Now, money-wise, this especially long transit of Venus in Leo could also mean that you're due to meet someone with enough creativity, brains, and enthusiasm to actually entice you into a long-term partnership. If that's the case, after you get over the shock of it all, be sure everything is on paper before you proceed too far, legally speaking.

The thing is, all Leo planets are terrific at inspiring others to follow their creative paths, but like the other impulsive fire signs, they're not always quite so good at the follow-through necessary to complete the projects. Loving Venus will inspire you to act the same, so while you might think you're madly in love, you should wait a bit to make things official. No running off to Reno or Vegas, no waiving prenuptial agreements, and definitely no announced commitments to parents or friends. You'll be in the mood to sign up, but let's just wait and see if it's the right thing for you. The good news is that right through August 11, generous Jupiter will also be in Leo and passing through that same house. So if you're romantically drawn to someone, the combined efforts of Jupiter and Venus, the heavens' traditional "benefics," certainly won't hurt your case.

Once Jupiter enters Virgo and your solar eighth house of intimacy and joint financial matters on August 11, you'll likely be feeling a lot more practically inclined in all situations involving money and other committed ventures. You might start up a new partnership, for business as well as romantic reasons, but backing away from someone you've cared about very deeply for a very long time is also a possibility. It won't be easy, but if they're draining you, pull the plug before you sink any further. You don't have to end the relationship. What you will need to do is let them know that you're not willing to put up with what they're doing—or not doing, in this case—any longer. Fortunately, you're one of the few signs out there that's good at not just issuing ultimatums but also following through on them.

The ever-present square between no-nonsense Pluto in Capricorn and your ruling planet, startling Uranus, will also continue to affect you in a major way. You'll tend to side with Uranus, as will all Uranian types, but if you try to shut Pluto out, he'll be all the more un-gentle with you. As soon as you feel things starting to shift and realize that you have absolutely no control over them, your best bet will be to make a quick getaway and call for help, even if it's just a shoulder to cry on. No, you don't cry much, if ever, but this year, Pluto might just dig in deep enough that you'll really need to. Give yourself this perk, guilt-free.

Neptune will continue her transit through your solar second house of finances and personal money matters, and since this lady is so good at dissolving boundaries and making us vulnerable in the process, it will be easy for others to take you for a ride. Don't let that happen. If something about a new friend or lover just doesn't seem right, look into it. It's lovely—and admirable—to accept others at face value, but occasionally they don't live up to our fantasies, much less our hopes, so doing a bit of homework behind closed doors this year is well within your rights.

The really big news of the astrological year is Saturn's sign change. He'll trudge back and forth between intense Scorpio and lighthearted Sagittarius until he's finally done with Scorpio on September 17. Now, remember, please, that this is the planet that best loves rules and regulations and always stands right behind the line painted on the floor in official places. He'll have a very different attitude about all that while he's in Sagittarius, though, a sign that never did know how to draw boundaries or establish limits. From June 14 through

September 17, Saturn will be in Scorpio and in the mood to help you lay down some laws that absolutely must be adhered to, come hell or high water. But for the rest of 2015, while he's in Sagittarius, Saturn will be a bit less likely to hold you accountable—at least, for whatever happens that's not on your watch.

One of the most positive things about Saturn's trek through Sagittarius is that this is a rare chance for us to glimpse the old naysayer in a good mood. Saturn is still the honorary authority figure wherever he goes, but in Sagittarius, he's a bit more likely to sit back, cross his legs, and shrug his shoulders at our mistakes, instead of doling out severe punishment. Your mission during 2015 is to rely on the fact that you've already done your job, or jobs, honorably and truthfully—so why not sit back, cross your legs, and enjoy the new friends your efforts have garnered you? Of course, Saturn is always Saturn, so you might be asked to take over the steering wheel from a member of your group who isn't doing a very good job at all. But since Saturn is in lighthearted Sagittarius, you'll be guaranteed, at the very least, a chance to open up the group to new experiences and to teach them a little thing in the process—and isn't that what leadership is all about?

What This Year's Eclipses Mean for You

There will be four eclipses this year, Aquarius, two solar (basically supercharged New Moons) and two lunar (a pair of supercharged Full Moons). The first Solar Eclipse will occur on March 20, bringing the Sun and Moon together in your solar second house of personal finances. Both luminaries will be in ultra-intuitive Pisces at the time, so if your gut tells you to invest in something, even if it's a major purchase, go for it. Just be sure to trust those antennae. If you feel you're being taken advantage of, step back, look things over, and think about the future.

The first Lunar Eclipse will arrive on April 4, all done up in partner-oriented Libra and your solar ninth house of far-off places, higher education, and new experiences. What a terrific time to plan the trip you've always wanted to take! Eclipses never fail to turn at least one small piece of us around entirely, but since you so love change, you'll end this adventure an entirely different person—and be quite happy about it. If you want to go back to school, this is a terrific time to do it. Pad that resumé!

The second Solar Eclipse will arrive on September 13, bringing the Sun and Moon together in Virgo and your solar eighth house of intimate partners and joint resources. Look over any paperwork regarding a loan or inheritance, and be sure your significant other is equally generous in sharing ongoing expenses. Take some time to think about exactly what it is you're looking for in a permanent partner, too. If your needs aren't being fulfilled, it might be time to make some drastic changes—but then, that's what eclipses are all about.

Later in September, on the 27th, you'll be allowed the opportunity to make a fresh start, thanks to the second Lunar Eclipse. This time out, the Moon will be in red-hot, fiery Aries and your solar third house of conversations and communications, so while you're always blunt and ultra-truthful, you might raise the eyebrows of even those who know you best with what tumbles out of your mouth. Of course, you'll enjoy this—and you won't make a secret of it, either.

Saturn

Saturn will dash back and forth between intense Scorpio and easygoing Sagittarius this year, traveling across the astrological state line that divides your solar tenth house of career and your solar eleventh house of groups, goals, and friendships. While Saturn is organizing your professional activities, from June 14 through September 17, he'll be wearing Scorpio, so any simmering power struggles between you and someone you think of as an authority figure will likely heat up, big time, and demand to be solved. Prepare yourself for an emotional battle, disguised, perhaps, as A Management Issue. Think about your areas of weakness, and work on them now. An intense grilling by higher-ups could be on the agenda, but if you show them you know what you're doing, it will eventually lead to a position of leadership.

The rest of the year, while Saturn is in Sagittarius and your solar eleventh house of groups, friendships, and goals for the future, you can expect to have a merry old time of it. You may be put in a position of added responsibility within your current circle, but you won't mind a bit. Mingling with several different groups, for different reasons, is also a possibility you'll enjoy—and a goal you should pursue. You can never have too many friends, and they can never get too much of you.

Uranus

You definitely have a better working relationship with this guy than most of us, Aquarius. Uranus is your ruling planet, so you're totally in tune with his energies. No matter what he tosses your way, you tend to grin about it, even if it's not quite politically correct to do so. If you were born between February 1 and 11, expect to be doing a whole lot of grinning during 2015. Uranus will form a sextile aspect with your Sun, activating your solar third house of conversations and communications with his very own invigorating and, okay, startling energy. Yes, you'll be especially blunt—but then, Uranus has been in this house for years, so everyone close to you will expect it. You might also decide to make some drastic changes to your daily routine, however, which might set some folks back. The neighbors, say, or maybe your siblings. It doesn't matter. You were born with a rebellious streak that doesn't quit. The only way Uranus will noticeably affect you this year is by making gosh darn sure that you show that streak to others—and doesn't that sound like great fun?

Neptune

If you were born between January 25 and 30, your Sun will be contacted this year by woozy, romantic Neptune, who never was very fond of reality. The aspect she'll be forming is a semisextile, which isn't known for being especially dramatic, but then, Neptune loves to work gradually and invisibly, much as a gentle stream inevitably creates its own path through rock. Your mission now is to listen to your intuition, which will be quite astounding. Record your dreams and insights, and be sure that you pay attention whenever you "just feel" something. You are a cerebral creature, so this might not initially be easy for you. But in the long run, if you listen to that small voice in the back of your head, you'll discover that finding the path to the true you is as simple as trusting your instincts.

If you're thinking of changing life paths and want to work for yourself, wonderful. And yes, eventually the Universe will provide. Until then, be sure you have a safety net—that is, a day job—before you leave that steady paycheck behind. Neptune does insist that we follow our bliss, but you'll need a solid financial foundation beneath you to keep chasing that bliss. By all means, connect with The One. Just don't disconnect with reality in the process.

Pluto

If you were born between February 2 and 7, you can expect a bit of a nudge from relentless Pluto this year. This poke won't be as intense or insistent as a square, but a semisextile from Pluto to your Sun is still plenty of reason to imagine you being in the mood to make some very deep and meaningful changes. With Pluto in your solar twelfth house of secrets, however, he'll be incognito, so you might not notice what's going on right away, which is part of his plan. Pluto endows us with the ability to be detectives and analysts. Even in an aspect most often described as "easy," you'll feel him urging you to dig just a little deeper and find out just a bit more. Heaven help anyone you're dating or even thinking of dating. You'll want to know absolutely everything about them, and if they don't bend under questioning, you'll do the footwork yourself to uncover the truth, the whole truth, and nothing but the truth.

Expect to do quite a bit of self-examination during your private moments—which, by the way, you should arrange often, regardless of your responsibilities. Any planet passing through the twelfth house inevitably turns up the volume on our psychic tendencies, but with perceptive Pluto on duty, you might be so sensitive to your environment that the harshness of reality literally hurts—physically, emotionally, and mentally. If you need a cave, find one and dig in—temporarily.

Aquarius | January

Planetary Lightspots

No fewer than four planets will hold court in your sign this month, Aquarius, and the Moon will join in on the fun when she becomes new on January 20. Since this entire cast is very, very fond of practical jokes and a medley of other surprises, one never knows what might come up. It's a given, however, that you'll be entirely responsible—and make no apologies.

Relationships

The New Moon will occur on January 20 in your sign and your solar first house of personality and appearance, heralding a major new beginning for you, in many ways. A whole new method of self-expression will be along shortly. A new wardrobe could be in order, but be sure to make adjustments to the inner you, too.

Money and Success

Investments will go very well for you around January 4 and 5, so if you're at all inclined to take a chance on a new business, this would be the perfect time to do it. Financial matters might not go so well on January 18 and 19, however, so steer clear and don't sign any official papers just yet.

Planetary Hotspots

On January 15 and 30, Mars and Venus will take turns squaring off with Saturn in Sagittarius, pitting your solar second house of personal finances against your solar eleventh house of groups and goals for the future. Squares act suddenly, so finding others who share your goals will come about just as suddenly, most likely through supposedly coincidental encounters.

Rewarding Days
3, 4, 5, 13, 14, 20, 22, 27

Challenging Days
1, 2, 15, 16, 29, 30

Aquarius | February

Planetary Lightspots

Several planets in Aries and your solar third house of neighbors and siblings could prompt you to spend a bit more time than usual with them. This is a great time to plan a block party, but getting together with the whole family would be just as rewarding. Avoid February 21, though, when tempers could heat up at the speed of a flash fire.

Relationships

By February 20, four planets will have made their way through adrenaline-loving Aries and your solar third house of conversations and communications, Aquarius. This pack is nothing if not game for just about any adventure, so challenge yourself. Return to school, or sign up with a whole new peer group. Take a chance on something exciting.

Money and Success

Wherever Venus goes, money is sure to become important. She'll spend most of the month in intuitive Pisces and your solar second house of personal finances, so you'll be able to smell a fraud a mile away. If your heart is engaged, however, you might decide to ignore the warning signs. After February 20, be sure you and you alone are in charge of your hard-earned money.

Planetary Hotspots

The New Moon will arrive on February 18 in your sign, urging you to trash everything that just isn't working and start over. It might be a friendship, job, or relationship that's reached its expiration date. No matter what you choose to toss out, rest assured that its absence will make room for more positive experiences.

Rewarding Days
2, 12, 18, 19, 24, 25

Challenging Days
1, 5, 6, 11, 20, 21, 23

Aquarius | March

Planetary Lightspots

The first few days of March will be fun for you, to say the least. Generous Jupiter will form an easy trine with your unpredictable ruling planet, Uranus, and between the two, one never knows what they might come up with. That includes sudden long-distance travel, but also the insatiable urge to join a class or find a new peer group.

Relationships

Thoughtful Mercury will set off for Pisces on March 12 and stay put in that dreamy, romantic sign. This will put him in your solar second house of money and possessions, so you might feel a bit overwhelmed with financial details at times and you might want to run for cover, but don't. Ask a capable friend to help you straighten it all out.

Money and Success

Talk about successful! There's not much you won't be able to accomplish around March 3, when benevolent Jupiter contacts Uranus, your astrological ruler. These two planets have the energy, ambition, and drive to get you started on a whole new path. Plus, if you're doubtful, they'll be happy to not so subtly remind you of why you're here.

Planetary Hotspots

Talk about hotspots, Aquarius. The Sun, our own personal ball of lifegiving fire, will storm the borders of Aries, where Mars is waiting. Now, Mars isn't only known as the red planet because of his color. His attitude is pretty darn fiery, too, so this collision in your solar third house of communications definitely won't be boring. Prepare for verbal fireworks!

Rewarding Days

2, 3, 4, 9, 24, 25

Challenging Days

5, 11, 12, 15, 16, 26, 27

Aquarius | April

Planetary Lightspots

Your solar third house of conversations will receive yet another astrological jolt this month, Aquarius, thanks to the New Moon on April 18. Now, you've had a whole lot of exciting, passionate encounters and communications since last month, but you might have thought it was over. Well, surprise! More unexpected news is en route.

Relationships

Jupiter's presence in your solar seventh house of one-to-one relationships has stirred things up for you—but in a very nice way. Jupiter is in romantic Leo, so whether you're single or attached, he's probably provided you with lots of chances to snuggle up with someone lovely. Well, yet another chance will come along around April 22. Prepare to be intellectually impressed. Yes, really.

Money and Success

You'll have three opportunities to return your financial state to a solid condition this month, right around April 12, 19, and 21. It's probably domestic matters that are tapping you out, so if you need to pull back and force someone to stand on their own two feet, no fair feeling guilty about it. You've done your part and then some.

Planetary Hotspots

The total Lunar Eclipse will arrive on April 4, activating your solar ninth house of higher understanding in a very big way. If you've been bored or restless lately—and when aren't you?—this would be a fabulous time to give your mind something new to mull over. Local politics, advanced education, or long-distance travel will scratch that itch very nicely.

Rewarding Days
1, 2, 12, 19, 21, 22, 26, 28

Challenging Days
4, 5, 7, 17, 18, 20

Aquarius | May

Planetary Lightspots

May 27 and 30 will be fun. Mercury will meet up first with passionate Mars and then with the Sun in your solar fifth house of lovers and playmates. They'll all be in flirty, easily bored Gemini, so if you're going to agree to a blind date or even accept an introduction, don't plan to stay for long. You can do this type of "interview" in three minutes or less.

Relationships

You've been having quite a big time lately, with both loving Venus and outgoing Jupiter in your solar seventh house of one-to-one relationships, so company probably hasn't been hard to come by. Finding one particular someone may still be a bit mystifying, but after May 21, the Sun in Gemini will send you lots of potential candidates, some of whom might actually be fascinating.

Money and Success

Pay attention to where you put your money, credit cards, and checkbook this month, especially around May 9 and 29, when it will be easier for someone dishonest to part you from your hard-earned wages. Use that great brain to separate truth from fiction, and dismiss anyone who's trying to "work" you immediately.

Planetary Hotspots

Your solar axis of home versus career will be activated by the Full Moon on May 3, Aquarius. This will put the Sun opposite the Moon, with both fighting for equal time. Tend first to the professional matter that's been so troubling lately. It won't go away unless you do your homework and figure out what's really needed.

Rewarding Days
5, 6, 16, 27, 28, 30

Challenging Days
3, 4, 9, 14, 15, 29, 31

Aquarius | June

Planetary Lightspots

Your solar fifth house of fun times and creative pursuits will open its doors to lots of lively Gemini energy this month, Aquarius. This pack of visitors will be quite welcome—especially once they start sending you off in the right direction to meet at least one interesting new someone. Whatever your hobby, think about turning it into at least a part-time job.

Relationships

You'll be on the receiving end of some wonderful attention for many, many moons, Aquarius, thanks to Jupiter's presence in your solar seventh house of relationships. This dramatic, theatrical planet always brings a parade along, so you won't have to lift a finger. You might need to sign a few autographs and pose for a few pictures, but hey, it could be worse.

Money and Success

Saturn rules careers and other professional matters. He's been in your solar eleventh house of groups, helping you to make contacts, but on June 14, he'll return to your solar tenth house of career—which is pretty much a double whammy. Yes, it's time to get serious about the life path you want to follow. Speak with mentors and advisors around June 6.

Planetary Hotspots

With all those fire and air planets hovering around in the heavens above you, it's a given that your month will often be surprising, thanks to your ruling planet, Uranus. Of course, you love surprises and sudden, last-minute direction changes, so you won't mind a bit. You might also be a bit more outspoken, but that won't be a hardship either.

Rewarding Days
1, 2, 5, 6, 8, 10, 16, 22, 28

Challenging Days
11, 12, 15, 23, 30

Aquarius | July

Planetary Lightspots

You'll be experimenting with ways to drastically change your appearance and personal presentation this month, Aquarius, so a new wardrobe or hairstyle might be in order. If you can wait, save your makeover until the Full Moon on July 31, when Venus will enter showy Leo and your solar seventh house of one-to-one relationships, guaranteeing you some admiring attention right away.

Relationships

Four planets in charming, romantic Leo will spend much of the month in your solar seventh house of one-to-one relationships, so if you're single, this is definitely the time to get out there and strut your stuff. Start right away, on July 1, when Venus, the Goddess of Love, will combine talents with generous Jupiter to help you knock the socks off anyone you choose.

Money and Success

July 18 would be the perfect time to sit down with an accountant or financial advisor and talk over money matters. If you need to, make an appointment with someone you know you can trust, either because of their reputation or your personal experience. Taxes, loans, and inheritance issues might come up now, too, so again, don't go it alone.

Planetary Hotspots

On July 25, your ruling planet, Uranus, will barge off into an edgy square with Mars, the heavens' spark plug. You'll probably be feeing pretty edgy yourself, so be careful driving and do your best to avoid arguments that could turn volatile. Honestly? This is one of those days that's better spent in bed—but no one says you have to spend it there alone.

Rewarding Days

1, 2, 3, 4, 5, 22, 23

Challenging Days

6, 11, 12, 14, 15, 18, 19

Aquarius | August

Planetary Lightspots

Leo just loves to play, so with a pack of Leo planets moving through your solar seventh house of personal encounters, there won't be any shortage of playmates in the vicinity this month. In fact, you'll probably run across a few new ones during the course of your errands on August 4, 7, or 15, and in some way, they'll be adventurers, romantics, or heroes.

Relationships

At any given time during August, one of five romantic, passionate celestial allies in Leo will turn up the heat in your solar seventh house of one-to-one relationships—and that's not to mention the New Moon on August 14. If you're attached, be careful not to make your partner jealous. If you're single, look to August 19 for a very sexy, attractive challenge.

Money and Success

The Sun and Jupiter will come together on August 26 in your solar eighth house of joint resources. If you've been waiting for the right time to have a heart-to-heart chat about the proper way to share both benefits and burdens, you should wait no longer. With both planets in meticulous Virgo, you'll also be able to provide pie charts, if necessary, to prove your point.

Planetary Hotspots

Jupiter will leave Leo behind on August 11 and make his way into your solar eighth house of intimate partners and joint finances. Over the past month or so, you've probably been casually "interviewing" potential partners, for both romantic and practical reasons. The right one might not make an appearance until after August 26, so be patient.

Rewarding Days

2, 4, 7, 13, 14, 19, 20

Challenging Days

5, 6, 12, 21, 22

Aquarius | September

Planetary Lightspots

After weeks of retracing her steps through Leo and your solar seventh house of committed relationships, Venus, the Goddess of Love, has decided to turn around and move forward, which means that you're ready to move forward, too. If you've been through a bad breakup and aren't quite ready to sign up again, don't. Devote the month to rediscovering your independent, creative side.

Relationships

You're already a shining beacon, Aquarius, the perfect example of how to have a relationship while still maintaining your personal freedom. But this month, you'll show even more of us how it's done. If you're with someone, though, it might be nice to treat them to a lavish night or weekend—just because you can.

Money and Success

Your solar axis of personal versus joint finances will be challenged on September 16 by the opposition between extravagant Jupiter and dreamy Neptune, possibly bringing along confusing money matters. If inheritances, disputes over shared possessions, or all-out arguments over finances come along, don't run from them. It's time to lay your cards on the table.

Planetary Hotspots

The total Lunar Eclipse on September 27 will get you talking, Aquarius—which, of course, isn't anything surprising for you. This lunation might convince you to restore communications with a sibling, though—which, depending on how you left things, might be a bit startling. Remember, there's no such thing as a last chance. Life offers us many of them.

Rewarding Days

5, 6, 8, 21, 22, 23, 30

Challenging Days

9, 16, 17, 24, 25, 26

Aquarius | October

Planetary Lightspots

Most of us might consider the Mercury-Uranus opposition on October 25 to be troublesome, Aquarius, but not you. No, you're truly Uranus's child. You love change and revel in it even more when it's of the unexpected, last-minute variety. You can expect lots of that around the 25th, so enjoy, but do be careful while you're traveling.

Relationships

On October 17, passionate Mars and excessive Jupiter will come together in your solar eighth house of intimate partnerships, urging you to put some fire back into your current relationship—or stray. The choice is yours, but if you have time and resources invested, you might want to think about behaving yourself. Otherwise, cut your losses now.

Money and Success

On October 8, Venus, the Goddess of Finances, will come together with the emotional Moon, who teaches us to operate from the heart. They'll get together in your solar eighth house, so preserving joint resources and inheritances will be important. Keep an eye on your taxes, but also on that deliciously sexy new person you're almost ready to settle down with.

Planetary Hotspots

The potent Full Moon on October 27 will occur in Taurus and your solar fourth house of home and domestic matters, so you'll be feeling a strong pull in that direction. At the same time, however, the Sun will be trying to turn your attention toward far more public matters, like your career. Bonuses and promotions will be available, but at what cost? Weigh things out before you decide.

Rewarding Days

7, 8, 9, 12, 13, 15, 23, 30

Challenging Days

5, 6, 10, 11, 17, 21, 22

Aquarius | November

Planetary Lightspots

Any issues you've had with your kids or your current sweetheart can be easily be put to rest on November 25, Aquarius, with very little effort on your part. Thanks to the Full Moon in chatty Gemini and a Mercury-Mars sextile, you'll be able to chat things over and arrive at a meeting of the minds. This has been a long time coming. Get it done now.

Relationships

If you're attached, loving Venus and passionate Mars will be happy to help you keep the excitement going between you two this month. You'll have to help, but how bad could dinner out and hand holding be? If you're single, get out there and look around on November 25. Someone with a great brain and a strong sense of self is looking for you, too.

Money and Success

Disputes over finances or property may come up around November 2. Check the details of every contract you've signed with an eye toward finding the truth of the matter. Don't be ashamed to ask for professional help, and do rest assured that around November 13, all parties concerned will receive what's fairly due.

Planetary Hotspots

A serious talk will be on the agenda for November 17—and this time, you won't be able to sidestep or push any pressing issues to the back of the line. It's time for the truth to emerge, and you know it, so why resist? You're at your best when you're totally honest. Speak your peace, and don't let anyone stop you.

Rewarding Days
5, 6, 10, 12, 13, 14

Challenging Days
2, 3, 16, 17, 21, 26, 29

Aquarius | December

Planetary Lightspots

The Sun and Mercury in Sagittarius will make this a truly memorable holiday season for you, Aquarius. You might even find that you have far too many invitations and not enough time—but it could be worse. Think about expanding your horizons through extended education, travel, and boldly going where you never thought you'd go.

Relationships

You're astrologically scheduled to meet some new people this month, and at least one of them might convince you to attend a meeting or a gathering of others they feel are your kindred spirits. Try not to allow your enthusiasm to bring you in too deeply too soon. Wait a few weeks and see if you're all truly on the same page.

Money and Success

A lucky break will come along between December 10 and 12, and while you may not find a pot of gold, there will be a financial reward waiting for you at the end of this rainbow—even if it's disguised as a competitor at first. Tap into your intuition. Have you just run into a future business partner?

Planetary Hotspots

On Christmas Day, the Full Moon in home and family-loving Cancer will occur, inspiring one and all to snuggle up and get close to loved ones. In your case, it might be that a coworker without many ties is on their own. Invite them to join you, not just for the holiday dinner but to other festive events as well.

Rewarding Days

1, 2, 5, 8, 12, 25, 30

Challenging Days

3, 4, 6, 10, 14, 19, 20

Aquarius Action Table

These dates reflect the best—but not the only—times for success and ease in these activities, according to your Sun sign.

	JAN	FEB	MAR	APR	MAY	JUN	JUL	AUG	SEP	OCT	NOV	DEC
Move			17		16, 17					27, 29, 30		
Start a class		24, 25	1, 2, 3	4		8, 9					13, 14	
Join a club	4, 5, 6, 22	19, 24, 25		2, 3		1, 2, 3			22, 23			30, 31
Ask for a raise	27	18			2, 3						10, 11, 12	10, 24
Look for work					16, 24, 25	24	15, 16					24, 25, 26
Get pro advice	2, 3									5, 6, 7, 23		
Get a loan			5, 6				18	12	13, 14	11, 25		
See a doctor				28, 29	27, 28						9	
Start a diet	12, 13		16									
End relationship	1, 19	6			14, 15		14	21				
Buy clothes		18	20							16		
Get a makeover	20	18, 19					30, 31					
New romance			3, 4	25, 27, 29		5, 22		7, 14, 15	6			
Vacation				22, 23, 26		10, 11			23			

Pisces

The Fish
February 19 to March 20

♓

Element: Water

Quality: Mutable

Polarity: Yin/feminine

Planetary Ruler: Neptune

Meditation: I successfully navigate my emotions

Gemstone: Aquamarine

Power Stones: Amethyst, bloodstone, tourmaline

Key Phrase: I believe

Glyph: Two fish swimming in opposite directions

Anatomy: Feet, lymphatic system

Colors: Sea green, violet

Animals: Fish, sea mammals

Myths/Legends: Aphrodite, Buddha, Jesus of Nazareth

House: Twelfth

Opposite Sign: Virgo

Flower: Water lily

Keyword: Transcendence

The Pisces Personality

Your Strengths and Challenges

Your reputation for being empathetic and always willing to take in strays of both the human and the four-legged variety isn't myth, Pisces. You are, indeed, extremely giving and perpetually prepared to give even more than you comfortably can to ease the suffering or discomfort of another. Whether you know the person, animal, or plant doesn't matter. If there's someone or something out there that's in need and you can help, you're more than up for the job, even if it drains you in the process. That said, it might not be a bad idea to tune in to your considerable intuition. Everyone thinks they're "psychic" and/or wants to be, but for you, it's a fact—and it only makes sense. You are, after all, the sign ruled by Neptune, the most ultra-sensitive energy in the heavens, so you have no physical boundaries. You're pretty much the equivalent of a psychic sponge. If whatever is happening around you is positive, you'll feel good. If it's not, you won't. In the latter situations, remember that self-preservation is a birthright for our species. If you need to, go. Right away. The places you do find comforting and welcoming are often metaphysical centers, where your more spiritual side can easily emerge. You also feel the need to "hide" from the world periodically, Pisces, and for that, you should make no apologies or offer any excuses. You need to retreat every now and then to recharge your batteries. That's all the explanation necessary.

Your Relationships

You love nothing better than romance and fantasy, Pisces. In fact, when you have a crush on someone—which is probably the way you still refer to it—you tend to hang back and admire them from afar. It's not that you don't want to meet them or that you don't have the guts to make your approach. The thing is, you don't want to knock them off that pedestal, and being with them one on one might do just that. It's not that you're critical. In fact, nothing could be further from the truth. Like Aquarius, your astrological next-door neighbor, you're open to one and all. But once you've seen someone as less than a god or goddess, the adoration often comes to an end, and the romance starts to wane. Since you're a mutable sign, you can easily become put off or distracted and move on, even before the relationship has really started. Your mission is to stop trying to find movie stars, models, and celebrities to love. There is someone quite wonderful out there right under your nose, and just because they aren't flawless or unattainable doesn't mean you shouldn't invest just a bit of time in getting to know them. Your ultra-sensitive heart is well known and easily seen, Pisces, so unfortunately, this does often mean that others will try to take advantage of you, so steer clear of anyone who seems to be a little too scheming.

When it comes to choosing a mate, you ordinarily do well with the other water signs, since we all feel comfortable right away with those who are astrologically built from similar ingredients. That said, since Scorpio just loves to scheme (and is pretty good at it), the other water sign, Cancer, might be a better match. They're just as sensitive as you, and just as private, the perfect recipe for quiet evenings alone at your place. What's not to love? You might also find refuge in the arms of a nice, stable Taurus or Virgo. The plus about the earth signs is that they sign up forever. Talk about security!

Your Career and Money

You're quite the artistic soul, Pisces, and plenty capable of infiltrating the ranks in any situation. Since a career in the arts often involves establishing connections with those who have already made their names in your field, this would suit you just fine. No matter where your tastes lie or where you end up, if you feel comfortable and accepted, you'll settle in nicely, as long as there are no loud noises or bright lights—or worse, constant friction among coworkers. None of those work well for you, and all are deal breakers. Now, when it comes to money matters, Pisces, your intuition doesn't always work just right, so you often are faced with famine because you tried to help someone else when life was handing you a feast. Don't do that anymore!

Your Lighter Side

The creation of some form of art, which translates into any form of self-expression that induces an emotion in others—well, that's what it's all about for you, isn't it? If you want to stay put at your current job, better make sure it allows you the luxury of believing in what you do, or at least feeling good enough about it that you don't feel bad when someone asks you how you earn your daily bread.

Affirmation for the Year
The work I do joyfully is the only possible work for me.

The Year Ahead for Pisces

Two out of three of the outer planets—among the mythological Titans—are being quite kind to you right about now, Pisces, so relax and enjoy the ride. To start with, Pluto is in Capricorn, forming a pleasant and stimulating sextile aspect with your sign. This means that all of Pluto's hidden gifts will be available to you this year, in a very big way—and Pluto's gifts are nothing to sneeze at. If you were born between March 3 and 8, you will be especially affected by this amazing force. You may become involved in a career that involves investigation, research, or translating a mysterious language into everyday keywords—and it might not even be a foreign language you're attempting to get across. Think about the puzzling speech of the law, not to mention that of business or mathematics—or astrology, for that matter. Any topic that insists that you dig deep, learn new talents, and teach others enough of the basics so you can get your message across will do just fine. Even if you don't do it for a living, though, you'll feel the need to dig deep.

If you're after total transformation—and you most certainly have been, or will be shortly—well then, you should aim toward a career/profession that will allow you to work with others who are extremely interested but still blank slates. You'll want to get them started on the right foot, and just as soon as you know they're hooked, you'll turn up the volume, so they just can't resist asking for more. Now, if anyone can do this, especially now, it's you. You have a natural skill that others often seem to lack—the ability to intuitively know what others don't know. Speaking of which, you will be especially good at sniffing out lies now. Basically, like advertisers, teachers need to know their audience, and you most certainly do. Use these temporary superpowers for good!

The most important thing for you to keep in mind over the coming year, and for many more years to come, is that your very own ruling planet—intuitive, dreamy Neptune—is currently right where she wants to be. (This would be number two of the three outer planets who are being kind.) She's wearing your sign—or should I say *her* sign—so she's on home turf for the first time in almost 150 years. In a nutshell, this makes you one of few people who'll experience her at her best and most potent, and be old enough and young enough at the same time to understand, appreciate, and remember her magic. If you were born between February 29 and March 1, this goes double, since you're also one of the selected few born under your sign who'll be astrologically involved in experiencing Neptune at her very best, both publicly and personally. It's all about hiding out and trying to shine at the same time, so you might be best served by choosing a lifestyle that allows you to be nothing if not discreet, peaceful, and devoted to your cause. No matter when you were born, however, you'll feel the effects of this subtle but potent planetary heavy hitter in your solar first house of personality and appearance. This might mean that you'll be in the mood for dim lights and soft music, so much so that anything too harsh will be something you'll want to run from. Do yourself a favor and listen to your antennae. Run, don't walk, away from anything that offends you or makes you physically flinch, regardless of the reason. That advice is kind of like preaching to the choir, though. You are on a spiritual mission at the moment and you most likely already know that you can't tolerate anything loud or lavish, so you won't be up for being disturbed, and if you're smart, you'll make an escape while you can.

Saturn will spend most of the year in Sagittarius and your solar tenth house of career matters and dealings with higher-ups, authorities, and elders, and while you'll be working hard, the rewards will be substantial not too far down the road, and you'll make a name for yourself in your chosen profession. Keep that in mind if you're asked to put in some overtime, take on a particularly tough project, or cover for someone who's dropped the ball. From June 14 to September 17, Saturn will return to Scorpio. If you were born during the early to middle part of your sign, you will get to enjoy the hard-earned and well-deserved stability you've been working toward over the past few years. You'll also find a positive way to put a lid on any habits you've found especially intoxicating and tough to stop, or a behavior that was fun in the past but is now non-productive and possibly harmful.

Of course, even the best of us can be caught off guard, and there will be temporary distractions, such as this year's meeting of the astrological minds in lavish Leo and your solar sixth house of work and work-oriented relationships. The astrological culprits behind these distractions are loving Venus and generous, risk-taking Jupiter, who'll be livening things up in this ordinarily businesslike house for much of the year. It's hard to think of you as not becoming involved very soon with someone you meet, directly or indirectly, through work. But even if you meet this person at the grocery store or post office or during the course of some daily ritual, you should know that there's something about you that will really hit them fast, and it will continue to keep them interested, too. If you want to keep them around, your mission will be to keep things exciting. That said, be careful when you decide to actually let someone know you've chosen them. Venus and Jupiter are normally pretty hard to forget, but they are impossible to forget in lavish, showy Leo. So from the moment anything that even remotely sounds like "I'm rather fond of you" escapes your lips, in the mind of your hopeful partner, you two will be "involved," and you will be off the market—in their mind, at least. If you're not ready to stop shopping around yet, be extremely clear, right from the get-go.

What This Year's Eclipses Mean for You

If you're attached, Pisces, you might find that your primary relationship is in a state of flux between mid-March and mid-September. The two Solar Eclipses scheduled for this year will see to it that you become totally and suddenly focused on the most important people in your life. On March 20, a total Solar Eclipse will occur in your sign and your solar first house of personality and first impressions. This will bring the Sun and Moon together, presenting a united front during a very powerful astrological meeting of the minds. You absolutely must remain true to yourself now, and remind yourself that you will never need to settle when it comes to love. You're worth waiting for, and are definitely worth the time it takes to really know you. But until you're sure of that, you won't attract the partner you deserve—so get sure! Fortunately, by the time the total Solar Eclipse of September 13 occurs, bringing the Sun and Moon together in your solar seventh house of one-to-one relationships, the Universe will have brought along some experiences that will build your self-confidence. Self-love needs to come before we can truly love anyone else.

On April 4, a Lunar Eclipse (Full Moon) will make its way into your solar eighth house of intimate partners, wearing partner-pleasing Libra. Yes, if you need to change your mind and take back those decisions you made six months or more ago, you'll have a chance now. This is the easiest time to start the separation process, but if you can't put it all to bed in April, you'll have six months to finish working out the details. Deciding how to proceed after the decks are clear would be better left until after the Lunar Eclipse on September 27 in assertive Aries and your solar second house of values. At that time, no matter what else has been going on, whoever or whatever you truly hold most dear will be clear to you. At that time, no matter what else has been going on, whoever or whatever you truly hold most dear in your heart will be your primary concern. The good news is that you'll be willing to step up and defend them—or it.

Saturn

Career-oriented Saturn will travel between intense Scorpio and casual Sagittarius this year, Pisces. This trek will bring him across the astrological border of your solar ninth house of new experiences and your solar tenth house of career—and it will happen several times, too. If you're overwhelmed on the job as the year begins, reach out with your subconscious as well as your physical presence and do something about it. Make connections. Learn something new. Mingle with those who can broaden your career perspectives. Saturn absolutely requires references. He also insists that you prepare—and prepare well—for his visits. If you haven't yet found yourself a life path to follow that fascinates you and inspires an almost obsessive devotion, you really should start looking now. A good place to begin might be the local community college, where a variety of subjects are taught. This will allow you the chance to see what's out there for career paths, then sign up for whatever resonates best with what you believe in, not just what you're capable of enduring for eight hours every day to earn a comfortable living. Saturn might also bring you another type of gift, however. He's a bit of a fan of relationships that involve an age difference, so if you've long been attracted to the boss, or if you're the boss and you're attracted to someone who works for you, well, it might be time to transcend the imaginary boundaries that separate you—which just so happens to be your personal specialty.

Uranus

If you were born between March 2 and 12, Pisces, you will enjoy a bit more personal attention from this startling planet over the coming year than others in your sign. Now, this might be fun, but it might also be financially upsetting. Since the aspect Uranus is making with your sign is a semisextile, if you pay attention, you'll see that while you are not quite motivated enough yet to get out there and pursue what you want without any regard for personal consequences or social repercussions—well, you're almost there. At the very least, the seed has been planted. You'll really need total financial independence now. See to it that you work that out. And speaking of freedom, let's talk about the fact that every metaphysical group you've been to recently has somehow featured a discussion on values. Yep. That's you, Pisces, right now. Forget what you used to think was important. Open your eyes to what's important in your life—and only yours—right now. It's tough to say how Uranus will choose to inspire you to think for yourself, but one way or another, you'll begin smelling roses—very soon.

Neptune

If you were born between February 29 and March 1, your Sun will be conjoined by Neptune this year, and since Neptune is your ruling planet, this will definitely be a year to remember. All those qualities you were given by virtue of this compassionate, spiritual, and sometimes confusing planet will be running on high, and you will be absolutely amazed at your psychic abilities. You might also become a bit too involved, however, with a person or a group that's really just using you because of your sentimental heart. Your mission this year will be to wade through the nonsense and make your way to that place of clarity that is only in your heart. Now, Neptune is the Queen of Altered States, so she also brings along a love for escaping reality. Some of her favorite ways to do that are through addictions. It doesn't matter whether it's television, pills, alcohol, or depression. You'll need to be on your toes this year. If you feel yourself becoming a bit too comfortable with any escape hatch, talk to someone immediately and change your life however you need to—to save it.

Pluto

Pluto will continue his trek through your solar eleventh house of future goals and current friendships, Pisces, which might just mean that you're due for another year of wondering whether or not someone really is your friend. But Pluto is actually creating a sextile aspect to your sign—a very positive, very productive aspect—so that probably won't be the case. Instead, you'll likely find that even those higher-ups and elders who seemed to be working against you were really just trying to coax you out of the shadows to see exactly how much you have to offer and what you're really made of. If you were born between March 3 and 8, this will most especially be the case. An added perk will be the fact that if you have done so much behind closed doors for so long without asking for any recognition, you truly deserve this. But you'll reap what you've sown over the coming year or so, Pisces, so no fair looking surprised when you're awarded exactly what you deserve. By the same token, however, if you haven't done what you're capable of, you'll receive notification from the Universe, loud and clear. It won't be a terrible experience, but you'll be made to understand that a terrific opportunity to completely change your life into what you want it to be has just passed you by, and you won't be happy about it.

Pisces | January

Planetary Lightspots

The Full Moon on January 4 will illuminate your solar fifth house of lovers, playmates, and dealings with children. What fun! Sounds like laughter and wonderful warm hugs. If you're not seeing anyone, what an excellent time to get out there and strut your stuff. If you don't have kids, how about taking someone under your wing?

Relationships

Venus will move into your sign on January 27, Pisces. This might mean you'll be especially intent on securing a partner or making sure your current sweetheart is reliable and faithful, but you might also be thinking about how much fun it would be to just keep dating those who occasionally cross the line between lovers and friends. Regardless, you'll be a romance magnet!

Money and Success

Wherever Venus goes, money follows, Pisces, so once she wanders into your solar twelfth house of Privacy, Please on January 3, you'll probably want to work alone, from home if possible. If you can, wonderful. Just be sure to put yourself on a strict schedule, and resist the urge to indulge too much in "secret" pleasures.

Planetary Hotspots

Assertive, aggressive Mars will enter your sign on January 12, Pisces, for the first time in almost two years. It's a given that you'll be a lot more feisty, but since others aren't used to seeing you this way, they'll understandably be taken aback if you have occasional bursts of temper. You know what, though? Too bad! It's your turn to vent.

Rewarding Days
4, 19, 20, 27, 31

Challenging Days
14, 15, 16, 28, 29, 30

Pisces | February

Planetary Lightspots

The Sun will take off into your sign on February 18, Pisces, which means your birthday is fast approaching—always a good time—but also that you're due to shine this month, most likely due to a creative pursuit you have finally perfected. You might also be looking for an escape hatch, but be sure not to overindulge in anything that might physically harm you.

Relationships

It's hard not to look at February 1 and stare, Pisces, and if you're single, you might also be stopping to stare. Venus, the Goddess of Relationships, will collide with dreamy Neptune that day. Now, this is the stuff that love at first sight is most definitely made of. If you feel it, don't let it slip away. Get that number.

Money and Success

There'll be a whole lot of planets moving through your solar second house of personal finances and money matters this month, and since they'll all be wearing impulsive Aries, you'll probably spend a bit more than you'd planned on. Refuse to be an impulse shopper, however, and don't let anyone talk you into a warranty if you know you don't need it.

Planetary Hotspots

Between February 19 and 21, several planets in red-hot Aries will storm the borders of your solar second house of values, Pisces. Now, these are extremely assertive types, so you might need to take a stand for what you hold dear, whether it's a person, an animal, or an ideal. Be prepared for a bit of a battle.

Rewarding Days
1, 7, 8, 18, 25, 26

Challenging Days
5, 6, 20, 21, 22, 23

Pisces | March

Planetary Lightspots

If you've been trying to restore contact with someone but haven't been successful yet, give it another shot around March 17 or 18. Remember, it's not always about what you say. It might also be about what you don't say. Let the past be the past, and if there's still a strong connection, focus on the future.

Relationships

The Full Moon will occur on March 5, Pisces, and she's chosen your solar seventh house of relationships and personal encounters for this highly emotional event. Expect to be especially sensitive—yes, even more than usual—for quite a while, and, just this once, for others to be equally sensitive to how you act and react.

Money and Success

You're not usually one to brag, Pisces, but between March 24 and 26, you may need to allow someone else to do so on your behalf. All your hard work will actually be recognized, and that raise, bonus, or promotion you were after will finally be within your grasp. About time, isn't it? Relax, smile pretty, and enjoy the attention.

Planetary Hotspots

If you've been thinking about making some changes to your physical self but you're having trouble committing to a diet or exercise regime, begin on the outside. A new wardrobe or hairstyle will make you look and feel like a whole new you, and might just inspire you to tend to your body and your health habits.

Rewarding Days

5, 6, 12, 13, 18, 23, 24

Challenging Days

10, 11, 15, 16, 26, 27

Pisces | April

Planetary Lightspots

Venus will be on duty in your solar fourth house of home and family as of April 11, and since this lady loves to love and be loved, this will be a warm and wonderful time. You might even be able to resolve a dispute between you and someone you really do care about. If you can hardly remember what actually happened, let it go!

Relationships

The Lunar Eclipse on April 4 will occur in your solar eighth house of intimate partners, Pisces, asking you to either commit or walk away. If your antennae don't twitch, you'll know it's right to stay where you are, maybe for the long haul. If they do, think about dissolving this thing early before it gets too complicated.

Money and Success

Several planets in impulsive Aries and your solar second house of personal money matters will make their presence known, inspiring you to get a little wild and crazy with your wallet, especially around April 9. Careful, though. Aries planets are also often in the neighborhood when sudden, urgent situations arise. Try to resist splurging until after April 14.

Planetary Hotspots

Mercury and the Sun in impulsive Aries will join forces with unpredictable Uranus early this month. Startling situations are often a result of this type of gathering, so you should prepare yourself for quite the surprise. You may need to dip into your savings to help someone close to you, but you might also be gifted with a streak of luck.

Rewarding Days
12, 13, 14, 19, 21, 22, 29

Challenging Days
5, 7, 15, 16, 17, 20

Pisces | May

Planetary Lightspots

The combined efforts of the Full Moon on May 3 and the New Moon on May 17 will activate your solar axis of travel, so if you're in the mood to hit the road or hop on a train, bus, or plane, give in and do it. It'll renew your spirit and create or revitalize at least one relationship. Let your mind and spirit run free.

Relationships

On May 7, Venus will tiptoe into your solar fifth house of lovers, play-mates, and relationships with children, all done up in ultra-sensitive Cancer. She'll be ready to shed some sentimental tears, pass out lots of hugs, and see to it that no one who makes your heart happy isn't very aware of that fact. You can also expect the same in return.

Money and Success

All those planets in impulsive Aries last month did their best to talk you into spending your money impetuously, so you're probably just now going through the credit card bills, Pisces—but not to worry. The New Moon on May 17 in Taurus, the money-magnet sign, will help you to find a fun, creative way to recoup any losses.

Planetary Hotspots

Mercury, Mars, and the Sun will all challenge Saturn via an irritating square this month, which will pit your solar fourth house of home and emotions against your solar tenth house of career and professional matters. Sounds like you'll need to do some juggling to please everyone around you, but with Jupiter in your solar sixth house of daily habits, you'll get used to it.

Rewarding Days
6, 7, 16, 17, 28

Challenging Days
3, 4, 9, 10, 25, 31

Pisces | June

Planetary Lightspots

The Full Moon in fun-loving Sagittarius on June 2 will get your month off to a lively start, and might also bring about some truly lucky breaks career-wise. Sagittarius planets love to travel, mingle, and laugh, so feed this lunation well with all of the above, and remember, an upbeat attitude makes lasting impressions that could come in handy soon.

Relationships

If you've been thinking seriously about settling down, Pisces, the easy trine between loving Venus and respectable Saturn on June 6 will provide you with the perfect astrological backup to ask questions and then maybe pop questions, too, if you like the answers. Think about the connection you have with a coworker—because they're certainly doing the same.

Money and Success

Right around June 22, when generous Jupiter makes an easy trine with unpredictable Uranus—who just so happens to be on duty in your solar second house of finances—your luck will be running on high. This is a great time to invest in a scratch ticket, but don't get carried away. This team is extremely impulsive.

Planetary Hotspots

On June 14, the Sun and Mars will collide in Gemini. This puts these two astrological fireballs of assertive energy in your solar fourth house of home, family matters, and emotions—so needless to say, tempers might flare, and yes, that does include yours. Think before you speak, no matter how long you've been holding it all in.

Rewarding Days

6, 7, 21, 22, 24, 25

Challenging Days

11, 12, 13, 14, 23, 29, 30

Pisces | July

Planetary Lightspots

All will be well in your world around July 21 and 22, Pisces, as the sky will be full of positive water energy. This is a great time to spend with family and friends, so if you're inclined to travel or entertain, try to reconnect with someone whose uplifting presence has been missing for far too long.

Relationships

Jupiter is settled into romantic Leo and your solar sixth house of work and relationships with coworkers, Pisces, which is plenty reason to imagine you in the arms of someone you see every day. If you haven't yet made your move, use Jupiter's meeting with loving Venus on July 1 to make this a month to remember.

Money and Success

With startling Uranus still making his way through your solar second house of personal finances, things may be a bit rocky for you at the moment. The good news is that on July 2, an opportunity to earn a bit more through a fun side job will come along, and you really should take it. Learning something new through interesting people just can't be bad.

Planetary Hotspots

On July 15, several planets will collide in your solar fifth house of lovers, fun, and playmates. The list includes the Sun, aggressive Mars, communicative Mercury, and the Moon, the Queen of Feelings. Needless to say, this much emotional passion could be tricky to handle. They'll all be wearing Cancer, however, so spending some physically energetic quality time with the kids is definitely in order.

Rewarding Days
1, 8, 9, 20, 21, 26

Challenging Days
6, 7, 11, 12, 14, 15, 24, 25

Pisces | August

Planetary Lightspots

After a year in Leo, Jupiter will amble off into earthy Virgo and your solar seventh house of one-to-one relationships on August 11—and that's when the fun will really begin. If you're single, expect a veritable buffet of new admirers, all of whom will be packing either an interesting accent or a ton of good stories.

Relationships

You probably did your fair share of arguing last month, Pisces, but taking a stand might have been exactly what you needed to do. This month, you'll be amazed at just how willing others are to at least try to see your point of view, even if they don't share your thoughts and feelings.

Money and Success

Venus and Jupiter will come together in your solar sixth house of work on August 4, Pisces, and while this would ordinarily be a good thing, with a square from Saturn set to block their enthusiasm, you'll have to work hard to get what you deserve. That goes for your paycheck as well as any raises, bonuses, or promotions you've been after.

Planetary Hotspots

Optimistic Jupiter and ultra-cautious Saturn will get into an edgy square on August 3, activating a battle between your solar sixth house of work and your solar ninth house of higher education. If you're feeling underqualified for a career or position you really want, this would be prime time to do something about it. Go back to school and learn something new.

Rewarding Days

6, 11, 12, 13, 15, 23, 26

Challenging Days

3, 4, 5, 7, 20, 21, 22, 31

Pisces | September

Planetary Lightspots

On September 17, Mercury will turn retrograde in partner-oriented Libra and your solar eighth house of intimate partners. It will be possible now to reconnect with someone you consider The One Who Got Away. If that's what you want, great. Why not at least give it a second shot? Just be sure you have new solutions to the problems that drove you apart.

Relationships

The Sun will join Mercury in Libra on September 23, Pisces, and since they're in Libra and your solar eighth house of intimate partners, there won't be much you'll want to do alone. If you're single, this would be a great time to rally the troops and get The Gang together. If you're attached, introduce your partner around.

Money and Success

On September 27, a Lunar Eclipse will plant a seed of change in your solar second house of money matters, Pisces, so buckle up and prepare yourself for what might be a bumpy ride. The good news is that when it's all over, you'll be equipped with a brand-new attitude, which will help you to find a different way of earning your daily bread.

Planetary Hotspots

The Solar Eclipse on September 13 will bring the Sun and Moon together in your solar seventh house of one-to-one relationships, Pisces, so you should probably expect some drastic changes. It might be that a business partnership is just not working. It might be a romantic relationship, too. Regardless, if you know it's time to move along, move along.

Rewarding Days

4, 5, 8, 22, 23, 30

Challenging Days

7, 9, 16, 24, 25, 26, 27

Pisces | October

Planetary Lightspots

The Full Moon on October 27 in earthy, practical Taurus will set up shop in your solar third house of thoughts and communications, Pisces, so your already keen antennae will be nicely grounded in reality. No matter what you're trying to decide, if you feel strongly that it's the right thing to do, follow through, no matter what anyone has to say about it.

Relationships

Venus, the Goddess of Love herself, will set off for your solar seventh house of one-to-one relationships on October 8, Pisces, and since Mars and Jupiter are already there waiting, you'll have a party—full of Virgos—on your hands. The upside is that this crew can't help but attract intelligent, responsible types. Just try not to be overly critical.

Money and Success

Financial matters could be tricky to handle around October 6, 10, and 22, and you may need to go over your books with a professional to untangle a serious snarl. The good news is that any joint money issues that have been troubling you will straighten out easily around the New Moon on October 12.

Planetary Hotspots

All those organized, meticulous Virgo planets in your solar seventh house of one-to-one relationships will most certainly see to it that there are no surprises for you in that department, Pisces. If you're attached, rest assured that it will be a drama-free month—provided you're willing to grin and bear a bit of well-meant criticism around October 10.

Rewarding Days
8, 11, 13, 14, 15, 23, 24

Challenging Days
10, 17, 18, 21, 22, 25

Pisces | November

Planetary Lightspots

The Sun will set off for lighthearted Sagittarius on November 22, the sign that most loves to laugh, just a day after chatty Mercury arrives. These two never fail to bring a merry entourage with them wherever they go, so your social schedule will probably pick up some serious speed. Sleep may be hard to come by, too—but why would you want to?

Relationships

Whenever magnetic Venus and passionate Mars get together, fireworks are always a possibility, Pisces. So on November 2, when they collide in your solar seventh house of one-to-one relationships, prepare yourself for some drama. No, you don't usually enjoy that sort of thing, but this time out, it could be fun. Just be sure it arrives through enthusiasm, not anger.

Money and Success

Venus will tiptoe into your solar eighth house of joint finances on November 8, all done up in Libra and bringing along her fondness for partnerships. If you have the chance to start a new business—especially if it's related to beauty, music, or art—you should seriously think about it. There may be some administrative snags around November 20, but they'll work themselves out.

Planetary Hotspots

The Full Moon on November 25 will illuminate your solar axis of career and personal issues. Now, this tug of war between the Sun and Moon could mean that you'll feel as if you're being pulled in opposite directions. Not to worry, though. Venus is on duty in Libra, the sign that best knows how to juggle. Be fair to everyone and they'll understand.

Rewarding Days

5, 6, 7, 10, 13, 17, 18

Challenging Days

2, 3, 19, 20, 24, 26, 29

Pisces | December

Planetary Lightspots

The New Moon on December 12 might inspire you to change jobs, Pisces, and maybe even your career. You're after something that will really fulfill you now—something you can really be devoted to. That chance could be right around the corner, but don't quit your day job just yet. Sit tight, arrange some interviews, and see what's out there.

Relationships

This holiday season looks to be quite positive for you, Pisces, as the Full Moon in family-oriented Cancer on Christmas Day shines her bright emotional light into your solar fifth house of lovers, playmates, and relationships with children. Talk about a merry old time! Gather the whole gang around the fire and enjoy the camaraderie and comfort food.

Money and Success

You'll need to work very hard to prevent yourself from overspending, and you'll probably be shopping for last-minute gifts right up until you leave for your holiday dinner. Impulsive Uranus is in your solar second house of money matters, and he'll be contacting several planets in excessive Sagittarius this month. Prepare your checkbook for a beating—or take a frugal chaperone along.

Planetary Hotspots

Thoughtful Mercury will set off for realistic Capricorn on December 9, and just about immediately, he'll bump into Pluto, who insists on all or nothing. They'll collide in your solar eleventh house of future goals, group affiliations, and friendships, so the right peer circle will be very important to you now. Fortunately, there'll be lots of opportunities to find them.

Rewarding Days
1, 2, 8, 12, 17, 25

Challenging Days
4, 5, 6, 14, 29

Pisces Action Table

These dates reflect the best—but not the only—times for success and ease in these activities, according to your Sun sign.

	JAN	FEB	MAR	APR	MAY	JUN	JUL	AUG	SEP	OCT	NOV	DEC
Move				22, 26	30, 31			13, 14, 15				25, 26
Start a class					2, 3							11
Join a club		7		21, 22						14, 15		5, 6
Ask for a raise			25, 26			1, 2		30, 31	27, 28			
Look for work		3, 4		2, 6	4, 5	5, 6, 7						
Get pro advice	22, 30	24, 25			14, 15							10
Get a loan						28			24, 30	6, 12, 13		25
See a doctor	30, 31				27, 28				12			12, 13
Start a diet		7, 8,										
End relationship			20				14, 15, 16		12, 13, 14	17, 25		
Buy clothes				6, 8		22, 23			22			
Get a makeover	27		20, 23					29, 31				
New romance	4	1, 25	5, 18, 20				21, 22	23, 26, 31		8, 15, 16		
Vacation												6, 13, 17

Notes

Notes

LLEWELLYN'S 2015

Astrological

CALENDAR

82nd Edition of the World's Best Known,
Most Trusted Astrology Calendar

Llewellyn's 2015 Astrological Calendar
Horoscopes for You Plus an Introduction to Astrology

Llewellyn's Astrological Calendar is the best-known, most trusted astrological calendar sold today. Everyone, even beginners, can use this beautiful and practical calendar to plan the year wisely.

There are monthly horoscopes, best days for planting and fishing, rewarding and challenging days, travel forecasts, and an astrology primer. Advanced astrologers will find major daily aspects and a wealth of other essential astrological information.

This edition features Christine Mitzuk's gorgeous artwork, inspired by the signs and symbols of astrology.

978-0-7387-2682-3, 40 pp., 12 x 12   U.S. $14.99

To order, call 1-877-NEW-WRLD
Prices subject to change without notice
Order at Llewellyn.com 24 hours a day, 7 days a week!

Complete Astrology
At-A-Glance

LLEWELLYN'S 2015

Daily
Planetary
Guide

Your Best
Opportunity Periods
from Jim Shawvan &
Forecasts by Pam Ciampi

Llewellyn's 2015 Daily Planetary Guide
Complete Astrology At-A-Glance

Empower your life with the most trusted and detailed astrological guide available. Take advantage of cosmic forces on a daily, weekly, or monthly basis with *Llewellyn's Daily Planetary Guide*.

With exact times down to the minute, this astrological planner lists ideal times to do anything. Before setting up a job interview, signing a contract, or scheduling anything important, consult the weekly forecasts and Opportunity Periods—times when the positive flow of energy is at its peak.

Even beginners can use this powerful planner, which includes a primer on the planets, signs, houses, and how to use this guide.

978-0-7387-2684-7, 208 pp., 5 x 8¼ $12.99

LLEWELLYN'S

2015

ASTROLOGICAL

POCKET
PLANNER

DAILY EPHEMERIS & ASPECTARIAN
2014–2016

Llewellyn's 2015 Astrological Pocket Planner
Daily Ephemeris & Aspectarian 2014–2016

Empower your future—plan important events, set goals, and organize your life—with *Llewellyn's Astrological Pocket Planner*. Both beginners and advanced astrologers can use this award-winning datebook, the only one to offer three years of ephemeris and aspectarian data.

Choose optimal dates for job interviews, weddings, business meetings, and other important occasions. Pinpoint ideal times to plant a garden, begin new projects, conduct self-reflection, go fishing, and more. Avoid planetary pitfalls by following the easy-to-read retrograde and Moon void-of-course tables.

Comprehensive and compact, *Llewellyn's 2015 Astrological Pocket Planner* also contains time zone information and space to jot down your daily appointments.

978-0-7387-2683-0, 192 pp., 4¼ x 6⁵⁄₁₆ $8.99

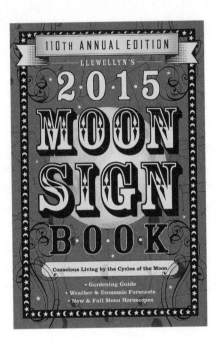

110TH ANNUAL EDITION

LLEWELLYN'S

2015

MOON
SIGN
BOOK

Conscious Living by the Cycles of the Moon

• Gardening Guide
• Weather & Economic Forecasts
• New & Full Moon Horoscopes

Llewellyn's 2015 Moon Sign Book
Conscious Living by the Cycles of the Moon

Since 1905, *Llewellyn's Moon Sign Book* has helped millions take advantage of the Moon's dynamic energies. Use this essential life-planning tool to choose the best dates for almost anything: getting married, buying or selling your home, requesting a promotion, applying for a loan, traveling, having surgery, seeing the dentist, picking mushrooms, and much more. With lunar timing tips on planting and harvesting and a guide to companion plants, this popular guide is also a gardener's best friend. In addition to New and Full Moon forecasts for the year, you'll find insightful articles on growing a tea garden, cultivating roses, organic and natural food labeling, the Moon and earthquakes, outer planets in water signs, and Greek lunar folklore.

978-0-7387-2686-1, 312 pp., 5¼ x 8 $11.99

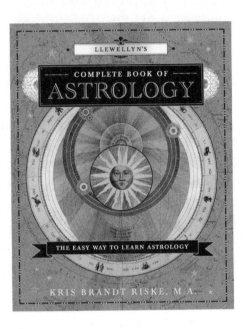

LLEWELLYN'S

COMPLETE BOOK OF

ASTROLOGY

THE EASY WAY TO LEARN ASTROLOGY

KRIS BRANDT RISKE, M.A.

Llewellyn's Complete Book of Astrology
The Easy Way to Learn Astrology
KRIS BRANDT RISKE, M.A.

The horoscope is filled with insights into personal traits, talents, and life possibilities. With *Llewellyn's Complete Book of Astrology*, you can learn to read and understand this amazing cosmic road map for yourself and others.

Professional astrologer Kris Brandt Riske introduces the many mysterious parts that make up the horoscope, devoting special attention to three popular areas of interest: relationships, career, and money. Friendly and easy to follow, this comprehensive book guides you to explore the zodiac signs, planets, houses, and aspects, and teaches how to synthesize this valuable information.

Once you learn the language of astrology, you'll be able to read birth charts of yourself and others, determine compatibility between two people, track your earning potential, uncover areas of opportunity or challenge, and analyze your career path.

978-0-7387-1071-6, 336 pp., 8 x 10 $19.99

LLEWELLYN'S

COMPLETE BOOK OF PREDICTIVE

ASTROLOGY

THE EASY WAY TO PREDICT YOUR FUTURE

☆ KRIS BRANDT RISKE, M.A. ★

Llewellyn's Complete Book
of Predictive Astrology
The Easy Way to Predict Your Future
KRIS BRANDT RISKE, M.A.

Find out what potential the future holds and use those insights to create the life you desire with this definitive guide to predictive astrology.

In her signature easy-to-understand style, popular astrologer Kris Brandt Riske offers step-by-step instructions for performing each major predictive technique—solar arcs, progressions, transits, lunar cycles, and planetary returns—along with an introduction to horary astrology. Discover how to read all elements of a predictive chart and pinpoint when changes in your career, relationships, finances, and other important areas of life are on the horizon.

Also included are several example charts based on the lives of the author's clients and celebrities such as Marilyn Monroe, Martha Stewart, and Pamela Anderson.

978-0-7387-2755-4, 288 pp., 8 x 10 $18.95

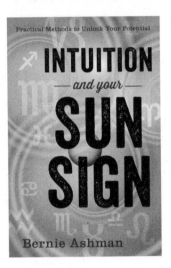

Practical Methods to Unlock Your Potential

INTUITION
and your
SUN SIGN

Bernie Ashman

Intuition and Your Sun Sign
Practical Methods to Unlock Your Potential
BERNIE ASHMAN

Your hidden spiritual and practical gifts come alive when you make the most of your intuitive potential. Astrologer Bernie Ashman reveals how to use a basic understanding of astrology to instantly tap into and use your varied intuitive gifts to overcome blocks and find the mental clarity you seek.

You'll need no astrological background to make use of this information in practical situations. Even more excitingly, you'll develop your own insights and intuition about others, letting you make better choices quickly and more easily and raising your self-confidence. Looking at someone else's Sun sign will allow you to communicate with them better, bringing improved harmony and understanding to your relationships. You'll master challenges, improve your imagination, achieve goals, and find personal empowerment.

978-0-7387-3894-9, 360 pp., 6 x 9 $18.99

To order, call 1-877-NEW-WRLD
Prices subject to change without notice
Order at Llewellyn.com 24 hours a day, 7 days a week!

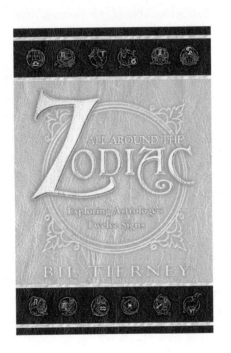

ALL AROUND THE

Zodiac

Exploring Astrology's
Twelve Signs

BIL TIERNEY

All Around the Zodiac

Exploring Astrology's Twelve Signs

BIL TIERNEY

Here is a fresh, in-depth perspective on the zodiac you thought you knew. This book provides a revealing new look at the astrological signs, from Aries to Pisces. Gain a deeper understanding of how each sign motivates you to grow and evolve in consciousness. How does Aries work with Pisces? What does Gemini have in common with Scorpio? *All Around the Zodiac* is the only book on the market to explore these sign combinations to such a degree.

Not your typical Sun sign guide, this book is broken into three parts. Part 1 defines the signs, part 2 analyzes the expression of sixty-six pairs of signs, and part 3 designates the expression of the planets and houses in the signs.

978-0-7387-0111-0, 480 pp., 6 x 9 $22.99

Bernie Ashman

SUN SIGNS
&
PAST LIVES

Your Soul's Evolutionary Path

Sun Signs & Past Lives
Your Soul's Evolutionary Path
BERNIE ASHMAN

Discover how to break free from destructive past-life patterns and reach your full potential.

Sun Signs & Past Lives offers an easy, foolproof way to pinpoint behaviors that may be holding you back from a rewarding life of peace and fulfillment. All you need to know is your birthday. Bernie Ashman divides each Sun sign into three energy zones, allowing easy access to innate strengths and the spiritual lessons for this lifetime. With his guidance, you'll discover how to transform these precious insights into action—reverse negative past-life tendencies, find healing, discover your life purpose, and get back on the road to empowerment.

978-0-7387-2107-1, 264 pp., 6 x 9 $16.95

GET MORE AT LLEWELLYN.COM

Visit us online to browse hundreds of our books and decks, plus sign up to receive our e-newsletters and exclusive online offers.

- **Free tarot readings • Spell-A-Day • Moon phases**
- **Recipes, spells, and tips • Blogs • Encyclopedia**
- **Author interviews, articles, and upcoming events**

GET SOCIAL WITH LLEWELLYN

Find us on

www.Facebook.com/LlewellynBooks

Follow us on

www.Twitter.com/Llewellynbooks

GET BOOKS AT LLEWELLYN

LLEWELLYN ORDERING INFORMATION

Order online: Visit our website at www.llewellyn.com to select your books and place an order on our secure server.

Order by phone:
- Call toll free within the U.S. at 1-877-NEW-WRLD (1-877-639-9753)
- Call toll free within Canada at 1-866-NEW-WRLD (1-866-639-9753)
- We accept VISA, MasterCard, and American Express

Order by mail:
Send the full price of your order (MN residents add 6.875% sales tax) in U.S. funds, plus postage and handling to: Llewellyn Worldwide, 2143 Wooddale Drive Woodbury, MN 55125-2989

POSTAGE AND HANDLING

STANDARD (U.S. & Canada):
(Please allow 12 business days)
$25.00 and under, add $4.00.
$25.01 and over, FREE SHIPPING.

INTERNATIONAL ORDERS (airmail only):
$16.00 for one book, plus $3.00 for each additional book.

Visit us online for more shipping options. Prices subject to change.

FREE CATALOG!

To order, call
1-877-NEW-WRLD
ext. 8236
or visit our website